D0811383

3 0120 02742624 6

FULL CIRCLE

JOANNA
ROWSELL SHAND

—

FULL CIRCLE
MY STORY

with Natasha Devon

JOHN BLAKE

Published by John Blake Publishing Ltd,
3 Bramber Court, 2 Bramber Road,
London W14 9PB, England

www.johnblakebooks.com

www.facebook.com/johnblakebooks ⨍
twitter.com/jblakebooks ⓑ

This edition published in 2017

ISBN: 978 1 78606 420 2

British Library Cataloguing-in-Publication Data:

A catalogue record for this book is available from the British Library.

Design by www.envydesign.co.uk

Printed and bound in Great Britain by Clays Ltd, St Ives plc

1 3 5 7 9 10 8 6 4 2

Papers used by John Blake Publishing are natural, recyclable products made from wood grown in sustainable forests. The manufacturing processes conform to the environmental regulations of the country of origin.

Every attempt has been made to contact the relevant copyright-holders, but some were unobtainable. We would be grateful if the appropriate people could contact us.

John Blake Publishing is an imprint of Bonnier Publishing
www.bonnierpublishing.com

'I would rather regret the things that I have done than the things I have not.'
LUCILLE BALL

CONTENTS

INTRODUCTION

When I look back on my life, there is very clearly one day that changed everything to come. It happened on a sunny Tuesday when I was fourteen years old, in Year 9 at school.

What's remarkable is how unaware I was, at the time, of the importance of that day. We had been told that talent scouts from British Cycling were coming into our all-girls grammar school in Surrey, and that if we wanted we could take part in a test. I remember writing my name on the sign-up sheet but not really being sure if I wanted to go.

Participating in the test would mean missing double maths, which for most people would be reason enough to give it a try, but I happened to quite like maths. I think the sunshine was a major factor in my decision – even now whenever the weather is pleasant I resent being stuck inside a building. The opportunity to be out on the playing field was a big temptation.

Deep down, I think I also had something to prove. At Nonsuch High School for Girls we had a tradition of selecting a small number of girls from Years 9 and 10 and training them to be the ball girls at the Stella Artois Championships (now the Aegon Championships) every June, the major tennis competition held at Queen's Club right before Wimbledon. Almost everyone wanted to do it, so the school would gradually de-select pupils based on ability, until they were left with an elite group to take to the event every summer.

I had known about the tradition of Nonsuch ball girls since the day I arrived in Year 7 – it was a big deal – but had decided not to go for it that year. I wasn't particularly good at throwing and catching (to be honest, I was horrendously bad at any sport requiring hand-eye coordination!), preferring race-based activities like running and swimming. Yet there was a part of me that envied the ball girls, who were massively celebrated in our school's culture. There were entire assemblies dedicated to them. They'd had this brilliant experience they could potentially brag about for the rest of their lives. So the cycling test was, I suppose, a way of proving that I was good for something. I knew I was relatively fit compared to my peers as I used to regularly be one of the few willing participants in the school cross-country running team each year but I'd never been on a bike beyond the occasional leisurely weekend rides with my dad at this stage.

As I approached, I saw that British Cycling had created a track on the sports field using cones. We had been told that they could provide us with a bike and helmet if we needed, but to bring along our own if we had them. I had brought my pink and purple cycle helmet, a bulky, colourful child's-style thing I had mistakenly believed was appropriate for racing. One of the coaches asked me what I was doing with it. Whilst he wasn't unkind, he simply seemed bemused as he took my helmet from me and provided me with one fit for proper racing.

We were told to race six laps of a 200-metre circuit, following the cones, in small groups of around six of us. Our field ran on a slight slope so the circuit had an element of downhill and then a slight climb. I remember distinctly racing ahead of the other girls as I powered up the gradual incline, but then braking as I hurtled down the slight slope, all too aware the fence was rapidly approaching and feeling out of control. I kept thinking I was going too fast, even as my teacher shouted out to me to stop using the brakes, because this was a race: going fast was the point.

Despite my erratic technique I had easily won the race from my group and returned to lessons feeling happy I had proved my sporting ability amongst my classmates. The traditional school sports weren't my thing but in terms of a race like this I had the fitness to beat the other girls. At the end we were given a card, stamped with the British Cycling logo, with our time written on it. We were told we could visit a website to enter our times to find out how we ranked in comparison to all the other teenagers who had taken the test. I remember walking home, clutching the shiny red rectangle and feeling excited about seeing my position. I've always liked the idea of stats, records and personal bests (PBs) – that's part of the reason why I'm attracted to races as opposed to team games.

The website was how I found out my time was third best in my school (and quite a long way behind the fastest girl). I started wondering if I could have gone faster if I'd had a tougher race. I'd won easily – could I have pushed harder if someone had been closer to me? At fourteen I was already analysing my performance and looking for improvements. The website also allowed you to see the times of boys from other schools in the area who had taken part in the test. Going to an all-girls school, it had never occurred to me at that point that boys might be naturally quicker or stronger (and it therefore made sense that their times were considerably faster than mine). I just remember thinking I was some way off the boys' times and that it was something for me to aim for.

It turned out that my time was just good enough for me to be called back to the second stage of testing, a few months later in September 2003. This time, the trial involved measuring how powerfully we could cycle on a static bike. I received a letter from British Cycling informing me I would be doing fitness tests on 'mountain bikes mounted on turbo trainers equipped with SRM cranks' and they would be testing 'endurance power, sprint power and maximum unloaded cadence'. I remember these words clearly as I took the letter in to my PE teacher Mrs Etheridge and together we tried to work out what it meant. The words 'turbo trainer', 'SRM cranks' and 'cadence' meant nothing to me. I looked up the word 'cadence' and found this to be a musical term. Now I was even more confused.

What all this turned out to mean was that we would be on static bikes and would be doing three fitness tests. The bikes had cranks which measured power output in watts and combined with measuring our body mass, they could work out a power-to-weight ratio and a fitness index. The maximum unloaded cadence test involved taking the chain off the bike and unlocking the resistance and us pedalling as fast as we could for five seconds. I was terrible at this, I needed some resistance to lean on. We then had a sprint test – again for five seconds but this time with the chain on the bike and the resistance on the turbo. A bit of resistance gave me something to kick against. Finally, a three-minute endurance test. The other cyclists groaned when we were told what to do but I didn't see the problem. It sounded simple:

pedal for three minutes as hard as I could. So I stuck it in the hardest gear and went for it.

This, I now know, was where I really made an impression on the coaches. In fact, I later learned that I had the highest score for endurance they had ever seen, for a girl of my age. They didn't tell me this at the time, because they wanted to check my test score hadn't been a one-off fluke. My sprint test had also apparently been impressive but my cadence test, as I had suspected, was abysmal, so there were no plans to send me to the sprint programme.

After my performance in the endurance test, I was one of two girls in my school to be invited to a final stage of testing in December 2003. This took place over two days. The first day involved a repeat of the tests on the static bikes as well as a cycling knowledge quiz. One of the questions was 'what are the differences between cyclo-cross and mountain biking?' I had never even heard of cyclo-cross. It was unlike me to struggle on a test.

The second day was when my lack of basic ability became apparent. We were informed we would be doing a group mountain bike ride in Epping Forest as a final assessment of our cycling potential, and this was an unmitigated disaster. I had been paired with a training buddy. His name was Alex Dowsett and he has since gone on to become a very successful professional cyclist. He must have stuck with me for all of about thirty seconds before he rode off and left me.

I had brought my bike along with me, which I had mistakenly believed was a mountain bike. I'd also worn tracksuit bottoms, thinking they were suitable attire. I therefore looked a total idiot when everyone else showed up with real mountain bikes radically different from mine, wearing Lycra. I spent most of that ride wandering around Epping Forest on foot, dragging my bike alongside me, with ripped trousers and muddy feet, thinking, *I hate this*.

It was obvious to me, the other cyclists and, perhaps most mortifyingly, the coaches, that I was by far the worst rider there. At this stage I was unaware of how good my score had been in the testing and so I thought that was it, this wasn't for me. I clearly wasn't a talented cyclist and that would be the end of it.

So it came as a complete surprise later in December when I got a phone call from Stuart Blunt, the South East region youth coach, telling me I had been offered a place on the South East region 'Talent Team' from January 2004.

The Talent Team was an initiative by British Cycling to nurture young cycling talent with the aim of developing future Olympians. There was a Talent Team for each region of the UK and these were mainly made up of young cyclists who were already established and winning medals at a national level and had been tested at their local clubs. However, there were a few of us 'from the schools' who had been identified as having raw talent, who British Cycling thought it would be worth investing in.

In total there were five girls versus three times as many boys on the Talent Team. Again, at this stage, I remember being bemused by the imbalance of it – I simply couldn't comprehend a world where the gender balance wasn't completely equal. At the time, we were approaching the 2004 Olympics in Athens and there were eight events for men with only half as many for women. I kept asking the coaches why. But I never received an answer I considered satisfactory, even back then, when my understanding of the cycling world was so limited.

I could never have predicted on that sunny Tuesday that the

test I had felt so uncertain about and so unprepared for would ultimately lead to me competing in the Olympics. Yet in an uncanny way the people around me forecast, even before I ever mounted a racing bike, that I was destined to be an Olympic athlete. Ever since I was a small child, people used to talk to me about the Olympics and this naturally led to me having a fascination with them whenever events were being shown on the television.

As a child, swimming was my thing and this was the event I always enjoyed watching the most when the Olympics rolled around. I had swum from a young age and competed at a pretty decent level until the age of around eleven, after I'd developed alopecia (or 'alopecia universalis'), of which more later, and my confidence was beginning to fail me. I used to become incredibly nervous before swimming galas and in the end it was too much for me to handle. Around the same time I developed a knee injury and used that as my excuse for stopping competitive swimming.

Even in spite of that, there were signs that I had the sort of nature that makes a good athlete. I was certainly determined and liked to subvert and exceed people's expectations of me. At ten years old I competed in the National Biathlon Championships, which involved running and swimming. Four weeks before the event I fell over in the playground and broke my arm. Everyone assumed I would drop out but I was determined to do it. I couldn't train with my swimming club in the pool but I went out running round the block every evening, with my arm in a sling. I had the plaster cast taken off my arm two days before the competition. In the end I came tenth. I never would have labelled myself as competitive at the time yet, I now realise, I absolutely was.

I had vague memories of watching the Olympics in Sydney

in 2000, but after I was singled out by British Cycling, I became properly immersed in the next Olympics in Athens. I watched the cycling events fastidiously, googling all of the names of the cyclists, and researched their times and achievements to date. That year, there were quite a few British medals, including golds for Chris Hoy and Bradley Wiggins, but the competition had been clearly dominated by Australia.

Looking back, I find it interesting to think of how my life might have been so different if that opportunity hadn't fallen into my lap and changed the course of everything to come. Yet it would be misleading to suggest my natural endurance ability meant everything was smooth sailing from there. In fact, the first few training camps I participated in as a teenager were a complete disaster. I'm pretty sure during this time the coaches thought they'd made a mistake in selecting me – I could see the doubt and irritation at my lack of basic knowledge and abilities, at first.

Yet, as on so many occasions during the decade-long career as an athlete that was to follow, disappointment spurred me on. I would prove everyone wrong. I would master my bike. I would succeed at this.

CHAPTER 1

MY OVERACTIVE MIND

I was born on 5 December 1988, the eldest child of Roger and Amanda Rowsell. Mum and Dad hadn't been married long when I arrived and, whilst they've never explicitly stated this, I'm fairly certain they weren't expecting me so soon.

Life was tough for my parents financially at the beginning and they had to balance several jobs to make ends meet. My dad's parents were in Southampton and my mum's in Shropshire, so they didn't have a support network of family around them where they lived in Cheam, Surrey, to assist in supporting them. My dad worked for HSBC, which at the time was called Midland Bank, from Monday to Friday. He then had a part-time job at an estate agent on Sundays.

Mum worked in a garden centre on Saturdays and for the rest of the week she was a childminder. I have vague memories of our house always being filled with other people's children when I was very small. Despite being an only child, the photos I have from that period show me that I was hardly ever on my own. Even though I don't have many concrete memories, I imagine this prepared me nicely for the arrival of my brother, Erick, twenty months later.

Erick was born in the summer. When we became old enough to have parties this was a bone of contention between us. I was always very jealous that the warm weather on his birthday meant he could have a bouncy castle in the garden. On my fifth birthday my parents arranged for a magician to come and do tricks at my party and whilst that was, even now, probably my favourite birthday ever, I was still resentful at missing out on a bouncy castle. December just isn't the time of year to bounce, unfortunately. Years later, when I got engaged, one of the first things I said after 'Yes' was 'We're having a bouncy castle at the wedding.' I'm pretty sure my fiancé thought I'd lost the plot but I was defiant about it and on the day, I bounced with joy in my floor-length wedding gown.

The house we lived at the time was link detached – this meant it was part of a row of small properties all joined together by garages. I remember it having a massive garden, although if I went there now, it probably wouldn't seem big at all.

The family behind us had a son who was about my age and we used to spend hours playing in the quiet street of our little cul-de-sac. That was when I first learned to ride a bike. I was given hand-me-down bikes from my aunts, who were just four and six years older than me. In fact, pretty much everything I had back then, including my clothes, was handed down from them.

We had two guinea pigs and a rabbit, which we kept in the garden. I remember one of the guinea pigs was called Bracken and the other guinea pig was white, as was the rabbit. I named them Snowy and Fluffy but used to use the names interchangeably.

Fluffy-slash-Snowy the rabbit was a boy, which I simply couldn't comprehend at the time. He was so pretty with his white fur and therefore, in my mind at least, unmistakably a girl. A few months after we bought him Fluffy-slash-Snowy 'turned' and became evil. He bit my mum's finger so deeply she had to go to A&E for stitches.

After that incident, Fluffy-slash-Snowy became more recalcitrant and harder to catch. I recall laughing as the whole family tried to fetch the rabbit from his run to put him back in his cage. Every time my parents got near him, my brother would yell 'Yay!', which would alert the bunny and cause him to scamper away. My mum was wearing thick gloves because of her fear of being bitten again. Soon after that I was told Fluffy-slash-Snowy 'went to live at a friend's house'. I suspect he was probably put down.

Even as a child, I always had an incredibly analytical brain, which I found incredibly difficult to switch off. Babysitters used to complain that I wouldn't go to sleep at night. I remember my aunties Adele and Naomi urging me to 'Just relax and let your thoughts drift away' and replying, 'But I'll forget my maths!' It would take them ages to reassure me that wasn't how it worked, that the maths I learned wouldn't disappear in the night, and to coax me to sleep.

I also had what I imagine was quite an annoying propensity to question absolutely everything. I have never, even as a child, had an ability to suspend my disbelief – I need to know exactly how and why things work the way they do. I remember on one occasion I was firing endless questions at my mum about Father Christmas: I wanted to know precisely how he managed to visit every single child in the world in one night. 'Magic' wasn't a sufficient response for me, I needed to understand the mechanics.

I was also curious as to how he fitted down those slender chimneys. And what about the houses without chimneys? And what about the children who speak different languages? How did he understand their letters?

In the end my mum got so frustrated she said, 'Oh, for goodness' sake, Joanna, Father Christmas isn't real! And while we're at it, neither is the Tooth Fairy or the Easter Bunny.'

I was distraught. It hadn't even occurred to me that Father Christmas might be imaginary, I just wanted to understand how.

Some athletes tend to have these sorts of over-active minds. We are constantly analysing what we have done and thinking of ways to do it better in the future. We never really have an opportunity to switch off from that way of thinking because everything we do, even if it's just resting, has an impact on training and therefore, ultimately, performance. In that sense it's helpful that I have always had the sort of brain which examines the details, loves data and leaves no stone unturned.

The downside, of course, is that I find it incredibly difficult to relax completely. I have to actively try to distract myself. Later in my life, at the Olympics, it became really important that I could switch off. By the time you get to the Olympic event you have done all the work and worrying might affect your performance negatively. During the 2016 Rio games, I obsessively played a game called Words with Friends. This is a little like Scrabble, with the option to play against people you know, randoms, or the computer itself. It certainly proved an excellent way to distract my mind from how my legs felt.

Although I had a tendency to be anxious and overthink things, I would generally describe myself as a happy child and I reckon I was quite well behaved too. Like most girls from my generation I had a couple of Barbie dolls and was really into the colour pink.

I was quite typical in that sense. The thing that really excited me, though, were Beanie Babies, which are adorable cuddly animals, fluffy and floppy and in all the colours of the rainbow. They sell for a small fortune on eBay now, I hear. The walls of my little bedroom were covered in wallpaper with a rabbit pattern and later covered over with pale pink paint.

When I was eight years old we moved to the other side of Cheam, closer to the primary school Erick and I attended. This meant that we could walk the short distance to school in the morning, which I remember being really happy about.

Cuddington Croft was a co-ed primary school and my recollection of it is overwhelmingly positive. I had lots of friends, including my best friend at the time, who was called Catherine. Catherine lived in the same road as me and had two older sisters, which explained why I always thought of her as being so much cooler than I was. Her sisters used to let her borrow their clothes and make-up, which made her seem really glamorous and grown-up.

My favourite memory of primary school is of a five-day trip to an activity centre, where we got to do various activities like rock climbing, abseiling, canoeing and zip wire. I was in my element. Other children in my class said they felt homesick but I don't remember feeling anything other than excited at the chance to try all these new endeavours.

The activity week was in Year 5. In Year 6 we went to Paris and that trip was deadly dull – it mainly involved walking around practising our very rudimentary French language skills on the locals and looking at cathedrals, I seem to recall. I would have called myself more academic than sporty, back then, yet I realise now I was always happiest doing something physical and was, secretly, a bit of a thrill seeker.

The other good thing about moving house was that it meant we were closer to Nonsuch, which would eventually become my secondary school. I can't remember exactly when I picked up on the idea that this was the 'big' school I simply *had* to go to, but I was very definite about it. I had a notion that it was the best school you could possibly attend and I think that came from some of the other pupils at Cuddington having older sisters there. In my head, going to Nonsuch was an honour and this idea was compounded by the fact that you needed to take an entrance exam to get in.

None of my desire to attend this highly selective grammar school came from the people around me; in fact quite the opposite. I remember spending hours working on practice papers for maths, verbal reasoning and non-verbal reasoning that would form the three exams. My parents never put any pressure on me to do this, I simply wanted to be the best I could be. I even attended a practice 'mock' exam at the local church to get used to working in exam conditions. The idea of attending Nonsuch appealed to my rapidly-developing competitive streak.

Going to Nonsuch changed my life, in so far as it is very unlikely I would have been able to take the cycling talent test anywhere else. Stuart Blunt, who was the coach charged with finding new young talent, has since told me that many local schools turned him down. I think perhaps those schools didn't consider the test important enough to justify their pupils taking time away from their studies. Of course I couldn't have known when I was in Year 6 that Nonsuch would provide the opportunity which would shape the whole course of my life, but I was always determined to go there.

Making the transition from primary to secondary school was hard for me for two reasons. Firstly, I was, and remain to this day, a naturally shy person. I find new environments and people daunting. The second, and perhaps related to the first reason, was that by the time I went to Nonsuch, to tackle the turbulent time of puberty, alopecia universalis had struck.

And so it was I took my first steps into the place that would be home to my teenage years, a time traditionally looks-and-love obsessed, with no hair at all.

CHAPTER 2

HAIR TODAY...

Throughout my childhood, I would get small patches of hair loss across my scalp. They would appear suddenly and re-grow after a few months. The hair that grew back would be white and very fine, like a baby chick, at first. I always found it easy to cover up these small patches, which were about the size of a fifty pence piece, with the help of my mum and some creative hairstyles.

I know now this is called 'alopecia areata' or 'spot baldness' and it's more common than most people realise. According to the NHS website it affects around two in every thousand people in the UK. As a small child, however, I simply assumed everyone had these small bald spots. After all, I had no reason to think I wasn't normal and you don't tend to go around inspecting other people's scalps.

I was about nine years old when the bald patches started to become larger and more alarming. Every time I washed or brushed my hair huge clumps of it would come out and every morning I awoke to find strands laying on my pillow. I found it very confusing and upsetting.

My parents had taken me to various doctors, who had prescribed creams for me to rub into the patches, but none of them worked. Now, it's my understanding that one of the leading causes of alopecia is the immune system fighting off hair follicles as it thinks they are a foreign body, so it's likely that applying products to the outside of your body won't do anything to fix it. As of today, there is no known cure and still very little research. Eventually, I reconciled myself to the idea that there was nothing that could be done.

Occasionally, someone at school would point at me and say, 'I can see your skull!' (they meant 'scalp', not skull. Had they been able to see my skull, I would have needed urgent medical assistance). I don't think the other pupils were doing this in a malicious way, it's in the nature of children to point out things which they consider to be out of the ordinary. I used to brush it off by simply shrugging my shoulders, or sometimes I'd fire a witty comeback like 'and?!'

I was just the right side of puberty for it not to knock my confidence too much, at that stage. As a nine-year-old I wasn't particularly bothered what I looked like so whilst losing my hair was undoubtedly distressing, I still got up and went to school every day. I carried on as normal.

Also, it didn't even occur to me to cut my hair short or to shave it off for the same reason. Many adults with alopecia choose to do this because they think it looks better, aesthetically, but I wanted to have long hair like the other girls. We had a mobile hairdresser who used to come to our home and she suggested I cut my remaining hair to shoulder-length and wear a thick headband at the front. In this way, I could cover up the bald patches at the front and also push my remaining hair back to give the illusion of more thickness there. Temporarily, it was a nice solution, but my hair was still falling out rapidly.

Alopecia universalis – total hair loss – struck when I was ten. Remarkably, I don't remember anyone at school commenting on it in any way whatsoever. I certainly didn't get bullied, which is quite amazing when you think how cruel kids can sometimes be.

Whilst other people pretended they hadn't even noticed, privately the complete loss of my hair had a huge effect on my confidence. I remember crying to my mum and asking her over and over again why my hair wasn't growing back. She offered to order me a wig catalogue (this was in the days before broadband), but I refused. In my eyes, wigs were something old ladies wore and they wouldn't be suitable for me.

As it turns out, I was wrong about this – there are lots of child wigs available. In fact, there's an organisation called the Little Princess Trust, based in Hereford, which takes donations of hair from the public and then makes special wigs, which are specifically designed for children who have alopecia, or have had chemotherapy. I really love that idea.

Without my hair, I relied on school and home feeling 'safe'. These were the places where people knew me and didn't give me those strange, sideways glances I sometimes encountered on the outside. Sheltered within the walls of Cuddington, I carried on as normal yet I shied away from doing anything outside of the sanctum it provided. Out-of-school clubs and parties were now out of the question.

I began to hate having my photo taken. I had never been particularly extrovert, but after alopecia struck, I retreated even further into my shell. When I look back at old photos from that time there are noticeable changes in my body language and the broadness in my smile compared with before the hair loss.

People always presume that alopecia is caused by stress yet as a ten-year-old I genuinely don't remember being stressed about anything apart from, ironically, the loss of my hair: I had a happy home life, plenty of friends at school and nothing in particular to worry about. It's a total mystery to me what triggered it, but after years and years of trying fruitlessly to figure it out, it's something I no longer dwell on.

I remember the only thing that made me nervous about going to Nonsuch, a school I had admired and dreamed of for so long, was how people might react to my alopecia. The prospect of being in a new environment with strangers terrified me and I spent the summer holidays prior to Year 7 worrying about how people might treat to me.

I needn't have fretted so much. Miraculously, once again, people were totally cool about it. People often find it difficult to believe when I tell them that, especially since Nonsuch was an all girls' school and teenage girls tend to have a reputation for being bitchy. Yet if there were any negative comments about my hair (or lack thereof), I certainly wasn't aware of them.

My dad always reckoned that the reason I wasn't targeted at school is that I was always unusually tall for my age and the other girls might have felt intimidated. I'm not sure about that, but it could have been a possible explanation. I'm more inclined to think it's because I was deeply non-confrontational. During my whole time at school I never once started an argument with anybody. I also made an effort to stay away from any gossip or bitchiness, and, ultimately, this was a tactic that paid off. It was also just a lovely school, in fairness.

Still, though, alopecia continued to affect how I felt on a personal level. We used to have regular school discos, with tickets being sold at lunchtime at the school shop. There used to be a mad dash on the day the tickets went on sale, with girls clambering over one another to ensure they got their hands on one.

Not only did I never buy a ticket to the disco, I used to dread people trying to persuade me I should go. Yet they never did. My friends seemed to just instinctively understand that it wasn't something I would want to do. They knew I was missing out, yet to my immense relief they never tried to pressure me. Worse than that, *I* too knew that I was missing out, but I just couldn't bring myself to take on the challenge of socialising outside of school.

I used to spend a lot of time looking at other girls' hair. It wasn't so much the hair itself I envied, it was that they could spend time styling and fiddling with it. Sometimes, girls used to bring straighteners into school and they looked like a fun thing to play with. I definitely felt sorry for myself, but I also made a huge effort to try and focus on other things.

The one thing I never allowed myself to say during this time was 'I wish'. The only wish I had was that my hair would grow back and I didn't want to jinx it by verbalising it. I was superstitious and, whilst I wouldn't say out loud I wished for hair, I also believed that if I actively wished for anything else then I'd use up my wishes and my hair would never grow back.

I lived in hope. Every day when I woke up I would feel my scalp, checking for new baby hairs. On birthdays, when I blew out the candles on my cake I'd make a secret wish for a lustrous set of locks like the other girls.

Back then I would have given anything, literally anything – my place at Nonsuch, my beanie baby collection, my left leg – for my hair to grow. I would even say the same was true until relatively recently. I've now reached a point where I've come to the conclusion that if all my hair miraculously came back, it wouldn't change my life one iota. Now, if I had the option of using my life savings in exchange for a treatment which would guarantee hair growth, I wouldn't do it.

It took a surprising turn of events many years later, in 2012, for me to reach a point of being cool with, even proud of, my alopecia.

In the meantime, I needed a distraction...

CHAPTER 3

THE CONTROLLABLES

Looking back, I never properly confronted all the feelings of confusion, frustration and despair I experienced when I lost all of my hair. Instead, I began to use school work as a coping mechanism. I became a perfectionist by nature, always wanting to get the best grade, an A*. I was hard on myself if I fell short of this target: if I got less than 90 per cent on a test then that was a fail as far as I was concerned.

School work not only gave my mind something other than alopecia to concentrate on, it was something which was directly in my control. The transaction was reassuringly simple in that the more work I put in, the better my grades.

In sport, athletes are often told by their coaches that they should 'focus on the controllables'. By this they mean that worrying about something outside of your control, like for example, how well another team is going to perform, is completely futile. Instead, our attention should be cast on the things we can control, i.e. our own performance.

Subconsciously, I believe my first couple of years at Nonsuch was the time in my life when I started to take on this way of thinking. I understood that I couldn't control whether or not my hair grew, but I could control how much effort I put into my school work. I'm not alone in having thoughts like this – lots of teenagers go searching for something which gives them a sense of control during a time when they don't feel like they have much. In fact, this is often one of the explanations given for eating disorders, so you might think that by comparison working really hard at school was a relatively harmless coping mechanism.

I still think this, to an extent. However, my teachers didn't agree. One parents' evening, a teacher told my mum and dad that she was concerned about me: I was working far too hard, in her opinion. This was a Year 9 parents' evening, the same year British Cycling came into my school, and the teacher in question also told my mum and dad I was 'too intense' and 'needed a hobby'. Little did she know that just a few months later, cycling would have dominated my life to the extent that I spent more time training than studying.

Having thrown myself into school and studiously avoided anything outside of it, it was a particular challenge for me when I realised I wanted to do my Duke of Edinburgh Award. I'd always been keen on the idea of completing the award, which was invented by the Queen's husband to help young people become rounded individuals and contribute to their community. Again, there's a lot of prestige attached to getting a Duke of Edinburgh, which comes in bronze, silver and gold, and involves adopting a service, a skill and a physical activity you wouldn't usually do during the normal routine of school, as well as the expedition. Not for the first time, my natural ambition and competitiveness overrode my shyness and I knew I had to go for it.

I had to get creative at that point – I wanted to be able to fulfil the criteria for the award whilst simultaneously avoiding a situation where strangers might see my hairless head. For my activity, I went back to Cuddington, my old primary school and another safe zone, to create an after-school club. For my new skill, I decided to improve my French and asked my parents if they would get me a tutor, meaning I could stay in the house.

For my service, I worked for a week in a charity shop – Cancer Research UK in Cheam Village. That was pretty scary, but I wore a hat the entire time and was hugely thankful when no one instructed me to take it off.

By the time British Cycling came to my school, I had successfully managed to avoid anything that took me too far outside of my comfort zone. Who knows, if they hadn't shown up, how long I would have continued that way.

Now, I had been given a once-in-a-lifetime opportunity and my overwhelming urge was to go for it. Yet it would be misleading to suggest this was an easy decision. Going to the cycling training camps would mean meeting new people. Perhaps most terrifyingly of all from the point of view of teenage me, it would also mean mixing with boys. When I had completed the initial three tests and the coaches told me I had been selected to come back and advance to the next level it was scary as hell and there was definitely an instinct within me telling me I had to find a way to get out of it.

Yet, at the same time, there was a voice in my head that told me it would be stupid to turn down such a chance. I'm now aware that the voice ringing in my mind was actually that of my parents, who have always told me to grasp the opportunities that life throws you because you don't know where they will lead. Mum and Dad had worked hard to teach me to just say yes and see where that took me before my natural propensity for overthinking crept in.

I'd also been told by British Cycling that I had raw talent. This idea motivated me to face my fears bit by bit, proceeding to each new round of the cycling challenge until it became somehow inconceivable that I would ever pull out. Even though, in theory, there were plenty of times when I could have abandoned British Cycling, there was something in me that told me there was no going back.

Part of me is surprised, looking back, that I kept pushing forward and went through to the training camps. Another part of me thinks it makes total sense, given that my life needed challenges to distract me from my hair loss.

People have since written in the press that alopecia gave me the drive to succeed as an athlete. In reality, it was more like the other way around: through the insecurity of alopecia, cycling had given me a glimmer of hope.

CHAPTER 4

CRASH AND BURN

In 2004, I officially became part of British Cycling's South East 'Talent Team', which was for under-sixteens. This meant I would be given £500 per year to buy myself suitable clothes and equipment, and would be expected to attend monthly training camps, which would each cover a different cycling discipline.

Apparently, British Cycling were torn between offering the single available place on their Talent Team to me and another girl from Nonsuch, Alice, who had also shown promise. I had registered off the charts in terms of what they had seen before in girls my age on the static bike, but Alice had been far better at the actual bike riding side of things. Understandably, they saw this as an important element of actually being a cyclist! They ended up taking both of us and it was a huge help to have a friendly face amongst all the new people.

If I was able to prove myself and rise through the ranks, I had the opportunity to proceed to the Junior National Squad, called the Olympic Development Programme. I had a major obstacle to overcome before that became a possibility, however. The obstacle being that, aside from my impressive power output, I was really quite crap at cycling.

My first training camp would be working on the mountain bike discipline (in which I had already shown such promise during that day in Epping Forest!) quite locally to where we lived, in Burgh Heath. It was a two-day training camp and for new members we would be issued with our first bike, a red Trek mountain bike, which I still have to this day, and some basic cycling kit. Each day involved a lengthy mountain bike ride as well as lessons and workshops about cycling.

For a start, I wasn't fit enough to do loads of riding in one go. For the length of a three-minute 'endurance test' I had been able to put in a lot of power, but I didn't have the stamina to maintain it. Going out for a mountain bike ride with the best riders in the region was nothing short of epic. I puffed and panted up the hills and longed for a break, but as soon as I would catch the group, they would set off again.

There were also things about cycling which the other, more experienced, young riders were completely au fait with, but came as a horrible shock to me. For example, when I was given my first pair of proper cycling shorts, containing a chamois to protect my nether regions, I was surprised to learn I was supposed to wear them without knickers on underneath.

Real cycling shoes were also a revelation and something I initially found difficult to fathom. They have a cleat on them at the bottom, which actually locks you on to the bike's pedals. To insert or remove the cleat requires a special twist of the foot. It's a really weird sensation the first couple of times you try it and I remember the uncomfortable feeling of knowing I couldn't put my feet on the floor to stop the bike, if I needed to. I was encouraged to use these at this first camp but it became glaringly obvious this would be a dangerous idea as every time we stopped, I couldn't unclip my foot and would go toppling over, potentially taking other riders down with me. For now I was put back onto flat pedals and trainers.

During that first ride I also got a puncture. Everyone else looked at me expectantly as if to say 'get on with it, then', becoming more and more incredulous as it gradually became apparent I couldn't even do something as basic as change the inner tube. It took me ages to even get the wheel out of the bike, my cheeks growing redder with embarrassment all the while.

My first ever trip to a velodrome wasn't much better. We were due to visit one of only two in the UK at the time, which was in Newport, South Wales. The boys at the training camp, who outnumbered the girls three to one, were incredibly excited about it. They were chattering animatedly about track bikes, about how they have no brakes, and how treacherous that would be on the slippery and steep sides of the velodrome.

Basically, those boys were showing off, trying to out daredevil each other in the way teenage boys are wont to do. Yet I was a total sucker for it – I couldn't imagine what it would be like to ride under those conditions and wound myself up to a state of high anxiety in the lead up to our trip.

When we arrived, I was given a bike with a fixed wheel, as are traditionally used in velodromes, to get me used to riding it. I just couldn't get my head around the idea of it having no brakes and was fixating on how on earth I was going to stop it. This gave me 'the fear' and the first thing I did after managing to get going on the bike was grab the railings with both hands to steady myself, which sent me crashing off to the right.

That was, technically, my first crash and it really hurt. Sometimes crashes at a low speed can be worse because you have no opportunity to slide and break your fall. I'd barely managed one lap of the velodrome before coming off my bike in front of everyone because I was so terrified. I have since been told that someone was filming the entire incident so I'm sure that will come back to haunt me one day! (Although perhaps, in light of the rest of my career, it will show that you don't have to be brilliant straight away to achieve things.)

All the other riders at the training camp, some of whom have gone on to become champions themselves, such as Alex Dowsett, were excited to grasp the opportunity of riding at the velodrome. To me, it was just so bizarre riding at a forty-two-degree angle and the wood the track was made of just didn't seem grippy enough.

Today, when I tell other cyclists about my first velodrome experience, they find it difficult to believe that I was ever that bad. People assume I must have taken to it like a duck to water, but that was never the case. I was slow. And embarrassing. And often quite dangerous.

Despite the various humiliations I'd suffered to date, I didn't need any persuasion to get back on the bike. That competitive drive within me knew that I had to do it and believed, despite all the evidence to the contrary, this was something I could master. Besides, I didn't want to be forever known as 'the girl who fell off and was never seen again'.

Initially, my determination was simply not to be the worst anymore, especially when another girl at the camp, who had also never ridden on a velodrome before, was able to do it first time. Now I literally had no excuse. After a time, when I was no longer the worst, and I could see how rapidly I was improving, the desire to be the best kicked in and it was this desire which would fuel my professional career.

But I'm getting ahead of myself – there were yet more total disaster stories from training camps to come. In March 2004 we travelled to a BMX track in Milton Keynes. We had to wear a full-face helmet, which was a new and deeply unpleasant experience for me, as were the realities of a BMX track.

I couldn't even master the most rudimentary BMX skills to the extent that I didn't even begin the course with both feet on the pedals – I certainly couldn't jump. In the end I just stood there at the base of the BMX ramp with one foot on the ground, like a total tit.

The next day, they entered us all into a BMX race, my first ever cycling race and the only thing at that point which could make my experience of the camp even worse. Because of the lack of girls, in spite of my very obvious lack of skill, all seven of us had to ride the three heats. I came last, last and last, respectively... And still progressed to the final.

As the seven of us lined up for the final, I knew what would happen: everyone else would race off and I would ride slowly over the bumps. The crowd of parents and other racers were watching. I wasn't even bothered anymore – they'd seen how bad I was, it couldn't get any more humiliating.

Except this time as everyone else raced off and I made my slow progress, there was a mass crash and nearly all of the other girls came down in a pile-up. Meanwhile I continued at my pace and got ahead of the tangle of bodies and bikes on the floor. I wasn't last anymore! Maybe slow and steady *could* win the race! I could smell the finish line and perhaps my embarrassment would be saved.

But no. The other girls untangled themselves, re-mounted

their bikes and despite my huge lead, they caught me and raced ahead. Once again, I was last.

I haven't been on a BMX bike since that camp. They're these tiny little things and to ride them requires all the skills I don't have and none of the ones I do. At least in the mountain biking I'd had periods of power and strength, although I suppose at least the BMX bikes had a single gear and a brake, which was their saving grace over the horrific fixed-gear track machines.

In April, we were off to Milton Keynes again, this time for road cycling. This involved trying another new bike and another new terrain. To absolutely no one's surprise, I crashed again. This time it was more serious than the one I'd had at the velodrome and I had to have a tetanus jab afterwards. I'd skidded at high speed and went sliding across the tarmac, resulting in what is called 'road rash' (a burn to the skin which is extremely painful because of the amount of nerve endings exposed).

There was some concern that my elbow had been broken, but as it turned out all of my wounds were superficial. I mostly remember being annoyed that I'd smashed and ruined the lovely purple watch I used to wear every day.

The crash didn't knock my confidence, only because at that point in proceedings there was no confidence to knock. I was as low as it was possible to be, an over-achiever by nature who was failing spectacularly at everything. I'd tried four distinct different types of cycling and hadn't yet hit upon anything I wasn't the worst at.

It's safe to say at this stage I wasn't showing any signs of being the talented rider British Cycling believed themselves to have discovered. But as we all know about perfectionists, we can't turn our back on a disaster unchallenged.

CHAPTER 5

'SOFT'

I don't remember distinctly thinking much at those initial camps. Perhaps I disassociated myself from them because they were emotionally (and sometimes physically) excruciating for me.

The first positive thing I recall registering during that time was the improvement in my fitness. I wasn't even training properly at that point, just attending the monthly camps and doing about three rides every week, here and there, in between.

The same summer I attended the training camps, I ran a 1500 metre race at a sports competition with other schools and beat the previously undefeated best girl from another local school by a comfortable margin. I'd had a cold and wasn't feeling great and yet I won the race with relative ease. Later, I was selected to represent my borough at the London Mini Marathon. I remember being surprised and overjoyed by how much fitness I'd gained.

I was, somewhat inexplicably, the only person who ever used to volunteer for long-distance running in my school and I'm not sure how I ever expected to do it, before the camps. I have always enjoyed running but my traditional method had been to show up, run, and hope for the best. Training with British Cycling showed me that regularly topping up your fitness reaped measurable rewards and, being the type of person who is intrigued by progress you can track and assess, this made me very happy.

I recall thinking to myself, *okay, so you're failing at cycling but cycling is making you better at other things and that is pleasing.* That might explain why I soldiered on, even after the disastrous BMX experience, which was by far the worst of the camps. I still shudder at the memory.

In July 2004, we visited the Herne Hill open-air velodrome. The velodrome itself was a subject of much contention for many years, with debates over the lease. The grandstand was unsafe to use but also a listed building. It was old, having being built in 1891, and then hosted the London Olympics, way back in 1948, and it's made of concrete as opposed to wood. However, it was nowhere near as steep as the Newport velodrome and the concrete didn't appear as slippery as wood. Also, it wasn't possible to use the facility in the rain so the combination of these factors already meant I had taken a liking to the place.

I'm pleased to say the facility is now thriving, with investment in new facilities and the track being resurfaced. It really is a gem of South London, hiding away behind the houses of Burbage Road. Back then it was our little secret amongst the cycling community with many local residents apparently not even aware of its existence.

Riders from the South East, South West and the Midlands were attending the Herne Hill camp and a quiet and steely resolve had grown inside me: this time, I was definitely not coming last. My personality was emerging and I was becoming competitive with the other girls.

Surprisingly, in the context of my previous solitary velodrome experience, I really enjoyed Herne Hill. I hadn't ridden on a fixed-gear bike since the horrible experience of Newport in February, but overall I had been gaining cycling skills. This time, the combination of the sunshine beating down on us and my new mood had produced a much more successful performance.

Up until that point my attitude towards cycling had been very much along the lines of 'Oh God, what next?' Now, I found myself wanting to race and hoping that the coaches would recommend me for the track nationals. It was a marked gear change, if you'll excuse the pun.

That autumn I was allocated a coach by British Cycling to prescribe me day-to-day training to fit in around my school work and I was seeing huge improvements now I had some regular structure to my bike riding between the monthly Talent Team training camps. My coach's name was Scott Bugden and here I have to thank him for his incredible patience with me for answering my neverending questions of why? I *had* to understand why I was doing training. At school I had always loved science so now the science behind training fascinated me. Thankfully, Scott had plenty of knowledge and was very good at explaining everything. I loved trying the latest sessions he was prescribing me, mainly on the turbo during the week as there were very little daylight hours around school, and relished this hard work. Weekends were spent riding my bike in Nonsuch Park on a Saturday to work on skills and racing in the London Cyclo-Cross League on a Sunday. After a few rounds I was leading the women's league and became totally focussed on winning the League overall.

As my attitude changed, so too did my priorities. Fast forward a year to the summer of 2005. I had begun racing my first full summer season, now aged sixteen and competing in the junior category. Studying was no longer the thing that took up most of my time. I took my GSCEs that summer and didn't get the perfect, straight A* results I had been aiming for. The Joanna from before all my experience with British Cycling would have been devastated by that. As it was, I was merely slightly disappointed. That same summer I won my first National Title – the junior girls' individual pursuit race at the National Track Championships (back at my favourite place, Newport) and that made it palatable to me that my studies were slipping.

I was incredibly proud to pull on the medal and red, white and blue striped jersey and take a lap of honour to the theme music of *Chariots of Fire*. My first happy memory of the Newport velodrome. My cousin Lauren, who was just four years old, was there watching and commented, 'Oh, wow! Jo's won a stripey T-shirt and a big gold coin!'

This was my first major step towards proving my doubters wrong. Everyone who had thought the Talent Team had picked the wrong girl. Everyone who thought my test scores were either a fluke, or irrelevant as I was so bad at actually riding a bike. All the people who had laughed at my crashes and my terror at the bikes with no brakes. I was now the best in the country at something. In the whole of the UK! And I had the medal, and National Champion's jersey, to prove it.

In August 2005, my dedication to cycling paid off when I was invited to a training camp with the Olympic Development Programme (ODP), the relatively newly formed Junior National Squad, which brought with it a whole new, more advanced, set of training camps.

My elation was short-lived. This first training camp as part of the ODP was what I can only describe as horrendous. I thought I'd finally made a breakthrough and was past the days of horrendous training camps, where I was the worst. But no, here we were again.

For starters, it took place after I'd done a week of racing at the Track Nationals and I was already tired when I arrived. The youth hostel we were staying at was at the top of a really steep Welsh hill and we had to ride from there to and from the Newport velodrome, every single day.

We had to ride wearing a rucksack with everything we needed for the velodrome, including a 'track pack' about the size of a laptop case, containing heavy chain rings, tools and sprockets. I have never been good at travelling light, but I later learned that everyone else had left their track packs in lockers at the velodrome, whilst I, oblivious that this was even an option, had lugged mine up that stupid hill every night. It was a silly little mistake, doing something I didn't technically need to, but it exacerbated my existing tiredness and meant my shoulders ached constantly.

Incidentally, there was one boy on our camp who found a sly way to negotiate the track pack problem: he put his belongings in a little wheely suitcase, which meant that there was no way for him to cycle with it on his back like the rest of us with our rucksacks. This forced the coaches to take it in their car and he was then able to ride to the velodrome unencumbered. I remember thinking this wasn't particularly sporting of him, but also pretty clever!

Every day meant riding to the velodrome for proper, hard training such as I'd never undertaken before. This time, it wasn't about learning new skills, it was about increasing fitness and pushing us to our physical limits. After that, we had to do a group road ride before finishing by riding back to the youth hostel.

I had expected to love this kind of hard training – I always relished hard work and despite my lack of skill in the early Talent Team camp days, I had always enjoyed a simple, good, hard workout. But overnight, I'd gone from being on my bike around four times a week to riding three times a day and I just wasn't ready for the increase in workload. Our road rides could be up to three hours at a time. Up until this point I had only joined the occasional club ride once a week, which was usually a maximum of two hours.

To make matter worse, lots of the boys in our group were out to prove they were the best. They were sprinting up hills and 'half-wheeling' each other, which is where one rider in the pairs you are placed in rides faster in an act of showing they are stronger (and therefore superior). I ended up riding quicker than I ever had before in an effort to keep up with the group and my heart rate monitor was reading values averaging in the 160s beats per minute for the whole ride, which was well into threshold territory.

Despite my hard efforts and rapidly accelerating heart rate, I was always getting dropped from the group and that did nothing for my state of mind. I had come here to prove myself and get a place on the Junior National Squad. That December I was to turn seventeen and I knew they only had one other girl of my age. What should have been an opportunity for me to shine kept going from bad to worse.

A lot of people on that camp concluded that I was 'soft'. Since then, 'soft' is a taunt which has followed me throughout my career, even after the Olympic golds. Though I was getting fitter, pushing myself further and training harder than I ever had before, people started to say that I didn't have it, mentally.

I was called in for a meeting with the head coach, Darren Tudor. He had an incredibly broad Welsh accent and initially the most difficult thing was trying to make out what he was saying. Eventually, I realised he was asking me to justify my poor performance. I answered honestly: I was knackered.

Darren and the other coaches didn't have a comprehensive enough understanding of my relatively short history with the sport of cycling. I'm sure they thought that I was being complacent, that I simply wasn't trying hard enough. In reality, the opposite was true.

My back hurt from the rucksack, my legs ached in a more ferocious way than they ever had before. I wasn't sleeping well, increasingly more stressed about the situation. My mood was low from constantly being left behind on the road rides. I now know that a day to relax and recuperate would have gone a long way towards instantly solving all of those problems, but at the time that wasn't presented as a possibility.

I'd also found it difficult being on a camp with a lot of competitive boys. Each time they had shown their superior strength and speed it had meant I would be out the back, grovelling my way up another Welsh climb alone. Today, at junior level, the trend is for girls to train as a separate group and have their own designated coach, which I think is a positive thing. I wish it had been that way when I was doing it. In hindsight it is amazing I carried on, given how tough these camps were.

My hair had grown back a little, although not fully, that summer. I would lose it all again by the time the next summer rolled around, but for the time being a small positive was I felt I didn't look as different as I might have done. Still, the boys were amused by how shy I was and used to tease me. I probably appeared an easy target: the weakest cyclist and the most inexperienced. Whilst at the time I wouldn't say I was bullied, some of the taunting got quite nasty and it undermined my already fragile self-confidence. I kept getting told by the boys it was 'just banter' but it isn't until now, many years on, I realise that it really wasn't okay and I shouldn't have stood for it. To me bullying isn't defined by what someone else calls it, but by how it makes the victim feel. It can be easy for others to describe something as just banter, but if it is hurting the recipient and it isn't two-way, then it is very much more than that.

Even in the context of my aching muscles, exhausted body and every small embarrassment I'd endured, the hardest thing to take was my motives being questioned by Darren Tudor. I knew some of the other riders had treated the training camp as a recreational jaunt – something they were doing because their mates were – but I wasn't one of them. I knew I wasn't there for a fun holiday (after all, a sopping wet Newport at the end of August really wasn't my idea of a vacation), yet this seemed to be the implication behind Darren's words.

After that I found every day, in some way, my commitment to the programme was being questioned. I could only respond by saying, 'I have told you I'm committed and I am.' But I don't think I was necessarily taken seriously.

At a time when no one else appeared to believe in me, it became important for me to disregard the criticism of others: I had to start believing in myself.

CHAPTER 6

THE TORTOISE BEATS THE HARE

When I think back to my experiences on the Talent Team, I am struck by how many people were better riders than me, initially. Yet so many of those more experienced cyclists dropped out of the process, whilst I soldiered on. Although I might not have had the skills yet, I was quickly learning that I had an inner determination and drive. I didn't know it yet, but it was that same drive which would one day make me a world champion.

It will come as no surprise to you to learn that my performance at the initial camp with the ODP wasn't enough to get me on the squad, like I'd hoped it would be. I did, however, continue to work with my local British Cycling coaches, Stuart Blunt and Scott Bugden, all through the winter. I think they were impressed with my perseverance. Expressing a wish to carry on even in spite of my shaky start was beginning to show them that I wasn't as soft or as uncommitted as some might have imagined.

In February 2006 I was invited back onto the ODP programme

and to attend yet another training camp. This time I was the only girl amongst four boys – Alex, Russell, Jonny and Matt. The camp took place during half term but the other girls' holidays fell on different weeks so they went on a camp the following week together.

Whilst I was a lot physically fitter than I had been on the previous camp, I was still suffering on the road rides. The boys were also continuing to pull what I considered to be some pretty underhand stunts. On one particularly horrible, wet and windy road ride they failed to indicate to me that there was a large stone ahead. Cycling etiquette dictates that riders should always try and signal to one another when there are approaching hazards, yet they didn't bother – whether through malice or apathy, I'm not sure.

I went careering into the rock and punctured my tyre. The coaches gave me that look I was becoming so accustomed to – the 'get on with changing it, then' look. Meanwhile the boys kept declaring loudly that they couldn't believe I had failed to notice the stone.

Whilst I was finding it tough, both physically and mentally, this time I could at least keep up. I was also getting precious one-to-one time on the track with coaches. Over the next few months I improved dramatically and there was a very quick transition from the ODP to being accepted onto the Senior Academy Squad.

When I look back to that time and try to work out why I ended up leapfrogging other riders who had initially shown more promise than me, I think perhaps it was an advantage that I came to cycling so late. Many of the other teen riders at the training camps had been practising their skills virtually since infancy and whilst in the first instance this gave them a head start, it also meant that they peaked too soon. Fresh to this art, I was full of abundant enthusiasm.

I was advancing at an incredible speed, but frustratingly I still couldn't completely shake off my reputation for being 'soft'. The label had arisen principally because of two things – the first being that I had made it very clear I did not enjoy riding in the wind and rain. My preference for fair weather conditions is something I maintain to this day and people still ridicule me for it. Crucially, however, now I don't give a damn. The second was that I was visibly upset when other people teased me or questioned my motivations.

The idea still prevails that to be an elite athlete you must develop a thick skin. After all, the adage tells us that nice guys finish last. I definitely didn't have a robust epidermis and I probably still don't, truth be told. If someone made a negative comment, even a seemingly off-hand one, I'd stay up all night thinking about it. I suppose, though, it depends how you define 'thick-skinned' because whilst on the one hand I was letting other people's negativity undermine me, on the other it wasn't stopping me from picking myself up and jumping back on the horse. Or bike, in this case.

I was still at school at this point, so training camps had to fit around the academic holidays. Darren Tudor was coaching me, mainly over the phone. He believed in me now, I felt, and I felt honoured to have instruction from the national junior coach, whose accent by that stage I was learning to decipher. I was cycling after school every day and occasionally even before – on some days my lessons didn't start until 10.20am, meaning I could fit in a cheeky ride before they began. I'd be on my bike by 6.30am, returning at 9.30 to shower and head to class.

I had one complete day off the bike every week, on a Monday.

Tuesday to Thursday was hard training. On Friday I'd taper down slightly, in preparation for spending Saturday and Sunday taking part in races.

Darren would instruct me to find specific terrains around my house to practise on, which sometimes proved a challenge. He wasn't familiar with Surrey, which is very different from Wales. I used to scour maps looking for the sort of roads he'd said I needed to train on that day. My main limiting factor was the lack of daylight during the winter. I didn't particularly want to be cycling along rough country roads in the pitch darkness and in February the light started to fade at around 3.30pm, when school kicked out.

There wasn't a velodrome nearby for me to train on, but I worked hard on the turbo trainer and rollers, and rode on the roads whenever possible. Additionally, I was racing nearly every weekend, sometimes in the UK and sometimes abroad.

I was rapidly becoming one of the best young riders in the country and was starting to see a pathway opening up in front of me. Soon I began to believe going to the Olympics was what I was meant to do with my life.

My brother Erick was also getting into cycling at this stage, which effectively forced our family to become avid fans of the sport. My parents' lives were absolutely dominated by cycling. Being in our late teens, that was the time when we were supposed to be going off and doing our own thing, but suddenly Erick and I were demanding much more of our poor mum and dad's time. We often had different camps or races at opposite ends of the country at the weekends, to which we frequently required a lift. Luckily, we had two cars – one a people carrier and the other much smaller – and Erick and I would constantly bicker about who got to take the larger vehicle.

Much more secretly, we used to each hope to get Dad as driver, because he was more hands-on with the bikes (although I feel obliged to add at this juncture that Mum had her advantages too – she was the better at navigation). There always used to be a protracted debate about whose race was 'more important' and who therefore 'deserved' the 'better driver'.

Taking a new direction and dedicating so much of my time to the bike meant forfeiting the rites of passage other teenagers take for granted. I hadn't been vastly popular at school and now I started to drift away from the couple of close friends I had made. Whilst they'd be spending their weekends at the shopping centre doing all the usual adolescent things, like trying on clothes and gossiping about boys, I'd have to go somewhere like Lancashire for a race. This was pre-social media so, whilst some of my friends did take an interest in my race results online, I had no real way of connecting with them and keeping in touch.

I also missed what I suppose now would be called my 'prom' but back then we called the 'May Ball'. It was the biggest event in our school's social calendar and I couldn't attend because I had a race the next day. Those missed opportunities made me even more grateful I wasn't talent spotted until a relatively late age. Each small resentment might have brought me that much closer to burning out and giving up.

Meanwhile I was making friends in the cycling world and this, to a large extent, compensated for the school friendships I'd had to surrender. Lizzie (then Armitstead, now Deignan) and I became very close. Over time, she would become my closest friend and be one of the driving forces that helped me to recover the self-esteem alopecia had robbed me of.

I didn't know an awful lot about nutrition, back then, so my main priority foodwise was to eat enough to give me the energy for my hugely increased quantity of physical activity. I'd even go so far as to say I developed a fear of not eating enough – I needed vast amounts to sustain me. I certainly wasn't aware of the importance of getting enough protein, so I used mainly to eat bowl upon bowl of pasta, thinking that I would fill me up.

I've always had a naturally slim build and these changes in diet and activity were making me put on weight. This was something I welcomed wholeheartedly. I knew how important it was to be muscular. If other riders or the coaches said my legs were 'looking good', I knew that meant they were toned with muscle and I basked in that compliment.

People ask me if there has ever been a conflict in having the body of an athlete and feeling attractive or feminine. The only answer I can give is that I have existed for many years in a world where success is attractive. The boys I was hanging out with were other cyclists, who thought it was cool to be fast and strong. Equally I thought my toned legs looked great in a dress.

What was causing conflict was my desire to stay on at Nonsuch and finish my A-levels. October marked the end of my ODP career and I had to send an application to become part of the Academy. The online application form asked me many deep and searching questions – what were my ambitions for the future? Was cycling a priority for me?

Whilst I had taken part in the Junior World Championships in summer 2006, I'd only been placed ninth and eleventh. In actual fact, that was a pretty good result considering the stage I was at, but I was gutted. It also meant I was only eligible for the lowest level of annual funding as part of the Academy – £6,000.

My application to the Academy programme had been accepted but this was a residential programmed based in Manchester. Some riders my age choose to leave school immediately post

GSCEs and dedicate themselves to the sport. That was a decision I considered, but I felt strongly that it was important to get to a certain level in my academic education, though, which would allow me to go to university later if I wanted to. So I took on the tricky task of trying to juggle my new-found vocation whilst continuing full-time study.

I ended up missing a total of twelve weeks of school that year, which included a ten-day training camp in Majorca, track competitions and road races. I also had a new coach, Dan Hunt. He was the women's endurance coach and combined us, the Academy, and the women's Senior Squad together for a couple of camps. This, along with Dan's general ethos, upped the intensity of my training still further.

It was very obvious to me that Dan didn't really enjoy coaching people who were still in school. As a sports scientist he found it difficult to juggle our inflexible schedules with his precise methods. He set me a particularly tough training plan, doing hours I have never done since, even as an Olympic athlete. At weekends I'd be riding for up to five hours. Yet I found that, despite the obstacles, I enjoyed the intense nature of the coaching. Dan certainly knew what he was talking about and the scientific nature of his training plans appealed to me.

One problem made itself apparent, however – in Surrey I didn't have access to a velodrome. So, when my A-levels were out of the way it was time to start the next chapter of my life.

Time to move to Manchester.

CHAPTER 7

THE 'STUDENT' YEARS

What followed my move to Manchester are what I always call my 'university years'. Although, of course, I wasn't actually at university in the traditional sense, that was definitely the sort of feel that period of my life had.

British Cycling arranged for groups of us enrolled at the Academy to stay in shared flats in Fallowfield, a very student-y area of Manchester. We paid them £3,000 per annum, for which in return British Cycling paid our rent and bills and arranged all of the logistics associated with them. This made life very easy for us, practically speaking.

On the day of my move, I loaded all of my possessions into my little Citroën Saxo and drove up North, all the while feeling incredibly excited at the prospect of my new life and independence. Little things about living away from my family home for the first time held a novelty for me, like the cool key fob we were given to allow us access to the building and the buzzer system for letting in visitors.

I'd enjoyed my trip to Asda to pick up crockery, cutlery and other small finishing touches for my flat immensely. Whilst British Cycling provided most of the basics, it pleased me to put my own stamp on the new territory and mark it out as my space.

The flat was shared between me and Katie Curtis, a Welsh rider the same age as me with a far more impressive list of wins who had also made the progression from ODP to Academy, with other male and female sprint and endurance cyclists occupying the wider block. Other young people living in the same area were, I think, always quite bemused by us, wondering why we were constantly hustling back and forth, carrying bikes and equipment. Our peculiarity was cemented by the fact that we used to refuse to keep our precious bikes in the designated area in the underground car park in case they were damaged or stolen, instead taking them inside with us, like pets. This was technically totally against the rules, but we didn't care.

Today, I live in what I would describe as 'real' Manchester and realise that Fallowfield was a good way of easing a Southern girl like me into Northern culture. Before moving, I'd considered Watford 'North'. When I first arrived at Fallowfield, I found everyone's accents completely unfathomable. I laugh when I think of that, now.

Our flats were smack bang in the middle of an area positively ripe for distractions from and obstacles to our training. We were directly above a Starbucks and a Wetherspoons. There was a McDonald's and a Nando's a few seconds' walk away, plus innumerable pubs and bars. The area had a reputation as a 'party zone'.

Looking back, I wonder whether this was a deliberate ploy on the part of British Cycling. We had to be up early each day for training and they had plonked us in what was probably the worst part of Manchester in terms of giving you the best chance of sticking to that routine. Of course, being able to resist temptation and focus is key to being a successful athlete and, in that respect, our new environment would certainly sort the women out from the girls.

Every Wednesday afternoon, we had an Academy education session, which covered a different aspect of life as an elite athlete. The most obvious of these was food and nutrition. I've found that a lot of people who exist outside the sporting world think that eating as a pro athlete must involve restricting yourself. In reality as a track rider, it's mostly about consuming high calories to sustain the massive amounts of training you're doing each day, although of course it's important to eat the right type of foods.

We would be permitted the occasional rare night out, after a big race, but then it was straight back into training. For a treat, we might have a takeaway once a month, but my big weakness was chocolate or cookies. Living opposite a Sainsbury's made the temptation incredibly high! At this stage in my career my food wasn't closely monitored by a nutritionist, but it was very much a sense of 'you're only cheating yourself' if you made bad choices. Occasionally, the cyclists in our block used to have a 'Come Dine With Me' style event, where we used to cook for each other and invite each other over. We were all keen on a dessert and that was never banned, just a case of everything in moderation.

Another Wednesday session involved learning how to avoid illness. This was something I knew woefully little about at the time. I remember I had thought on the various training camps I'd attended leading up to that point that the other riders were being freakishly OCD-like in their attitude to catching germs. They were all using alcohol hand gels virtually every time they touched anything.

In this session, I learned that being obsessive about germs is in actuality an essential part of elite athleticism. Not only did we have to use alcohol hand gels, they had to be the right ones (foams were better than liquids as they lasted longer) and used in the correct fashion to completely coat every millimetre of our hands.

Illnesses, even mild colds, are anathema to athletes. Not only can they prevent you from performing your best on the one day you have to showcase your abilities, they can interfere with training. Some people train through a cold but having done this myself, I would now never train when ill at all. Usually, I find this prolongs the illness and I feel so lousy, I am not even getting quality training done anyway. I take illness as a sign my body has had enough and needs a rest. Unfortunately for me, throughout my career, and despite my new-found obsession with hand foam, illness always seemed to plague me. I had been told alopecia was due to my immune system fighting off my hair follicles thinking they were a foreign body, so I wondered if a combination of this, plus fatigue from training, meant I was never very resilient to all the little bugs. Either way, hand foam never left my side for the rest of my career!

We learned about the proper way to stretch, which is a way to limit the chances of sustaining the other main obstacle to an athlete's performance: injury. I was taught how to use a foam roller to keep the 'IT band' supple (a process called myofascial release – which gives a similar affect to a deep tissue massage) and minimises the risk of knee injury.

There was a session on how to interact with the media, but I missed that one. I don't think that's hindered me since, particularly. When you're interviewed directly after a race, high on adrenaline, filled with lactic acid and reeling from victory or defeat, all you can really do is give an authentic reaction. I'll never know what I missed, of course, but it might have come in handy during the press furore in 2012 surrounding my podium appearances without a wig.

We tackled the less obvious things, too. We were encouraged to improve our French because it's a widely spoken language in the cycling community. The UCI (Unione Cycliste Internationale) is based in a French-speaking part of Switzerland and were also given some advice on managing our finances.

Basically, those Wednesday afternoon classes helped me to organise my life.

For leisure, I did anything where I could be sitting, like going to the cinema. People are quick to assume that athletes are super-active all the time – that we must be always running up flights of stairs instead of taking lifts, for example. In reality, the opposite is true – we always, *always* take the lift. If you're not training, the rule is that you must be resting as fully as possible. In fact, we have a saying: 'Don't stand when you can sit, don't sit when you can lie and don't just lie when you can be asleep'.

I didn't find it particularly challenging to block out the takeaways and nightclubs, or to rest properly when I was supposed to. Like most of the people there, I realised I was being given a rare opportunity and so I grasped it with both hands. Later, I'd reflect that if you couldn't hack it at Fallowfield, you stood absolutely no chance in an Olympic Village, which was party central, so this would be good preparation.

Many, however, didn't make it. Initially, Katie and I were sharing with another female rider but one day we came back from a race to find her and her belongings had disappeared. We never saw her again.

The flats themselves had a combined living and dining area

and a couple of bedrooms each. In ours, one of the bedrooms was much larger than the others and had its own ensuite. When each occupant came and went there were always big discussions about who would get it, which would be settled with a draw.

The flats weren't well insulated and many of the windows didn't even seem to close properly. We had electric heaters, which we'd crank up to the maximum before we left for a training ride so that the place would be warm and cosy when we returned, often chilled to the bone. One day, we got an email from British Cycling saying our electricity bills were unacceptably high. I think that generally got ignored and we continued to use the electric heaters and the tumble dryer, which generated plenty of heat in itself.

A lot of people complained about the quality of the flats, but personally I loved them. Perhaps they were a little basic and maybe the fact that the windows didn't work wasn't totally ideal, but for our first taste of freedom in the big wide world I considered them very decent. The best thing about them was that they were only a fifteen-minute ride to the track. To find decent routes for road riding on the outskirts of Manchester was a little harder, but since I was primarily there for the velodrome, that didn't bother me so much.

For the first time, I had the opportunity to structure my day around training, after spending so much of my life doing things the other way around. Our days began at 8am, so we'd arrive at the velodrome at 7.30 to get the bikes set up. Most days we would be finished by 5pm, although sometimes it was later if we raced track league. We used to joke that we were like vampires in the winter, never seeing the daylight, but actually I enjoyed having the opportunity to focus solely on our increased training volume.

It was a huge advantage to have such unencumbered access to a nearby velodrome. In Surrey, the nearest one had been a two-and-a-half-hour drive away. Being able to visit the track so frequently really escalated my abilities.

My parents were still very supportive at this time and, as well as ferrying the things from home I had forgotten and suddenly realised I needed to and from Manchester, they'd come and watch races whenever they could. My dad in particular really got into it, despite not having much interest in cycling historically.

I had a few small hiccups. Smartphones hadn't yet been invented, so I would use a TomTom sat nav, stowed in my back pocket, to find my way out of Manchester. The other riders had told me that Wilmslow was the place to head for if I wanted to get to the Cheshire lanes so I entered it into my TomTom and told the other girls to follow me. The TomTom ended up taking us straight down the A34, one of the busiest dual carriageways heading out of Manchester. My fellow riders were deeply unimpressed.

If I had to go back and give my eighteen-year-old self some advice, I'd probably tell her not to take everything quite so seriously. From the very beginning I was incredibly driven, determined not to let the party environment turn my head and devastated when my performance wasn't perfect. I should have had more of an awareness that mistakes are a necessary part of learning; you simply cannot grow and develop without them.

This was also the period of my life when I had the conscious realisation of just how much I wanted to make it to the Olympics. Other riders took the decision to continue their education and go to university and whilst this had always been part of my life plan, the urgency of the impending 2012 London Olympics meant that I felt it was more important to focus on sport at that moment.

The coaches had made it very clear from the start that they were there to spot Olympic talent. Every subconscious notion I'd harboured during childhood about one day being an Olympic athlete seemed to crystallise at that point.

It's weird when I look back to all the times people said 'You could go to the Olympics one day' when I was running and swimming during my childhood. I didn't take it seriously and I used to respond by saying 'yeah, maybe', or something along those lines. But the opportunity that fell into my lap at Nonsuch and finding cycling had in fact brought me closer to the destiny others had predicted for me.

I guess that was when I started to believe there was such a thing as fate.

CHAPTER 8

THE CHIMP PARADOX

'The Uni Years' (as they shall henceforth be known) introduced me to a man who would go on to be incredibly influential upon my career, as well as the innermost workings of my mind – Professor Steve Peters.

Steve is probably most famous for having written *The Chimp Paradox*, a book which is considered seminal by many eminent psychologists and has sold millions of copies across the globe. In it, he introduces his reader to three key components of our brain – parietal, frontal and limbic.

The parietal brain, says Steve, is most like a computer, efficiently taking care of all the things we do without consciously thinking about them and keeping us functioning at a basic level. The frontal brain is the part that makes us a human being and contains elements like our personality, our values and our morality. The limbic brain is purely emotional. It doesn't have any concept of right or wrong, it just registers emotions and responds. This is the part of the brain Steve famously nicknamed 'the chimp'.

The chimp's needs are simple – basically it wants to feed, breed and either fight or flee from danger – and its reactions are extreme and distracting when those needs aren't met. Because the chimp is distinct from our individual personalities and our personal ethics, which are contained in the frontal brain, we are not responsible for how it might react to something. However, Steve argues, we are responsible for how we, then, in turn respond to our chimps. In essence, if you keep your chimp happy, it won't dominate your outward behaviour.

According to *The Chimp Paradox*, the more sophisticated parts of our brains, the human and computer parts, can't operate properly unless we have met the needs of the limbic brain first. So, whether you're intent on attaining your brain's intellectual or creative potential, or in my case performing under pressure as an athlete, it's incredibly important to have a good relationship with your inner chimp.

I first met Steve Peters when he came in to do one of our regular Wednesday afternoon Academy education sessions. He was ostensibly there to teach us how to mentally prepare for the pressure of elite sport. In actuality, we spent far more time quizzing him about the high-profile murder cases he has worked on throughout his totally fascinating career. I found him to be as straight-talking as he was intriguing and I liked him a lot.

British Cycling arranged for me and the other riders to have access to some one-to-one sessions with Steve over the course of the next year, despite the fact that the Beijing Olympics were fast approaching. He was ready to talk with us about absolutely anything, whether how to tackle pre-race nerves or the best way to handle a teammate who was being difficult. He even heard us out on any issues we had with the coaches and staff. Usually, he brought our problem back to his chimp analogy. Occasionally, he'd say things that seemed harsh, but contrary to my 'soft' reputation I actually liked that aspect of him. I enjoyed having a perspective from someone who existed outside of the incestuous and close-knit world of cycling.

Steve taught me about the brain's 'flight, fight or freeze' mode. He explained that this used to be a very useful function of the mind, back when we were cave people and regularly had to survive the reality of potentially deadly predators around every corner.

Back then, we'd encounter danger – let's say a tiger for the sake of argument – and rather than dithering and hesitating about the best way to tackle the situation (which is a bad survival choice because it would probably result in the tiger eating us before we had the time to respond) our bodies would immediately flood with adrenaline, the conscious, logical mind would shut down and we would automatically have the overwhelming urge to run away from the tiger, freeze so it won't see us or (less likely) take it on in a fight. That is what the flight, fight or freeze mechanism was invented for.

Whilst the world has changed unrecognisably (after all, it was rather unlikely I was going to come face-to-face with a tiger on the mean streets of suburban Manchester), our instincts remain the same. Each time we are put into a stressful situation in the modern world, the chances are our brains will put us into flight, fight or freeze mode. This is a problem for a lot of people because their instinctual response to stress isn't serving them well because it's not appropriate for the modern situation they find themselves in. This is especially true of professional athletes.

In a race or game scenario, fight, flight or freeze is probably the last thing you'd want. Whilst the adrenaline coursing around our bodies can help us take our performance up a notch, we also need to have clear judgement and to be fully in control of our bodies' responses. If we're unable to achieve these things, it will most likely equal a disastrous result.

Steve taught me that the best way to avoid flight, fight or freeze is to change the blood flow in the brain, directing it to the frontal lobe. He took me through a 'mental warm up', which I could do trackside before a race in order to make this happen. This was, incidentally, the first time I was introduced to the concept of 'focussing on the controllables', a mantra I've referred to before and will again. It has served me incredibly well throughout my years of pro cycling.

Steve also taught me that to avoid a fight, flight or freeze response (or 'silence the chimp', as he always calls it), you have to address whatever it is your mind is telling you is a threat. You simply can't try to ignore fears, your brain will only shout them louder. Instead you must take your worries out into the open and face them.

In the case of a race, it's likely your mind will start presenting you with all the worst-case scenarios, asking questions like, what if I can't perform? What if another team goes faster? What if I fall off and crash? What if I DIE?! It's important to eliminate those fears in order to release them.

Steve said the best way to do this was to write down all the worries circling around my brain. Seeing them written down would not only get them out of my head in the most visual and physical way possible, it would help put them into perspective. After all, some things simply look ridiculous once they are written down. If I really wanted to 'exercise my chimp' then the best thing to do, he told me, was to go through each fear one by one and say out loud why it was a stupid thing to fret over. I'd reassure myself by saying 'obviously you are not going to fall off and come last. You have done this a thousand times before'.

Another top tip Steve gave me was to phone someone who was a bit removed from the situation, say a family member or friend who hadn't come along to watch the race. I've found this to be an invaluable distraction as an athlete. When you hear the voice of someone who is existing in a 'normal' world outside of the velodrome or track, you realise there is more to life than riding around in a circle really fast. My dad became my go-to person to call and come my first World Championship, even though he was due to come and watch, he spent the morning on the phone to me.

I've practised Steve's techniques so many times now, they are second nature to me. I don't do the mental warm up consciously any more, it's simply a ritual I go through automatically (probably stored in my parietal brain, actually), as natural as doing a physical warm up or stretching. I've since been told that I am one of the riders who deals best with pre-race nerves and the pressure to perform. I credit Steve with a large proportion of my abilities in this area.

In those early days at the Academy, Professor Peters and his chimp taught me to see races as opportunities as opposed to threats. It was exactly the advice I needed.

CHAPTER 9

TEAM PURSUIT

Moving to Manchester coincided with some big news in the world of women's cycling – the team pursuit, up until now just an event for men, was going to be introduced for women at World Cup and World Championship level. Unfortunately this was too late to make the Beijing programme (where there were seven events for men in track cycling but just three for women – a fact that boggled my mind we could have this level of inequality in 2008), but it was a big step forward for women's cycling at World level.

From late 2007 I threw myself into training for the team pursuit. Up until that point everything I had done had been focussed on the individual pursuit, which was the Olympic event. The difference between the two events, aside from one taking place in solitude and the other as part of a team, has to do with strategy. In an individual pursuit you're basically just trying to get around the velodrome over the required distance as quickly as you possibly can.

In team pursuit, you are working towards an optimum maximum speed which all three of you in the team can realistically maintain over the distance of three kilometres. If you are at the front, in 'man one' position, your job is to put in massive amounts of power and get everyone up to that speed. You will then usually 'swing up' and drop to the back of the team to allow the second rider, who has benefited from you taking the brunt of the wind up until that point and is therefore more energised and fresh to continue to maintain the pace. The three of you proceed to swap positions at regular intervals, as per a strategy devised amongst the team and your coach beforehand.

The race takes place over a total of twelve laps and on average each cyclist will lead for a lap before changing. That's the theory, anyway. In reality it often doesn't pan out like that. The idea is that having accelerated up to speed in lap one, you maintain a steady speed for laps two to twelve. Your coach will time you to a tenth of a second for each lap and will take steps forwards or backwards to indicate if you are too slow or too fast from the sidelines.

For a team pursuit competition all teams will ride with the track to themselves in the qualifying round to set a time and then the teams with the fastest two times will race against each other for the gold and silver medals, and the third and fourth fastest teams will race against each other for the bronze medal. Or at least this was the case in 2008. The regulations have since changed but for the purpose of writing about my upcoming competitions, this was the procedure.

The individual pursuit and team pursuit require slightly different physical abilities. Although both take place on the same bike and both over a distance of three kilometres, the individual pursuit is a constant, sustained effort for around three and a half minutes. In the team pursuit, by having two other teammates sharing the workload on the front, you are able to cover the same distance quicker. It also benefits an athlete who is better at putting out a high burst of power for a lap, then spending two laps 'recovering' in the wheels. I use the word 'recovering' in single quotes here, as it is by no means easy. But the power requirements in man two or man three position will be on average about 30 per cent lower than on the front.

It's important to understand each person's strengths and weaknesses in the team. Some riders are really good at starting fast but will tire quickly, others have the stamina to maintain speed in the race's dying stages. On the day of the competition, we'd also have to take into account how we were all feeling, physically and mentally. If one team member wasn't at their best for whatever reason, we had the option to adjust the formation accordingly.

Team pursuit is an exact science: if you are at the front and bringing the team up to speed from a standstill, you have to try not to go so hard your body fills up completely with lactic acid from the exertion, which might cause your legs to seize up later in the race. Thereafter, the art is being able to adjust your speed by minuscule fractions of a second, according to the signals you are receiving from your coach. On lap twelve, it's the hardest you'll ever work in your life and by the end of the race, you are always completely spent. Riders often do a couple of victory laps before the elation wears off and then stagger off the track from exhaustion.

My training at the velodrome began in the winter, as is traditional – a track cyclist's life typically involves being on the track in the winter months and on the road in the summer. These are broken up by a series of World Cups between November and February and the World Championships in March.

All winter, I trained for six days per week, twice per day. I hadn't expected much from my first team pursuit sessions – after all, I'd never done it before – yet my coach told me I took to it 'like a duck to water'. I was finally finding my niche.

Lizzie had sustained a fairly major injury and Katie Curtis was poorly with a stomach ulcer that winter, so once again I found myself in the position of being the only girl. There were eight male academy riders living in Manchester and using the velodrome and so I ended up training with them.

Fortunately, the men, many of whom I had first known as boys in various training camps, were starting to mature by that point. I no longer had to endure endless teasing and found that trying to keep up with them as they tore around the track was dramatically improving my race times. For them, it was just training but for me, I was in race gear and desperately hanging off the back of the group and it forced me to up my game. Until that point, my forte had been power output. Now, I was developing speed.

The individual pursuiters for Beijing were Rebecca Romero and Wendy Houvenaghel. I joined them on training camps and some occasional sessions on the track in Manchester when they were around between various other competitions. Becs and Wendy were older and more experienced than me and took me under their wing, passing down tips and techniques which would improve my performance from advice about recovery to pacing efforts in training.

In the past Becs had been a rower and had won an Olympic silver medal in Athens 2004. Wendy had even more of a dramatic career change, having previously been a dentist in the RAF. She'd never done an Olympics before but was winning a lot of races domestically, had represented England in the Commonwealth Games and now progressed to qualifying for Beijing. There was a lot of buzz and excitement around the both of them: having had no British female cycling medallists at the previous Olympics, the women's endurance squad was looking very strong.

Becs made it clear that what she really wanted was a chance to win the individual pursuit. She was without doubt the most single-minded and driven person I have ever met. This made her interesting to observe and in many ways an excellent teammate. Her speciality was shouting at us in a very motivational way during training on tough days climbing never-ending mountains in Majorca. She would yell things like 'Come on! To the next tree! You're nearly there!' as we grovelled up climbs.

I found Becs utterly fascinating, because she didn't care at all about pleasing people, or what others thought of her. She wouldn't let the universal requirement to be polite jeopardise her race, ever.

An example of this was during a training camp when a group of male and female GB cyclists were sat down at dinner. The women were at one table and the men at another (don't ask me why). There was a member of staff sat on our table at dinner, who was at the time working for Steve Peters, and she was suffering from a cold. There was one remaining place at the table when Becs arrived, next to her, and she was expected to sit there, which meant that most dreaded of all things for a professional athlete: proximity to germs.

Becs walked into the room, saw where she was expected to sit, shrugged in an exaggerated fashion and took herself off to sit at the boys' table. There was no apology or explanation – nothing was going to come between her and her performance. I respected her for this and learnt a lot from her.

In March 2008, the World Championships were being held in my new hometown, Manchester. As the host nation we already had an automatic place in the Women's Team Pursuit, despite not having ridden at any of the World Cup rounds that winter, which usually act as qualification. It had been obvious all winter that two of the three places in the team would go to Wendy and Becs as they were head and shoulders about everyone else, but that third spot was up for grabs.

There were many other female cyclists who were trying to break into team pursuit after it had been introduced. Wendy and Becs' coach, Dan Hunt, had been working with them since 2006. Word had reached him about me being 'soft' and I don't think he was particularly enthusiastic about me as a choice for the team. Once again, I was having to prove myself amidst doubts about my abilities.

All my sessions desperately chasing the men's Academy riders around the track had paid off and I was team pursuiting well. I was developing good leg speed and all the time bettering my skills at riding in close proximity to a rider in front. We had very few women's training sessions together – with it being Olympic year, the focus was very much on Beijing and the Olympic events. But when we did train as a women's group, this was my opportunity to prove myself to get the third spot.

Fortunately I proved my worth, and it was confirmed I would be representing Great Britain at my first ever senior World Championships, just nine months after leaving school and relocating to Manchester. I was aware this was going to be a big one. A home World Championships, in Olympic year, with a huge amount of expectation on the GB team to deliver. I'd like to say I was ready, but in reality I was a nervous wreck.

Wendy was very different from Becs and was more of a maternal figure, at least when I first knew her. She was thirty-three at the time, which meant there was a big fourteen-year age gap between her and me. Wendy's contribution to the team came out more on race day itself than in training, when she told me to 'lean' on her if I found myself in difficulty. I found this particularly comforting when she said this in the pits just before we began to warm up. Even in spite of all my advice from Steve Peters, I was shaking with nerves and needed that extra reassurance.

There was a massive and obvious rivalry between Wendy and Becs, and they took it with them all the way to the Beijing Olympics. Yet, being in the position of riding the team pursuit together meant we were forced to cooperate, which must have been strange for them. I didn't get involved in the dynamic between them and I can't say I really understood it that much. Just as when I was at school, my instinct told me to stay out of any potential confrontation and try to be friendly to everyone.

Since we hadn't gone through the normal qualification process for the Manchester World Championships and had qualified a team pursuit team via a host nation place, we would be riding first in the qualifying rounds. This put us at a potential disadvantage. If you are the last team to ride in the qualifiers you can see how fast the other teams are riding and make last-minute adjustments to your team strategy accordingly. If they're faster than you, you need to match their speeds – unless you qualify in the top two, you cannot go on to race for gold. If they are slower, it means you can win by a comfortable margin and conserve your much-needed energy for the next round.

In the absence of a team's time to use as a yardstick, Dan had selected a time for us. It was faster than we, or, as far as we were aware, anyone had ridden up to that point.

I braced myself for what would be my biggest challenge to date.

CHAPTER 10

DISASTER AND TRIUMPH

I'd gone through my whole mental routine and succeeded, at least partially, in silencing my chimp. All that was left was for me to try and hold it together amidst the thunderous, deafening roar of the home crowd, a totally new experience for me at the time.

The World Championships were a big deal – I'd already met famous cyclists here I'd only ever heard of in legends heretofore. Brightly coloured branding was everywhere, providing another assault on my senses, and making the previously familiar Manchester velodrome look like an entirely different venue. There were four and half thousand spectators who had flocked to Manchester that year and about 99 per cent of them were British. The noise they made every time Britain was mentioned was totally overwhelming.

I was in 'man two' position, sandwiched between Wendy at the front and Becs at the rear. Having just about held myself back from being sick before we lined up, the beeps were now counting down, ready for us to start. Still a little shaky, we got away from the line cleanly and settled into our formation. Wendy rode the first one-and-a-quarter laps, bringing us up to the required speed before swinging up and putting me in the lead. As we entered the banking and turned to the left, I had a terrible realisation: my handlebars were loose.

I thought about signalling to the coach but it was too late – the race was underway. We had talked through the regulations about a mechanical mishap but we hadn't discussed this! I was on the front of the team, with loose handlebars, and I had no choice but to keep riding.

The dimensions of a velodrome are designed in such a way that you don't really need to steer to go around each bend. If I were going at Chris Hoy's speed it may have been more of an issue, but at the bottom of the track and on the front of the team I could at least still ride around the oval-shaped track. But this wasn't an individual pursuit on my own, it was a team pursuit. After my lap on the front I needed to swing up the track, change direction and swing back down to join the rear of the team – an extremely technical and precise manoeuvre. But moving my handlebars made absolutely no difference to the direction of the front wheel! Panic had well and truly set in, yet I continued to race around the velodrome, rapidly approaching the end of that lap.

Let me try and impress upon you how panic-inducing this development was: I was riding the most important race I'd ever ridden in my life and *my bike was broken*! It's like that dream some people have where they are sitting their school exams and they look down and suddenly realise they are naked.

This development should have spelt calamity, yet at the same time I became conscious that my bike wasn't going to do what I was asking it to, I experienced an unprecedented shot of adrenaline. I've never experienced anything quite like this since and the closest thing I can describe it as was like getting an electric shock. I credit this adrenaline with the fact that somehow, throughout the course of the race, I managed to achieve exactly what I was supposed to. I used the weight of my body to manoeuvre the bike up and down to execute the change and somehow with a combination of adrenaline and desperation not to let my teammates down, I rode, technically, the best I ever had up to that point.

I still don't know how I managed it – I didn't feel like myself at all. But thanks to a strong team effort, we rode a time of 3:25.7. Dan Hunt had set us a target time of 3:25. I can't stress this too strongly: it was a miracle, to have come within seven-tenths of the target time under such circumstances.

In the immediate aftermath of our miraculous race, the challenge was how on earth I was going to dismount if my handlebars weren't working. People I speak to often aren't aware of exactly how much effort it takes to get off your bike when you're in huge amounts of pain, even after a normal race. What usually happens is that you gradually slow down before descending to the very bottom of the track, then steer off before being caught by a mechanic.

I began to feel quite scared when I realised I was going to struggle to steer off the track and then ride around on the flat inner area with no banking to allow me to turn the corners. I made my way off the track in the home straight, kicked back on the pedals as hard as I could to slow myself down quickly, and thankfully a mechanic was there ready to grab me. It was then that my legs gave way.

The excess adrenaline I'd produced to get me through the race had dissipated and suddenly, my legs, which were choc-full of lactic acid, simply refused to work. I was pretty much dragged by the mechanics and carers back into the track centre, where I collapsed onto the floor in the pits. Unable to move or speak, I was just lying here. Dan was getting more and more exasperated, and quietly asked me to 'stop causing a scene' – I think he thought either I was just being embarrassingly dramatic (and therefore very un-British), or all his previous reservations about me not being able to hack it were coming true. As far as he was concerned, everything had gone according to plan and yet here I was collapsing after the qualifier. He must have been wondering how I was going to manage the final.

At this point I wasn't able to get my breath back to speak and explain what had happened – I was trying to articulate what had gone wrong, but burbling nonsense. No one was particularly interested in trying to listen to me. Anyway, they had other riders to take care of and many more races to come.

I remember feeling a mixture of frustration and completely gutted in the aftermath of that race. I'd worked so hard and yet to all the people who mattered it looked like I was living up to my 'soft' status. It seemed to take forever for me to regain my composure, get the right people's attention and get the problem with my bike sorted. In the end it was Wendy that I was finally able to speak to and explain the problem, and she was then promptly able to alert Dan and the mechanics and get the bike fixed. Thankfully Dan now understood the situation and reassured me the bike would be good to go for the final and that my legs would come round too.

It's safe to say in spite of achieving a time which allowed us to race for the gold, I was not having a good day. It was made yet worse when we were called for a random drugs test between the qualifying rounds and the final. I'd only done a couple of drugs tests at that stage in my career and I don't enjoy them at the best of times (I suppose it would be quite strange if I did enjoy weeing in a pot in front of a total stranger, but there's no accounting for taste). To have a drugs test at such a juncture was highly unusual. Normally, riders are requested to attend drug testing after the finals. There has only ever been one other time in my career since when I have been requested to provide a sample between rounds. This was at the World Championships in 2012 when we broke the world record in qualifying and in order for the record to be ratified, all team members needed to provide a sample.

I find it difficult to pee in front of people, especially into a disproportionately tiny container, which is what a drugs test involves. To make matters worse, after the drama of what followed the qualifying round, and multiple nervous bathroom trips beforehand, I just didn't need the toilet now. I was drinking more and more water to try and encourage the right reaction from my body, but my bladder was refusing to fill, to the extent that I was in danger of becoming over-hydrated for the final.

Eventually, when I'd finally drunk enough that I'd managed to provide a sample and sign all the relevant paperwork, there were only ten minutes to go until the start of the warm up for the final round. This was very far from ideal. Despite this, we raced well (all handlebars in full working order!) and beat our opponents from the Ukraine by a huge margin. We recorded a time of 3:22, which was a new world record, taking a whopping three seconds off our qualifying time. But a gold medal and world record of course meant we had to endure yet another drugs test!

This time, not even the peculiarities of pot peeing with random witnesses could temper my exhilaration. I couldn't believe it: I was a world champion and I had won a rainbow jersey.

To me the rainbow jersey was a mythical, magical thing. I'd already seen cycling legends like Chris Hoy and Bradley Wiggins win one. In cycling, the rainbow jersey is presented to the winner of a World Championship event and then needs to be worn by the reigning world champion whenever he or she competes in the same discipline again over the following year until the next World Championships. It is a highly distinctive white jersey with horizontal coloured bands of blue, red, black, yellow and green around the middle, the same colours as the Olympic Rings. Wearing this jersey helps make the reigning champion easier to spot by spectators and competitors alike but is mainly a huge honour for the rider. I would say the presentation of the rainbow jersey means more than the medal in the cycling world. I would now need to wear mine whenever I raced a team pursuit for the whole of the next twelve months. (Admittedly not the actual presentation one... a skintight version would be made!). When I was presented with mine, it put a stop to all the lingering feelings of alienation and of not quite fitting into the world of cycling I'd been experiencing.

The Manchester World Championships changed all that. For whatever reason, perhaps because of a natural ability, maybe my relative age, or perhaps because we were all fairly new to the discipline, I'd been able to match Wendy and Becs' performance when we rode together in the team pursuit. For so long I'd been battling people's expectations that I wouldn't be able to cope yet here I was, having just created a brand new world record, and the proud owner of a rainbow jersey!

I'd taken the journey from uncertain teenager to world champion. Finally, I had proof that I deserved my place in the world of elite cycling and had done enough to silence the people that doubted me (at least for now, they never shut up for long).

I returned to training with a renewed enthusiasm, finally feeling like I truly belonged.

CHAPTER 11

LOVE AT (NOT QUITE) FIRST SIGHT

After the Manchester World Championships, I allowed myself to take one, solitary, totally blissful week off.

I went home to my parents' house in Surrey and pretty much slept for the entire week. It wasn't the most exciting way to spend my first, treasured bit of holiday, but it was exactly what I needed after the excitement and exertion of breaking my first world record.

After I'd had my rest and recuperation, British Cycling asked me to join Team Halfords Bikehut, an all-female squad who would be racing the Tour of Flanders. The race, which takes place annually in Belgium, is probably the most important women's road race on the UCI calendar. The route is both famous and prestigious, and taking part was presented to me as a great opportunity.

The Tour of Flanders for women is held on the same day as the men's race and for the men it is one of the five 'monuments' of cycling. The first men's edition was held in 1913 and in 2004 a women's event was added for the first time, covering a similar course to the men but a shorter vesion. For women it is in the top tier of racing, now called the Women's World Tour, and takes in a challenging course of the famous cobbled climbs of the Flanders region of Belgium. These are incredibly steep climbs and although short at just a few hundred meters in length, reach gradients of 20-30 per cent.

Looking back, however, I know my participation was simply to make up the numbers so the team could start the race. The team was based around Nicole Cooke, the current National Road Race Champion and favourite for the gold medal at the Beijing Olympic road race that summer, and a team of six riders needed to be named on the start sheet. On reflection, I'm not sure I really needed to be in Belgium at all, that spring. Having had a track-based winter and then having taken a week off, a few weeks of training on the road, building up my mileage, would have been ideal. But I didn't have the conviction to say no. Maddeningly, I wasn't paid a penny for racing with Team Halfords Bikehut, a professional team.

Another reason for my reticence was the terrible memories I had of having ridden Tour of Flanders the previous spring. It was my first experience, not only of that particular race but of elite women's road racing abroad generally, and I was incredibly enthusiastic and excited in the run-up. I remember in anticipation trying to find suitable terrain to train on back home in Surrey. The course is notorious for including several very steep inclines as well as difficult-to-navigate cobbled sections, so I attempted to find the Surrey equivalents. It wasn't easy, but I'd felt reasonably certain I was adequately prepared.

As it turned out, my self-assurance was totally misplaced. The only way I can describe my first Tour of Flanders was as a baptism of fire. The initial shock came when we began the race in a bunch of approximately two hundred riders. I'd never done that before and was completely out of my depth.

I knew it was important to try and avoid finding yourself at the back of the bunch at all costs. In fact, if you want to do well, I'd say it's imperative you are in the top twenty riders. If not, it's highly unlikely you'll ever make it to the front. Furthermore, in constricted spaces bunches produce a 'concertina' effect. If this happens, you can find yourself pushed back further and stuck amongst the slower cyclists indefinitely.

I must have been told a thousand times in the run-up to my first Tour of Flanders how important it was to make my way to the front of the bunch as early as possible. The notion was impressed upon me so much that I'd begun rolling my eyes and saying, 'Okay, I get it!' every time it was mentioned. Yet somehow all those warnings failed to give me any kind of indication of what it would be like being in a bunch of some two hundred riders, all desperately clawing to try and get in the top 10 per cent, having been given the exact same advice. You have to experience it first hand to really understand.

The race was 140 kilometres. Within the first forty, two riders collided and crashed right in front of me. I did my best to avoid them, but it was impossible; I came down hard and managed to land on my face, which forced my top teeth through my bottom lip. The forks on my bike were snapped in half and my helmet was smashed. I, however, was still shocked and dazed, and for some reason thought I should continue to ride the race. Somehow, I had failed to register just how badly I'd injured myself and jumped onto a spare bike. It only began to hit home a few kilometres later when I took a swig of water and it stung like hell where my teeth had slashed open my bottom lip. There was also blood streaming from my nose and eventually I had to come to a stop. That was when I was put in the broom wagon.

The 'broom wagon' is the name given to the vehicle which trails behind cyclists during a road race and 'sweeps up' any stragglers who obviously aren't going to make it. They can't keep the public roads open indefinitely on race days so there is an obligation for the organisers to pick up anyone lagging behind. As you would expect, there's quite a lot of shame and stigma associated with this happening to you in the world of cycling and I distinctly remember thinking, *I can't believe I am in the broom wagon, how embarrassing!*

In the context of that experience, you can understand why I wasn't brimming with enthusiasm at the prospect of joining the Tour of Flanders the following year, 2008. Additionally, a week off the bike resting is by no means the best preparation for a race of this magnitude.

All the preparation for Manchester had left me with what are known as 'track legs' – I'd trained to be powerful, strong and fast over a short distance. 'Road legs' are what is needed over a huge distance such as the Tour of Flanders. It is actually possible to have legs suitable for both road and track and for the two to complement each other, but I didn't want to specifically train for the road at that point. The week of rest following Manchester was utterly non-negotiable in my eyes; I'd earned it. Besides, I was knackered.

Bearing all of this in mind, it's fair to say I didn't ride the Tour of Flanders wanting to win. I was a little indignant, feeling I'd been forced to participate for no visible benefit, and simply wanted to get it over with. Because of a combination of my lack of physical preparation and resentful attitude I did about as well as I thought I would – which is to say 'not very'. I accept as a cyclist it is often your job to ride races you don't want to ride, in support of your team leader, so I admit this attitude wasn't a good one to have. But it was all part of the steep learning curve I was still on, just nineteen years old and only nine months after leaving school.

After that, perhaps surprisingly, things began to improve. In fact, during my first year of being a full-time cyclist I went on to win a total of four races in Belgium and won two national titles on the road. I surprised myself by getting into my stride and doing well on the road. I'd still say that first year was probably my best season for road racing, even now.

In Belgium, women's cycling is huge. It's given much more gravitas and respect than it was in the UK at the time. The Belgian races are called 'kermesses', which is Flemish for 'festival' or 'fayre'. When the kermesse comes to town, a bike race is also held in conjunction with the festival. I really enjoyed the warm festive atmosphere and the big crowds. Kermesse races for women were usually between eighty and one hundred kilometres long and took place over relatively short laps, between three and ten kilometres. The race would be a fixed number of laps, starting and finishing in the town centre and taking in a loop around the local roads.

As a track cyclist, I was finding these shorter road races suited me well.

Whilst in Belgium I also met Daniel Shand, with whom I would one day fall in love and marry. Actually, that last statement might not be quite right. Dan lived in Littleborough (just outside Manchester) and being a cyclist himself, he used to visit the Manchester velodrome to train sometimes. According to him, we had bumped into each other on a couple of occasions going to and from the track, although I have absolutely no recollection of this.

I had gone out to Belgium to race with Lizzie. Her boyfriend at the time, Adam, was sharing a house with a few other riders, which included Dan. They were renting the house from Jos Ryan and Tim Harris, who are quite famous in the cycling community since they own a number of houses in Belgium and give riders first priority to rent them during race season.

I'd arranged to go and pick up another one of Dan's housemates in my car and to take her to a race. On the way to the house my trusty TomTom had died (we're still pre-smartphones, remember). I had absolutely no idea how to get around an unfamiliar town in a foreign country without it and was starting to panic.

The first person I saw on entering the house was Dan. I said, 'Oh God, my TomTom is broken and I can't get to this race without it!'

That was our very first conversation (or at least the first I remember). Dan still maintains to this day that my satnav wasn't really broken and it was all a ruse to play a damsel in distress and engage him in some chat.

Especially as it turned out all I needed to do was turn it off and back on again.

CHAPTER 12

DOWN UNDER

As the road season ended in September 2008, the track season began, with the European Track Championships in Poland. Once again, I rode the team pursuit, which allowed me to wear the glorious, coveted rainbow-striped jersey during the race, and we won.

I also rode the individual pursuit in Poland, getting a bronze and a new personal best time. I quickly worked out that, had I attended, my time in the individual pursuit would have been good enough for seventh at the Beijing Olympics (where Becs and Wendy had just won gold and silver, respectively).

That winter would be my first full season racing as a track rider. The previous winter the riders preparing for the Beijing Olympics took priority, but this year was all about us younger riders gaining experience. Each winter a serious of World Cups take place around the world, which act as qualifying events for the World Championships. I'd never competed at one before, but this year I would be competing at three – Manchester, Melbourne and Copenhagen.

The December trip to Melbourne was the one I was most excited about. As an idealistic nineteen-year-old, the idea of travelling so far was a thrilling prospect. As I write this, aged twenty-eight, I have come to recognise how much long-haul flights and jet lag can interfere with your performance on the track, especially as you get older. I hadn't experienced that yet, so it didn't occur to me at the time to be anything other than totally keen.

Before Melbourne, I'd only ever raced in Europe. I'd been to Athens as a junior rider, to Belgium often, as well as to France and even Bulgaria. Melbourne would be my first experience of a long-haul flight.

We were told we would be arriving on the Tuesday, with the race taking place on Thursday. Older riders warned us we would be facing terrible jet lag but the coaches seemed totally unconcerned. This was my first clue that the Melbourne trip wasn't going to be a super-serious one, at least as far as they were concerned.

We were also to travel with a very small team – just our coach, Simon Cope, our manager, Shane Sutton, and three riders – myself, Lizzie Armitstead and Katie Colclough. Usually, you'd also travel with an entourage in tow, consisting of a carer and a mechanic at the very least.

Back then, every nation had to be represented in the World Cup, even if it was for just one event. (Since then the rules have changed.) It quickly became apparent that the Melbourne trip was simply an attempt by British Cycling to give us young riders as many and as varied experiences as possible. This was never meant to be an occasion where we demonstrated a serious performance (although, as it turned out, we did). And so it was that we flew out to Melbourne experiencing the unusual sensation of having minimal expectations placed upon us, ready for maximum fun. In reality, our visit panned out in the exact opposite way to the one you might have expected, considering how little was evidently expected of us.

The actual travelling was less exciting. In my naivety, something I'd failed to grasp about world travel as a professional athlete is that you don't actually get to see that much of the world. You get to see the inside of a hotel, a couple of roads, a velodrome and then perhaps have one day to do a quick bit of shopping, if you're lucky. Globetrotting, in this particular instance, is therefore much less glamorous than it sounds.

On arriving in Melbourne, our coach, Simon Cope, took us out for a road ride, partly to wake the legs up but also to help adjust ourselves to the time and climate differences. My feet had swollen from the long flight and I still remember the epic struggle to squash gigantic feet into tight cycling shoes.

I quickly realised why the other, more experienced riders would try and avoid going as far as Australia. Our usual instructions were to rest as much as possible when we weren't training. If we weren't sleeping, we'd often read or watch box sets, with our feet elevated to direct the blood flow away from our tired legs. In fact, I've often thought that if cyclists had a Fitbit, in contrast to everyone else their aim would be for the number of steps they took to be as low as possible by the end of the day.

By then I'd become so used to this way of life I'd even try and avoid doubling back on myself in the supermarket, taking great care to select everything I needed the first time I went down each aisle – that's how important it was to conserve energy. Later, in the run-up to the London and Rio Olympics, we would be taken to the Celtic Manor in Newport for two weeks to experience the gold standard of recovery time. Celtic Manor is a place where everything is taken care of for you, from your meals to bike repair. You don't have to lift a finger. That's ideally how you'd prepare for a big race.

Melbourne was the antithesis of everything we'd been told was good for race preparation. We were instructed to keep up and moving to combat jet lag but I was a little unsure, always conscious that I was wasting unnecessary energy.

As soon as we arrived I was desperate to go to sleep, but forced myself to stay awake until 9pm, Australian time. I woke up with a start just an hour later and found it impossible to get back to sleep. It was infuriating, that first experience of jet lag, and I reflected broodingly on how it might impact my performance on the track as I sat around waiting for the breakfast buffet in the hotel to open, at 6am.

The first day of racing I surprised myself to win the individual pursuit. The total hours of sleep I'd had in the last two nights I could have counted on one hand! Hardly ideal preparation. I had also never won an individual World Cup event so it was brilliant for me to show my potential this early on in the Olympic cycle. At this point the individual pursuit was still the Olympic event and I had my work cut out if I wanted to race it in London 2012 as we already had Becs Romero and Wendy Houvenaghel, who were the top two riders in the world.

Lizzie, who had rapidly become my best friend, had raced and won the scratch race. This is quite a basic sort of race in terms of rules, in that it takes place over forty laps of the track and the first over the line is the winner. It usually involves around twenty riders, one or two from each participating country. The scratch is a lot more psychologically tactical than anything I was used to; the most important skill involved is the ability to read your rivals, something Lizzie has always been a natural at.

Lizzie also participated in the points race. This takes place over one hundred laps, with a mass start. Every ten laps there is a sprint. If you gain a lap, you are awarded twenty points, plus you get four points for every lap you complete. The winner at the end is the person with the most points (as the name of the race would suggest). Points races really aren't my thing – I'm more accustomed to having to focus on putting in pure power and would prefer not to have to think more than is strictly necessary during a race.

The great thing about being so close with Lizzie was that whilst in Melbourne we were riding the team pursuit together and our skills are cyclists were completely different. It was perfect – we each understand the cycling world well enough that we can provide support to one another, yet we were never direct rivals, unlike Wendy and Becs.

Unfortunately for Lizzie, she crashed during the points race and needed stitches in her elbow. I had assumed this would mean she wouldn't be able to line up in the team pursuit the following day and as we had no reserve rider, that was us finished for the weekend. So I took myself out sightseeing in Melbourne and completely switched off from race mode. But it is a testament to her resilience that despite the stitches in her elbow she returned to racing on the final day and along with myself and Katie Colclough, we won the team pursuit against a strong Australian squad, who pushed us all the way.

Melbourne was a lesson for me in how not all races need to be taken so seriously and in actual fact, a happy head can result in fast legs! The races in Melbourne were the most relaxed I'd ever been in and this was also the most successful I'd ever been – my first ever gold medal at world level in the individual pursuit as well as the team pursuit gold!

Our flight home from Melbourne wasn't until midnight on the Sunday, which gave us another day to explore the city after racing. We didn't know where the 'must see' areas were so ended up in a fairly generic shopping centre. I bought a new camera, believing I'd left mine at home, only to discover my old one later in the bottom of my bag. My dad still teases me about this to this day, asking me if I've remembered my camera whenever I go… well… anywhere.

In February 2009 there was another World Cup in Copenhagen. This was a much more popular destination for British riders than Melbourne, since it involved a far more convenient, short flight, and a huge squad of male and female riders went over there for what would be the last World Cup of the season.

This time, we flew home as soon as we were done so there were no sightseeing opportunities. At just a month out from the World Championships everything was getting more serious. The trip was a success – I won another gold for team pursuit and a bronze for individual – making me the overall World Cup winner in both events. But I didn't even have time to get the faintest impression of Copenhagen as a place.

The track season concluded where it started – in Poland, now with the World Championships. I finished fourth in the individual pursuit in a new personal best time and much to the surprise of many, was very happy with this. Of course I would have loved a medal, but with some of the Olympic riders from around the world who hadn't competed at the World Cups now returning to competition, I hadn't expected to make the finals so this was a great start to the week. But as Steve Peters taught me, focus on performance rather than result. My performance of a personal best time in this incredibly pure test was a marker of how well I was progressing and that was what really pleased me.

We then successfully defended our team pursuit world title, with the line-up being Wendy Houvenaghel, myself and Lizzie Armitstead. The nerves I felt before this title defence were even more than they had been a year ago – defending felt like so much more pressure! The overwhelming feeling when we won was pure relief. No happiness and barely any celebration, just *phew*! I was angry at myself about these feelings and from that day vowed never to feel relief at a victory again: we were the best in the world but that should never be expected or normalised, and instead should be celebrated just the same as if it were the first time. This is a policy I am pleased to say I maintained throughout the rest of my career. I had feared losing and this was more of a motivator than the desire for victory. But from then on I changed and saw every race was an opportunity to win rather than a threat to lose.

Throughout this period, things were progressing with Dan. We had made friends on Facebook and were regularly exchanging messages, which I would then forward to Lizzie for dissection and analysis. She was my advisor in all my dealings with Dan, whom she fervently (and correctly, as it turned out) believed would be the perfect partner for me. Actually, she wasn't so much an advisor as a strategist – the puppet master in our blossoming romance.

CHAPTER 13

FRIENDSHIPS AND FIRST DATES

Whilst I was pushing myself to ever-greater and more impressive feats on the track and road, in private I was still shy and unwilling to take risks. I needed someone who would nudge me out of my comfort zone if I wanted to build a social life for myself outside the world of elite sport. Enter Lizzie, stage left.

Throughout our friendship, Lizzie had always been my polar opposite. Whilst she is outgoing, bubbly and incredibly opinionated, I have always been too much concerned about upsetting people to assert myself, which meant my tendency was to hide away in the shadows. Lizzie enjoyed the psychological aspects of racing, sizing up other riders on the road and trying to anticipate their next move, whereas I clung to the idea that only my performance mattered because only mine was controllable. I was into numbers, power outputs and personal bests, whereas Lizzie's interests were more human.

In the light of her ability to read people, I suppose it made sense that Lizzie always seemed to have an instinctive radar for the times when I needed a push in the right direction. She was like the sister I never had, swooping in to guide and advise me when I was flailing, so it therefore made total sense that she would micromanage our plan to ignite a romance between Dan and me.

At first, this was confined mainly to Lizzie and I co-writing replies to the Facebook messages Dan would send me. There was a long period, over the winter of 2008 and early 2009, when I was travelling a lot with the track team, when I wouldn't have the opportunity to see Dan in the flesh. This meant the Facebook messages were crucial.

Dan was never talking about anything particularly out of the ordinary in his messages to me, most often he'd get in touch to congratulate me on a race result, but Lizzie and I both detected a flirtatious undertone. I used to scour the messages for confirmation Dan liked me in more than a friendly way and always used to be delighted if he ended with an 'x'. Lizzie would advise me on how long to wait before replying and how I should phrase certain things.

It was when I returned to Belgium the following year, 2009, that we could step up the plan. Lizzie teamed up with Jos (the owner of our rented accommodation) and Jos's mum, Kathleen, and between them they made it their mission to make sure Dan and I got together.

Lizzie began engineering inventive ways to ensure Dan and I had time alone together, in a way which must have been, in retrospect, embarrassingly obvious. For example, she'd claim she had no room in the car to give me a lift home from a race and 'subtly' suggest Dan should take me instead. He always complied.

Before too long, everyone in our friendship group was in on it and even I was excluded from foreknowing the details of some of their schemes. I remember there were times when we'd all arrange to meet up to do a road ride together at 9am, only for Dan and I to discover we were the only ones who had shown up. Looking back, I'm sure he must have known there was skulduggery afoot, but he took it all in his stride, relishing our time together.

Eventually, Dan asked me out on an official date. We went to Averbode in Belgium, a place famous primarily for two things – its beer and its ice cream. I remember agonising for ages over what I should wear, calling in Lizzie to help me decide. I'd only brought a very limited wardrobe with me over to Belgium for the summer (I was to be spending most of my time in cycling Lycra, after all) and tried every single item I had more than once for Lizzie and I to inspect and scrutinise.

In the end, we decided jeans and a white vest top were the way to go – classic, universally appropriate, flattering on my athletic frame and not 'trying too hard'. The idea that I should look as though I hadn't given my attire much thought is hilarious when you consider how long we had spent selecting that particular 'casual' ensemble.

I still remember the flavour of the ice cream I devoured copiously on our date (whilst the beer was forbidden, being still so young and having a freakishly high metabolism I was completely unconcerned about any potential consequences for maintaining my ideal training weight and dived into the ice cream). The flavour was called 'Speculoos' and it was divine. You know those little 'Lotus' biscuits you sometimes get, wrapped in plastic on the side of your beverage in coffee shops? Well, in Belgium they have the flavour of those biscuits in spread form, a bit like Nutella but way better, and they call it Speculoos spread. This was the ice cream version of that flavour.

As you would expect, we talked mainly about cycling. Riding

was ultimately why we were in Averbode eating exotic flavours of ice cream in the first place, after all, but since Dan was a road racer and I was a track rider, there was enough difference in perspective to ensure the conversation never became dull.

So was it love at first sight with Dan? Sort of. The first time we ever had a proper conversation, the day my TomTom failed me the previous summer, I remember he shot me this broad, cheeky grin. He probably won't remember doing it consciously, and I certainly don't think it was a deliberate ploy to make me go weak at the knees, but that was certainly the effect it had. Unusually, for someone who is naturally shy, I basked in the attention he was giving me.

As we chatted, I reflected on how good-looking he was. Not only that, he didn't seem quite so 'laddy' as the other male cyclists I knew. He was thoughtful, considerate and easy to build a rapport with. I knew then that I liked him.

Years later, when we got married, Dan said in his speech that he was instantly attracted to my 'bonnie face'. I had absolutely no idea what that meant, although I had a vague notion of it being a euphemistic way of suggesting I've got fat cheeks. Afterwards, I remarked to Lizzie that it was a strange turn of phrase and that 'Bonnie' sounded like the sort of name you might give to a dog. I think, in retrospect, I was being a bit oversensitive (and mean, Bonnie's actually a lovely name for dogs and humans). At any rate, at least it proved that the instant attraction I felt for Dan was mutual.

Things progressed quickly after the Speculoos ice cream date. Someone in Dan's rented house in Blauberg moved out and the room I had been staying in at Jos's house had another guest waiting to move in, so I moved into the shared house in Blauberg. We never planned to effectively move in together so soon, but this happy, coincidental turn of events meant we could spend far more time together.

The summer road season is generally nowhere near as busy as the winter season spent on the track. During winter, we'd be at the velodrome for lengthy training sessions twice a day, five days a week, plus all the extra things like physio appointments, sports massages and meetings would quickly occupy any spaces in between. (I'm mainly writing this for the benefit of my brother Erick, who was convinced my life as a track rider involved practising a three-minute dash around the velodrome a couple of times a day and the rest of the time was spent sitting on my arse!)

In Belgium, no race was more than an hour-and-a half drive away and we were racing between twice and four times a week. In between races we would train, but road training was much more flexible in its nature than what we would do for the track. We could go out on our bikes any time during a free day. Usually we'd choose the morning, which would mean some free time in the afternoon.

Flanders is very flat, but the French-speaking part of Belgium in the South, Wallonia, is much hillier. Since Dan and I both enjoyed the challenge of hillier terrain (oh, how things have changed!), he took to driving us down to a route famous for its climbs near Liege, so we could train together.

In August, my parents came to Belgium to watch me race and that was the first time I remember publicly referring to Dan as my boyfriend. It was a big deal for me, as my parents' approval was important.

I had won the race, which was a good start, and afterwards we all went out for an Indian meal to celebrate. The meal was uneventful, with everyone being super-formal and polite to each other. I don't actually remember that much about the dinner, which is a good thing – if that first introduction had gone badly it would be forever etched on my memory.

The biggest step forward was when I officially changed my Facebook status from 'single'. The social networking site had been the thing that first brought Dan and I closer, so it seemed significant somehow when I was able to make those few clicks which told all my friends I was 'in a relationship with Daniel Shand'.

I was in love and now I had declared it to the world.

During the summer of 2009 getting together with Dan wasn't the only big change. This was also the summer that I learnt to sprint. I'd won races in Belgium before and had enjoyed four victories in 2008, but all of these were solo wins. Training rides with Lizzie Armitstead and Tim Harris were where I first started believing I could win bike races in a sprint. We used to sprint for the yellow town signs when out training. Every time. Local knowledge helped so you knew when they were coming. At first I kept getting beaten but Tim gave me some great pointers and by doing more and more, I got better and better, physically faster as well as technically better.

I had never really worked on my sprint in training, I had always been told I was a 'diesel' engine and knew I took a while to get up to speed. For the first time I realised I was neglecting a huge trainable area just because of a label that had been assigned to me and I started to believe I could win if a race came down to a sprint.

That summer I won five races in the eight weeks I was out there and picked up more primes (cash prizes given to intermediate sprints during a race) than I ever had before – not bad for a diesel engine! (Perhaps a happy head helped with this too – as I have said, I am a firm believer in happy head, fast legs.) Whilst you may think a few kermesse wins isn't particularly significant, this was also the start of me believing I could really develop my peak power. I had never really looked at this as a trainable area – I knew my initial numbers had been good when I'd first tested with British Cycling, but I also knew I was bigger than most of the other girls and power-to-weight ratio meant my sprint was nothing special. I was a diesel engine. But now seeing the huge difference some training had made, I realised this was a huge area for development, and that development would help on the track.

I was already a twice World Champion in the team pursuit but always from riding the man two position. After this summer I never won a World or Olympic title from any other position than man one. I saw I could make man one in the team pursuit my own as there was so much room for development on my peak power. Tim Harris may have thought he was helping me win kermesse races, but in fact he sparked the change in my development from a diesel engine to a fast team pursuit rider who, come Rio, was able to accelerate a 108-inch gear from 0 to 40mph in just a lap and a half.

Before I knew it, the summer road season was over and I was back in Manchester and throwing myself wholeheartedly into the intense winter training regime. My confidence was boosted by my new-found sprinting legs and new relationship status, but now we were approaching a new scary scenario – meeting Dan's family. Dan had a twin sister, Natalie, and an older sister, Keeley, both of whom I was quite terrified of meeting. I'd also never met his mum, Jeannette, or his step-dad, Gary. I desperately wanted them to like me, but my natural shyness meant I always found it difficult meeting new people.

The one family member I had met was his dad. Kev was a

keen club cyclist and a regular at the Manchester velodrome for public training sessions and races. He had also been racing out in Belgium that summer so already knew about me. When I say 'knew' about me, I don't just mean as in Dan's girlfriend, I also mean he knew about my alopecia. As hair loss can be so closely linked to cancer, meeting new people can all too often result in misunderstandings. At what point do you reassure people you don't have cancer? Do you just not mention it at all? Do you wait for them to mention it? Does it even matter?

Fortunately for me, Kev had done a brilliant job of explaining my condition to Dan's other family members before I met them. Kev is a great people person and wherever he goes, he always seems to know someone. As a fellow cyclist, he understood my lifestyle and he did an amazing job of welcoming me into his family.

I'm pleased to say meeting the rest of Dan's family went well and although my confidence was beginning to blossom, I'd had enough of being 'that girl with no hair', but that was about to change.

CHAPTER 14

GETTING WIGGY
WITH IT

Lizzie Armitstead and I had both moved to Manchester at the same time, during 'the uni years', and that was when she had taken it upon herself to show me how to apply make-up. The condition alopecia also meant I had no eyebrows or eyelashes but Lizzie showed me the difference that eyebrow pencil and eyeliner could make in the absence of hair. I was stunned by how different I looked, with the eyeliner giving the impression of eyelashes: my eyes were so much more defined. Lizzie also took me shopping for clothes that suited me more than the ones I was wearing and were generally more stylish. All of these things boosted my fragile self-esteem no end, coinciding nicely with meeting Daniel Shand.

At this stage, my hair had also briefly grown back again. To other people, it would have looked sparse and thin during that year, but because I was used to having no hair at all, to me it seemed like a lustrous mane and gave me a lot of confidence. So

I was distraught in the autumn of 2009, just a month into my relationship with Dan, when all my hair fell out again.

During the summer of 2009, whilst getting together with Dan, the small amount of hair I had gave me a lot of confidence compared to nothing at all. So when it all fell out, I went back to rock bottom. Dan was supportive but I don't think at this stage he quite understood the impact of hair loss. He told me it didn't bother him at all, but that didn't mean it didn't bother me. I'd never looked into wigs before but now I was like 'enough's enough'. However, for some reason I couldn't even bring myself to google the word 'wig' – I had a total mental block about it. Like so many times before, Lizzie instinctively knew I needed a rocket up my backside to help me overcome my fear.

One day, she told me she had found a place at the Trafford Centre called Hot Hair. They sold wigs and hair extensions but weren't a shop in their own right, instead having a stand in the middle of Selfridges, which Lizzie said might make the prospect of a visit less daunting. I was hesitant at first, but she eventually persuaded me we should go together.

We spotted the stand in the beauty department straight away and I kept getting within a few feet, only to lose my nerve. The Hot Hair display was completely out in the open and I was mortified at the prospect of taking my hat off in front of all of the random people going about their shopping. I kept circling the stand, getting within a certain distance before dashing off. Lizzie was trying to persuade me to bite the bullet, but I'd procrastinate by telling her I liked the look of a dress, or those shoes and asking her what she thought.

Lizzie ultimately realised I was never going to pluck up the courage to have a conversation with the sales assistant, so she called upon her own endless reservoir of confidence and did it herself. When she came back, she reported that there were screens around the stand which allowed you to try on the wigs completely in private, away from the prying eyes of curious passers-by.

I said I was still worried about the prospect of taking my hat off, even if it was just in front of the sales assistant. Lizzie reassured me that this was what they did for a living and they had probably seen 'loads' of people with alopecia before.

Now I have more knowledge of wigs, I realise that Hot Hair are, or certainly were, really more a brand for people who want to change their look for a special occasion – a night out, or fancy dress. For that reason the salesperson had probably never seen anyone with alopecia before. Luckily, I had no inkling of the scope of the wonderful world of wigs at the time, so Lizzie's words reassured me enough to stop dawdling.

Lizzie also said she'd try on some wigs too, so I would feel less alone (she really is the best friend a girl could ever have). She has long, thick, dark hair but was trying on blonde, bobbed styles to try and make me laugh and relieve some of the tension.

I ended up settling on a dark wig which reached just below my shoulders. This surprised some of my friends and family. They assumed that since I was used to having no hair at all, I'd go for something blonde and short, which would make the transition less startling. Yet I was taken with this particular piece. I enjoyed the feeling of it being a complete and dramatic transformation. I wanted to feel like a completely different person, perhaps someone who could be less shy socially and stand up for herself a little better.

Having gone from never wearing a wig to now having purchased one, my big question was at what point should I start wearing it in front of my British Cycling colleagues? Out and about on my own was fine. No one knew me as I walked around the supermarket and I loved feeling more normal. Although I did irrationally feel that people would be staring at my hair and kept wondering to myself if they could tell it was a wig. Wearing it in front of everyone else for the first time was a bigger deal, though.

Shortly after I bought that first wig, in the autumn of 2009, I travelled to Melbourne again for a competition, this time as part of a far larger team. I wore my new hair to the airport and, as I approached the assembled team, everyone stared. How I wanted the ground to swallow me up! I was acutely uncomfortable as we traversed the airport concourse, convinced even the people who didn't know me were staring. As we approached security, I tried to swallow my anxiety. I'd always worn hats to airports before and had sometimes been asked to take them off at passport control. What if they told me to remove the wig? I would be humiliated.

Luckily, they didn't, and afterwards one of my teammates said, 'You look nice, Joanna.' The comment addressed the elephant in the room and suddenly everyone was asking me about the wig. They weren't being rude, simply curious – asking what it was made of, if I could wash it, and where I had got it from. Now, it wouldn't phase me in the slightest to answer questions of this nature, but back then I was trying to reply in hushed tones, so as not to draw attention from the surrounding passengers. I didn't want people who didn't know me to know I was wearing a wig (although, in retrospect, it was probably obvious). To me it was still a shameful little secret.

I speak to a lot of people with alopecia now through support groups organised by Aderans Hair Centre, who make the wigs I now wear, and in my role as an ambassador for the charity Alopecia UK. Some women find it really difficult the first time they wear a wig in public. It's natural for people to ask questions – hair is often a staple of office small talk, I understand – so comments like 'Oh wow, your hair looks great, where did you have that done?' can actually become rather awkward.

I know people who have done extensive research to provide a detailed backstory in this eventuality. They'll look up local salons and the names of their employees, even the numbers assigned to different hair colours, so that they can have a convincing tale at the ready for when their new hair comes under scrutiny. I don't judge people for feeling this way because I remember clearly having those types of thoughts. Obviously, I couldn't have pretended to my colleagues that my wig was real but if I had that option in a normal job, I probably would have taken it.

Now I am entirely open about wearing a wig and I actually find the more open I am about it, the cooler other people are about it. If I speak in hushed tones and seem embarrassed, other people also seem to react awkwardly. My attitude is like a mirror and however I react to questions is reflected in the other person's response.

A lot of people tell me I don't 'need' a wig. They say I am beautiful 'the way I am'. In fact, when I first told Dan why Lizzie and I had been to the Trafford Centre to buy that very first wig, he wasn't impressed at all. But, ultimately, it wasn't about him. Whilst I am regularly told by people I look lovely with no hair and shouldn't be ashamed, it's easy for me to convince myself they are 'just saying that'. Wearing a wig gives me a confidence boost and most importantly, gives me back control and that's why I do it. With a condition like alopecia, which takes something away from you, it is so nice to have an element of control back.

Having said that, it is reassuring to know Dan was attracted to me when we met for the first time, when I had very little hair which was rapidly thinning, and before I'd even googled the word 'wig'.

CHAPTER 15

FALLING FACE FIRST

The big news, in December 2009, was that the Olympic events would be changing at the London 2012 Games. The outdated scenario of seven events for men and just three for women in track cycling, which had been the case at Beijing 2008, would be a thing of the past. The whole programme was completely overhauled, with the loss of the points race, Madison and individual pursuit, in favour of two new sprint events for women and two new endurance events too – the omnium (which is a little like a heptathlon for cycling and involves being a great all-rounder) and the team pursuit.

This new programme would result in five men's events and five women's events. I was over the moon about this equality, and the prospect of the women's team pursuit being part of the London programme was truly amazing. At this point I was a two-time World Champion and current world record holder in this event. And now all of a sudden there was the chance of competing in a women's team pursuit at a home Olympic Games!

The addition of the team pursuit meant the loss of some of the most iconic races not just for the men, but for the women too. I had originally been talent spotted for the individual pursuit, yet the adding of women's team pursuit to the Olympic programme meant, very controversially at the time, removing this event for both genders. The event I thought I'd been training for would no longer exist, come London 2012.

To be honest, if the events had looked the way they now did at the time British Cycling came to Nonsuch, I am fairly sure I would never have been selected for the Talent Team in the first place. The team pursuit requires so much skill, and when I was first talent spotted, I had brute power in abundance but none of the skills you would associate with a team pursuiter.

Now in life whenever I think I can't do something, I look back to this time, and how I would never have dreamt in a million years I would become the best in the world at an event like the team pursuit. Even in those early stages of my career, I had already come so far in terms of the transformation from the girl dragging her bike around Epping Forest just a few years before. I was now hoping to go to a home Olympic Games as a team pursuiter!

Male Olympic hopefuls, in particular, were disgruntled by the changes, since the number of cycling events for them had been reduced from seven to five, to make room for the increased number of female races. What were once popular events had been lost and many cycling fans weren't happy about it. Gutted as I was at the loss of the individual pursuit, the most pure event in track cycling in my eyes, I can't say I agreed with those who weren't happy: more equality is always a positive thing in my book (and this *is* my book, after all!).

Whilst I was, and still am, very happy that the Olympic events were overhauled between the 2008 and 2012 Games, I still think it is a travesty we don't have the individual pursuit, or indeed the kilo, in the Olympic programme. There has been a move away from timed events with an opinion they don't make good TV viewing. I completely disagree with the view that timed events are boring to watch and anyone who says so needs to watch back the men's kilo final from the Athens Olympics!

***

In the winter of 2009 I started to help Dan out a bit with his training, using what I'd learned from having access to the best coaches British Cycling had to offer to help him improve his performance. Dan had never had any professional direction before, structuring his training mainly around things he had gleaned from the internet, so my assistance had a dramatic effect. A lot of men might have felt emasculated, having their girlfriend instruct them in this way, but Dan is above such things and embraced the opportunity wholeheartedly.

At the start of 2010, after he had decreased the overall volume of his training but increased the intensity, he won his very first race of the season. He had signed for the new British Team Raleigh, which regularly took him abroad to race. This would still be my number one piece of advice to anyone wanting to enhance the effectiveness of their training – quality over quantity.

Just as Dan was thriving, I was conversely having one of my worst stretches of cycling yet. We'd won a silver in the World Championships in March 2010, which is of course an excellent result by most people's standards, but the teenage girl in me who used to beat herself up when she didn't achieve an A* at school found it hard to accept that she hadn't won gold. But the disappointment hadn't just come from myself: this was the first time a British women's team hadn't won the team pursuit at the World Championships and losing out to an Australian team, with an average age far younger than ours, made it even worse. We were all gutted. And to make matters worse, this was the first World Championships since the announcement of the team pursuit becoming an Olympic event. Suddenly, just over two years out from the London Games, we went from being world leaders to being on the back foot.

Then, in the summer of 2010, I had a serious crash. Despite the season, predictably, considering we were riding from the velodrome in Manchester to Cheshire, it was pouring with rain. Myself and another female rider were cycling side by side. The road was slippery and, as I broke sharply to avoid a hazard, I crashed and landed face first.

The women's team had been given a new coach, Paul, who was in the process of actively recruiting more female riders in preparation for the 2012 Olympics and the accompanying increased number of women's cycling events. He scraped me off the road and put me in what was essentially the boot of his car to wait for an ambulance. I remember looking at people and having no idea who they were. There was a girl called Claire Galloway, a medical student who was now trying out for the team pursuit team, who came to check me over in the immediate aftermath of the crash but I couldn't place her at all; I was clearly badly concussed.

My two front teeth were dangling by a thread and I'd also broken my nose. I was taken to Macclesfield Hospital. During the journey, a paramedic refused to believe I had been wearing a helmet when I crashed in light of the severity of the injuries I had sustained. I remember in my confused fug, I was still able to express how angry and indignant this allegation made me:

I had definitely been wearing a helmet and I hated being accused otherwise.

The staff at Macclesfield had been keen to keep me under observation overnight, but as soon as I got to the hospital and had been given a preliminary check-up, all I could think about was getting away and having my teeth fixed. It would probably have been more medically sensible for me to follow the doctor's advice and stay, but in this instance my vanity won.

Dan was in Portugal at the time. The connection fee from mobile to mobile for European phone calls was 75p. I remember this so distinctly because he and I had discussed it before he left: we didn't want to pay the 75p connection fee more than once per day! We therefore had an agreement that we would only call each other once each day, at an agreed time.

When I called Dan to let him know about the crash, I was genuinely worried he wouldn't pick up, because of the whole 75p thing. Thankfully, he seemed to sense it was an emergency, spoke to me and then called his mum to arrange for me to stay at her house, as I couldn't be left alone, concussed, overnight.

Paul drove me to Dan's mum's house, where I stayed the night, and the next day my dad drove up to Manchester to collect me and then take me to the dentist. Jeannette Shand, now my mother-in-law, is one of the most caring people I've ever met and ideally suited to her day job as a nurse. I felt happy to be staying at her house and I knew I would be cared for, but I think even she was a little surprised when she saw the state of me that night.

Once my dad had taken me to a dentist, the procedure that followed I would still say is amongst the most painful of my life. Using no anaesthetic or painkillers whatsoever, the dentist literally shoved my two front teeth back into their original position and applied a brace to make sure they stayed there. I was waving frantically in the chair to try and indicate that I was in pain, but the dentist didn't seem to care.

As a result of the crash my face had swelled up to the size of a football. It was quite spectacular, in a strange way, the capacity my face had to swell. My nose was broken and I was regularly getting nosebleeds. My teeth were still extremely painful and it was months before I could bite into something like an apple again. For the time being it was a liquid diet only.

The accident forced me to take time off the bike. After a week, frustrated by my enforced sedentary state, I started riding on turbo in an attempt to get back into the swing of things. I kept getting more epic nosebleeds, perhaps my body's way of trying to indicate that I had returned to training too soon, but I ignored them, believing it was better to persevere.

My pig-headedness cost my dearly: coming back to the bike too soon led to me contracting glandular fever. I remember trying to train and managing just a few minutes before I would collapse, sobbing with exhaustion. Tests were done, but initially they indicated that nothing was wrong with me, which made me think my total lack of energy must be psychosomatic, or perhaps a side effect of the trauma of my bad crash. I became incredibly frustrated with myself. Mentally and physically depleted, I started to think maybe I was 'soft' after all. Eventually, a subsequent blood test revealed I had glandular fever.

The illness was completely debilitating and forced me to rest throughout all of August and September. There had been talk of me going to the Commonwealth Games in Delhi during this time, but owing to the state the illness had left me in that was now out of the question. This was a real shame, not only because I would have loved to have represented England at the Commonwealth

Games (an event which still included the individual pursuit), but also because this would have been my first and only chance to experience a multi-sport Games before potentially going to the big one in London 2012.

Later in the autumn I finally returned to training. Two weeks later, I had another crash.

I was at an open track session, which any member of the public could pay to access. Another cyclist was riding high on the track but punctured and slid down into my path as I was racing around the bottom. Riding at speed, I hurtled straight into the fallen cyclist and over my handlebars. I had stretched my hands out in front of me to protect myself from the impact, which pushed my arm up into my elbow joint and fractured it at the top.

Weirdly enough, it wasn't the top of my elbow but my wrist that hurt most, at the time. I was advised by the first aider at the track to go for an X-ray, but I wanted to go home and clean myself up first. They put my arm in a sling and I headed home only to find one of the random drug testers had turned up, meaning I then had to try and wee in a pot one-handed. This was no easy feat and as I contemplated the complex manoeuvres and angles required, I remember thinking that the past few months had been a catalogue of disasters – I couldn't seem to catch a break. I really needed to go to hospital yet here I was, sitting waiting to wee in front of someone else.

Having taken my usual amount of time to produce a sample (hours!), I stayed home and went to bed, deciding I would visit the hospital in the morning. I woke up to find it wasn't my wrist that hurt anymore, but now my elbow. Apparently this is quite common in such injuries. Dan took me to hospital and the X-ray revealed my elbow was indeed broken.

Additionally, I still wasn't feeling my best after the glandular fever. In fact, whilst I did eventually manage to train myself back to fitness, I'd go so far as to say I haven't really ever been the same since. Unfortunately, both of these setbacks coincided with an important meeting with British Cycling, ahead of the London Olympics.

When I arrived at the meeting, I discovered that I was one of twelve girls who would be competing for just three places in the team pursuit. So far in my career, I had been used to being one of only five or six female riders, but now the pool from which British Cycling could select was considerably larger. On the one hand this was a good thing, since I definitely wasn't in any fit state to race that winter and there were now plenty of other people who could do it in my stead. On the other, it had reduced my chances of competing at Olympic level. There would now be a selection battle and past results would count for nothing. And at the start of that battle, following glandular fever, my still-sore front teeth and broken elbow, I was the least fit I'd been in years.

Ultimately, I decided the situation was one of Steve Peters' 'uncontrollables'. The only thing I could have any direct influence over was whether or not I picked myself up and threw myself back into training, following my series of pitfalls. And dust myself off I had to, if I had any chance whatsoever of making the World Championships team the following March. This was crucial, not just for the journey to make Team GB for the London Olympics, but also as my funding from UK Sport was decided solely on World Championship results. If I didn't make the team I'd drop down from the highest funding level, grade A, to a grade C. This would effectively halve my income and put me in a far more strained financial situation in the year to go until London. Motivated as I was to win, funding was always a huge factor every year when it came to the World Championships.

It was now November 2010, and a group of eleven girls were training together in Manchester, all focussed on making the London Olympic team. Number 12, me, was unable to join the team whilst my elbow was broken and it would be a few weeks before I would be able to ride on the track again, so I had to watch on, often from a turbo trainer in the track centre, as the other girls repeated drill after drill on the track. Two of the new girls that had joined that winter were the previously relatively unknown cyclists, Laura Trott and Dani King. It became clear very quickly that they were extremely talented and this excited the coaches. I felt in some people's eyes I was already written off, my series of injuries sidelining me whilst others progressed rapidly.

I can't deny, at this stage, that I felt some jealousy towards the group and a little panic, but amidst that unpleasant cocktail of emotions was a steely determination: I *had* to make it onto the team.

CHAPTER 16

BOUNCING BACK

The World Championships in March 2011 were in Apeldoorn, Holland.

Despite my best efforts to get back to full fitness, including taking myself off to Spain over Christmas with Dan and us both missing out on seeing any family over the festive period, it was just too big an ask. The previous six months of illness and injury had taken their toll and when it came to selection trials in Manchester, my legs just said no.

The one small positive I could take was that despite starting with a group of twelve girls to select from, I had made the final four, just not the final three. This would mean I would be travelling out to Holland and fulfilling the role of reserve rider. I would be required to warm up with the team and be on standby should anyone become ill last minute, and also be ready to step in for the final, should anyone underperform. The team can be changed up until one hour to go so I needed to stay ready.

The three selected riders were, unsurprisingly, Wendy Houvenaghel, Laura Trott and Dani King. Wendy, like me, was already a two times World Champion and her experience combined with the youth of Laura and Dani made for a strong line-up. Being a reserve rider is a horrible experience and a lot of cyclists have spoken about how unfair it feels. It's what I imagine it must be like being the understudy for the main role in a play. You have to prepare just as thoroughly and learn all your lines, all the while knowing that your only chance to be in the spotlight is if the person who's supposed to play the part befalls some kind of misfortune. It's humiliating to know that you weren't someone's first choice.

As a reserve, you have to warm up in the track centre just as you would if you were on the main team and then watch someone else ride the race. I stood on the sidelines as Wendy, Laura and Dani set the fastest qualifying time. After the qualifier, Paul called a team meeting and announced he would be making a change to the line-up. My heart skipped a beat as I thought I would be in with a chance. But the change was simply to swap the starting positions of Wendy and Dani. The team went on to win the gold with a dominant performance over the USA. Of course I was happy for them, and for Britain too, but it was undoubtedly the lowest point of my career.

I was only twenty-two years old at the time, still young by most people's standards, but I had heard rumours that some people thought I was past my peak. I knew I was being compared unfavourably to Laura and Dani, who were just eighteen and nineteen respectively, fresh and full of enthusiasm as well as talent. No one said anything to me in so many words, but I could tell from the way people spoke to and acted around me that they thought I was a lost cause. Devastatingly, I also knew my lack of participation meant my funding was definitely going to be halved.

I appealed the decision, citing the series of illness and injury that had hampered my training so badly, but to no avail. The rules were clear in black and white. A medal equalled A-level funding. Fourth to eighth place equalled B-level funding. Below eighth place equalled C-level funding. I hadn't even competed so it was straight to C.

To add to the pressure, I was acutely aware that we had only just over a year to go before the London Olympics. There was no doubt in my mind that my non-selection in Holland had been caused by a series of bad luck and timing, but how could I convince everyone it was an unfortunate blip and not an indication of everything to come?

Others might have crumbled at this point, but just like so many times before the fact that people were making it so clear that they had doubts about my ability only served to fuel my personal reserve of self-belief. The obvious lack of faith in the idea that I would bounce back from my horrific season made me all the more determined that I would prove everyone wrong. It's really fortuitous that my brain is wired to respond in this way to doubters, because at this stage it was more important for me to find some inner resolve than it had ever been. Before that, though, what I really needed was some perspective after being immersed in all the shocks and disappointments, as well as a break to clear my head. As ever, the time I had in which to shoehorn a holiday was limited, but I did manage a last-minute booking for a week in Lanzarote with Dan. It was exactly what I needed and did me the world of good.

Firstly and most importantly, Lanzarote provided me with some much-needed sunshine. I regularly describe myself as being 'solar powered', since it feels to me like I can soak in optimism, energy and, ultimately, extra fitness directly from the sun's rays. The winter had been a terrible time for me to try and work my way back to peak fitness following injury and illness for that very reason, when daily battles with rain, ice or even snow make matters even tougher.

Secondly, this was an opportunity to shake myself free from any adverse psychological side effects arising from the events of the last few months. It was the first time Dan and I had ever gone away on a holiday together and I was determined I wouldn't do anything remotely work related the entire time so I switched off my phone and cut myself off from my life, for a while. I will admit that I peddled on a pedalo in the sea on one of the days we were out there, but that was the extent of anything even vaguely cycling related. The rest of the time we mooched about, relishing the hot weather.

Properly switching off was something I was never very good at doing as a cyclist and getting myself actually away on a holiday was the only way to do so. I knew my funding would be halved so the logical part of my brain told me a holiday was a silly thing to do, but it is one of the best decisions I've ever made.

After I returned, revived and refreshed, it was time for some pure, hard graft. I started hitting the gym, which up until that year I had only ever done under duress, seeing it as fairly pointless and unenjoyable, to improve my leg strength. I had a severely deflated bank balance, but used my savings to fund a couple more trips to Belgium to spend some time racing the kermesse scene again. This was, I believed, the best place for me to get fit. I was racing on the road, but it was all about training for the track. The fuel and channel crossings were expensive, but I felt if I didn't go then it would cost me more.

Above: Looking rather pleased with myself at the beach.

Below: Being 'Big Sister' to my shiny new brother, Erick!

Above: Sadly my career as a ballet dancer never really took off. . .

Below: Running cross-country at school. I managed to beat the favourite with room to spare. Somehow, this still wasn't the sport for me, though.

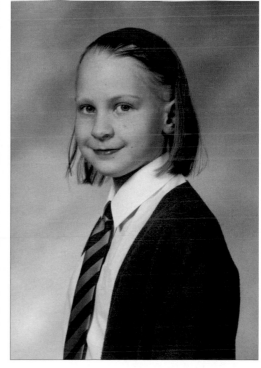

Above: Me, pictured riding an outsized, furry bicycle that didn't always go in the direction I wanted. Room for improvement.

Below left: Little did I realise that I'd already found my perfect mode of transport years ago – my shiny red trike!

Below right: My last primary school photo, in which you can see the early onset of alopecia.

Above: Competing in the 2008 Capernwray road race, which takes place by the beautiful Lake District.

Below: Another road race victory in Belgium, 2009.

Above: An early date with Dan, the man I would one day marry. Bruges, 2009.

Left: Another incredibly important person in my life – Lizzie Armitstead (now Deignan), my friend team-mate and all-round partner in crime.

One of the most incredible days of my life: before, during and after the Women's Team Pursuit final at the London 2012 Olympics. As well as taking gold, Dani, Laura and I managed to break the world record – again.

© Getty Images

Above: A victory hug from Dan after that amazing day.

Below left: A postbox was painted gold for every gold medal won at 2012. Here is mine, in my home town of Cheam in Surrey!

Below right: With multiple Paralympic gold medal hero, Sarah Storey, after the London Games.

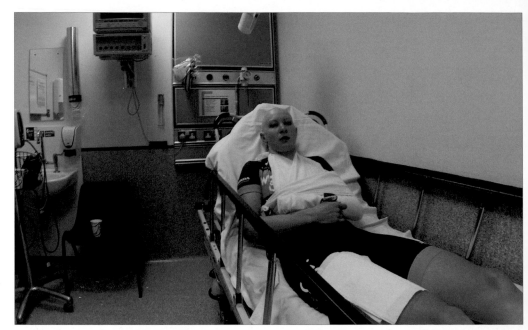

Above: Not all fun and games: laid up in A&E with a broken collarbone after a real wipe-out in August 2013. I'd gone right over the handlebars, in front of thousands on live TV.

Below left: Collecting my MBE from Buckingham Palace. © *Getty Images*

Below right: At a 'warm weather' training camp in Majorca. Whoever said being a professional athlete was all glitz and glamour?!

In September 2011 it was time to see whether my combination of racing miles and gym work had paid off. It was the National Track Championships and I was riding the individual pursuit.

As I've already mentioned, the individual pursuit is very straightforward compared to team pursuit, in that the aim is simply to ride twelve laps as fast as you possibly can. Whilst in some respects this means there is less to think about, it also means there is nowhere to hide if your fitness or performance isn't up to scratch. There is almost no luck involved in the individual pursuit, it is all about pure power combined with pacing ability.

It was therefore an immensely satisfying and, if I'm honest, a bit of a surprise in light of my most recent track races before the summer, when I not only qualified fastest, but achieved a new personal best by a huge margin of five whole seconds. I completed the race in a time of 3:30.4. Three minutes and thirty had always been a meaningful time for me since it was one I had been working towards. Being, as I am, so motivated by numbers, the significance of that time gave me a huge confidence boost.

I had been up very first in qualifying, the race organisers clearly not ranking me amongst the favourites, and had the painfully long wait to see if anyone else would beat my time. I call this a painful wait but I actually decided this was the best position to be in. Everyone else had seen my time and now had the worry of whether they could they better it. Their performances were of course completely out of my control so I actually quite enjoyed the relief of having got my ride out of the way and knowing I'd done everything I could. Steve Peters had always taught me to base my contentment on performance rather than result. I was over the moon with my performance to break my personal best by so much. Either way, my training had worked and whatever anyone else did, I was in the shape of my life.

First and second place in the qualifiers then had to race each other for the gold and silver medals, whilst third and fourth competed for the bronze. I remained at the top of the leader board and found myself racing against Laura Trott for the gold medal. Wendy Houvenaghel, the Olympic silver medallist from Beijing and multiple World Championships medallist, had qualified third. I raced the final again, completely focussed on my own performance – I knew I had another good ride in me. And I produced the goods to replicate my time from the morning and win the gold medal. This was a visible turning point – a statement to the coaches which told them I was here, I wasn't past it, I was back from the brink, and I was definitely on form.

Of all my wins as a cyclist, to me this is one of my most valued. On paper it is actually one of the lower ranked races, simply racing against the other British riders as opposed to the rest of the world. There were no TV cameras or roaring crowd, but it marked a huge turning point and gave me a vast amount of self-belief. All the training I had done that summer I had never really known if I was improving. When you get fitter, training doesn't get any easier – in fact, it usually just means you can push yourself even harder. Every day I worked hard, and rested hard. Most of this was done on my own, based at my parents' house in Surrey, as well as the roads of Belgium, only returning to Manchester when I had to join the rest of the team. I was hoping my hard work would pay off, but when in the middle of a hard training phase you never really see the benefits until you rest up a little and let the form come through.

This first race at the National Championships had allowed me to come back with a bang. I went on to cement my new status as 'the girl who bounced back' by also winning gold in the team pursuit.

But the cherry on the cake was when I achieved a bronze in a bunch race – the points race. The tactics required for bunch racing had never been my thing and I hadn't been expecting a medal at all – I simply wanted to get stuck in and race hard. All my hard work was paying off in a way even I could not have anticipated.

All in all, I'd say that was a very good week indeed.

CHAPTER 17

DUTCH COURAGE

M y new-found success and accompanying buoyant mood were tested when the next place I had to compete was back at the scene of the disastrous World Championships, just seven months earlier – Apeldoorn, in Holland. We even stayed in the same hotel, which immediately brought back memories of how terrible I had felt, both physically and mentally, the last time I was there. Even as I write and think about that hotel now, I shudder slightly.

The event was the European Championships and would be one of just three remaining major events before the London Olympics.

The velodrome in Apeldoorn has a reputation for running slow, meaning people don't tend to achieve their best times on it. It would have been so easy for me to consign myself to defeat before we had even raced, but I was determined to try and change my luck in Holland, and for that I was going to require some (Dutch) courage. (Sorry!)

I tried to bring my focus away from where we were geographically and onto the physical process at hand. Instead I occupied my mind with the concerns like how I would prepare, the best way to train in the few days leading up to the race and how I would keep active without overdoing it. I concentrated my internal monologue on mundane questions like 'Should I do more, or less, than yesterday?'

Most of all, I tried not to be sidetracked by the fear of someone else taking my place on the team pursuit. The worry of being a reserve, or worse still of not going to competitions at all, was a constant and overbearing presence in my mind as a team pursuiter. We don't have specific trials for competitions, the coaches make their decision based on a bank of evidence they have built up by analysing our performances over the entirety of the season. Every single training session and race you participate in ultimately counts towards the coaches' decision about whether you should be allowed to race in the next one.

Of course, this leads to frequent differences of opinion and protests from riders that they have been eliminated unfairly. Personally, however, I have never felt that this way of doing things was particularly unjust. Looking back over my career, whilst at the time I might have felt apprehensive about the selection process, I always believed it was based purely on performance: the fastest team would ride, simple as that.

That didn't mean I wasn't fearful at the time, however. I would say I experienced a high level of fear going into each competition, always because of selection. It goes with the territory of doing a job where months of effort ultimately only count in a few minutes. But would I even get the chance to participate in those few minutes? Selection was out of my control. All I could do was be the best I could be and I couldn't do anything about it if other girls would be faster. But this meant I developed an even greater fear of setbacks such as illness and injury. I would do anything I could possibly do to minimise risks, all because selection meant so much.

That summer, by overcoming the obstacles of the previous season, I had shown the coaches my commitment to the programme. Now, it was up to my legs to do the talking.

How do I cope with that level of pressure? The answer is I'm not sure. I think it might be wired into my fundamental character. Even at school I remember liking the idea of exams – that everything you had learned over the course of the academic year ultimately came down to this one chance to demonstrate it under timed conditions. I do know that's quite peculiar, by the way!

I suppose another element of the answer would be that most of the pressure I'm under comes not from the people around me, but from myself. I am an inward-looking athlete and my own biggest critic. There are disadvantages to this way of thinking, in that I'll mentally self-flagellate when my performance hasn't been absolutely perfect. The plus side is that I'm far more concerned with my opinion of myself as an athlete than I am with what other people might think of me. It's that part of me that keeps going in the face of extrinsic disapproval.

Looking back, I can see that I was thinking in this way from my very first training camp. Let's face it, no one thought I would make a very good cyclist based on what I was exhibiting in the early stages after being scouted at Nonsuch, and with good reason. Yet, there were these little glimmers of hope that showed me I might have a natural aptitude for cycling. These small flashes of hope were like carrots dangling in front of me and I continued to follow them, even when other people were giving me the stick.

My tactic of doing everything I could to shut out the bad memories of Apeldoorn paid off and along with Laura Trott and Dani King, we won the European title and also rode even faster than the team had gone at the World Championships earlier that year, when I had been in reserve, despite this race coming during a training phase and not having a full taper (when training volume is backed off for a major competition in order to peak).

I had continued to do a lot of gym work, which other riders were sceptical of. Traditionally, if you were an endurance rider, gym work wouldn't be part of your training repertoire, but as team pursuiters we are actually more like sprinters in that we are trying to be fast for a lap at time whilst on the front, so building muscle became a priority. Improving my strength in the gym was working for me, and in spite of anyone else's reservations, I was determined to carry on with it.

In February 2012 it was time for the Olympic test event at the brand new London velodrome in Stratford, East London. The track had only been finished a few months before then and it wasn't open to the public.

They were holding the test event in the form of a World Cup, which struck me as a strange decision. Why invite the rest of the world to have a test run on the new velodrome, the very same one we would be competing on for Olympic medals in just a few months' time? But perhaps that is an unfair judgement on my part. We Brits are, after all, all about fair play, and in that context it was a fitting gesture.

The event was huge and attended by lots of media, keen to see what form we were on so close to the Olympics on home turf. It was therefore extremely unfortunate that, under the gaze of the world press and the scrutiny of such expectation, the qualifying round didn't go particularly well.

I was in 'man one' position for the team pursuit and started way too fast. Later, everyone would blame this on the crowd. The velodrome seated 6,000 spectators, who were all cheering wildly for Britain, which people thought would be enough to distract and over-excite me. There was probably an element of truth in that: the enthusiastic home crowd did cause me to get a little carried away, but it was mostly because I couldn't feel my legs. Now let me explain…

Training works by overloading and then resting to allow adaptations. When we near an important competition we will 'taper' back our training, meaning we are not overloading as much as usual. Usually, we cut out the volume and just keep in some high-intensity efforts. You want to have just the right amount of work in your legs. Obviously, you don't want to be knackered for a big event, but in an ideal world you would want to ache, slightly. The pain in your legs connects you to them. You can feel every push and turn, and this helps your mind to tune into your legs to the extent that you can adjust your timing to tenths of a second, as required.

On this occasion, I'd got my taper a little wrong. My legs felt so fresh, it was an alien feeling, usually being accustomed to a heavy training fatigue. I'd not included enough work in the week before the race and as a result, felt no pain in my legs whatsoever as I lined up.

Because I was so fresh on this occasion, I shot out round the track like a bat out of hell. The team fortunately didn't split, which can sometimes happen when the first rider is too fast, but we were all far too fatigued by the end of the race to keep up the pace I had set. Our legs full of lactic, forcing them round for the remaining laps as they locked up in pain. We qualified in second place, very narrowly missing slipping down to third.

After the race, I'd exerted myself so much that I vomited, a lot. I remember we were taken to the mixed zone, which is where journalists from various outlets congregate to ask athletes questions. Jill Douglas from the BBC asked me a question and all I could do was shake my head and try not to splatter her with sick – I was too exhausted to utter a single word. Fortunately she understood and moved on to one of my teammates.

As luck would have had it, the finals were the next day. This was highly unusual (finals were most often held on the same day as qualifiers) but it did give me a little time for recovery and reflection.

The following day, we sat in plastic chairs next to the track and watched as the Australian team won bronze and set a new world record in the process. A lot of cyclists would react badly in that situation. If you see another team get up and ride faster than the time you and your coach have projected for yourself, it's really easy to panic and assume all your training has been done at the wrong pace. Yet I've always been advised that to make a last-minute change to the line-up or your performance plan would be ill-judged in those circumstances. To do so would be an emotional, rather than a logical, decision.

The Australians were not able to ride for the gold, after qualifying third in the opening round, according to the rules. Yet they were faster than we had been and that didn't bode well for the impending Olympic Games. I, however, chose to see it as a challenge. As soon as I saw Australia's time I just knew, in my gut, that we were going to ride faster. The crowd were behind us and conditions were good.

During the final race, I started too fast again. I still hadn't reined in my freshness enough, despite all the effort I'd put in during the qualifier. But that's me being characteristically overcritical of my performance. The start wasn't as bad as last time and not only did we win the gold, we broke the world record that had been set by Australia just a few minutes before.

Whilst the gold medal ride hadn't been perfect, it was undoubtedly a huge improvement from the day before. We beat our rivals, Canada, by just eight-tenths of a second. To us, that felt like a huge victory, even though objectively it wasn't the biggest margin. By setting a new record, we were telling the world that we were a team to be reckoned with, ready to push the boundaries.

That was our first of six world records that year.

CHAPTER 18

SPOTLIGHT

It was during the London World Cup in February 2012 that the press became excited for the first time about me standing on the podium without wearing a wig. In fact, the three days between the close of the competition and flying out to Majorca for training camp were entirely taken up with me trying to manage all the media attention being focussed on me.

Having won team pursuit gold on the Friday night, I went on to win individual pursuit gold on the Saturday night. The individual pursuit, whilst not an Olympic event, was still often incorporated into World Cup programmes and had been a great chance for me to race alone. After the excitement of the world record-breaking ride in the team pursuit I had got all of about three hours' sleep but was still buzzing when I raced the individual pursuit qualifier on the Saturday morning. My stomach still hadn't settled and this time, despite a relatively well-paced ride, I hadn't even made it off the track before vomiting again!

I was able to get a bit more sleep before racing the final on

Saturday evening and this must have been broadcast live on a prime-time BBC channel. I was over the moon to win the race and returned to the podium, my second time of this competition, to collect my gold medal – as usual, without wearing a wig. But nothing could have prepared me for what ensued.

I found the reaction of the newspapers strange, not to mention unfamiliar, because I'd won a lot of medals up until that point. Of all the times I'd ever been on a podium, only two of them I had worn a wig for – I didn't like the look, it just didn't seem right in that brief period following a race to quickly put a wig on. I'd stood up there with no hair plenty of times before and no one had batted an eyelid. Perhaps it was because of the hype surrounding the impending Olympics that the British media were particularly hungry for unique stories.

There was a very brief time when I was concerned about appearing on a podium with nothing to cover my head. This was a detail I had forgotten until I looked over some diary entries from 2006, when I rode the Junior European Road Championships as a teenager. This was long before I started wearing wigs, when I used to just wear hats out and about. I remember, when I looked over the regulations for the competition, there was a clause in there which stated no one was allowed to wear a cap when collecting their medals. This is rare in road cycling – if you look at pictures of cyclists on podiums, both male and female, you'll see they often wear caps, often with their sponsors' logos on them.

I've never admitted this to anyone before, but there was a small part of me that hoped I wouldn't win a medal in the Junior Euros, so I wouldn't have to suffer the indignity of everyone seeing my head. I wouldn't say I sabotaged myself exactly, but there was a tiny voice in my head before the race began which told me that to come fourth wouldn't be such a terrible result. When I did finish fourth, therefore, there should have been a portion of me which felt relieved. In reality, I felt crushing disappointment. British Cycling seemed to be winning everything that year. I was expected to medal and everyone was asking me what went wrong. I was ashamed, thinking that all the investment the coaches had put into me up until that point had come to nothing.

It was on that day that I realised defeat was a thousand times worse than any embarrassment I could feel standing on a podium wig-less. The voice in my head disappeared and I became focussed on winning, unencumbered by insecurity about alopecia (at least when I was competing). Since then I'd stood on podiums with nothing on my head many times.

My wins in the team and individual pursuits in London had been shown on BBC television and were subsequently picked up by the *Daily Mail* and *The Sun*. I was thrust into the spotlight for the first time in my career. The newspapers sent photographers to my parents' house to take pictures of me with and without a wig on. This was done with my consent and prior arrangement, but I can't say I was particularly comfortable with it. Although no one said anything, I could tell my mum and dad weren't best pleased having press at their house either, especially as *The Sun* photographers stayed until well past ten o'clock at night. After the photographs emerged, I was invited onto what was then *Daybreak*, the breakfast news show on ITV.

As I remember it, our coaches at British Cycling weren't particularly happy with me doing all of these interviews. Their perception was that I was revelling in all the attention I was getting when I should have been focussing on my training. In reality, nothing could have been further from the truth. I was deeply uncomfortable answering questions, especially when they related to when I had first lost all of my hair, aged ten.

My whole life I had used distractions, whether it was over-achieving academically at school, or training on the track, which prevented me from having to confront my true feelings about having alopecia. This was my way of functioning, but that didn't mean that I was coping. When something traumatic happens to you it's impossible to be truly okay until you have worked through the difficult emotions and come out the other side. I hadn't gone through this process yet, so I was still a little unsure about how I felt. Standing on the podium wig-less had been interpreted as a gesture of defiance, so the perception was that I was a lot more confident than I was in reality.

I remember when I appeared on ITV's *This Morning*, Eamonn Holmes popped his head around the door of the make-up room, saw me and said something along the lines of, 'Oh, you're wearing a wig! I thought the whole point was that you weren't ashamed of having no hair.'

To me the whole furore was bizarre. I realised I'd spent the six years since 2006 convincing myself that no one was really bothered about my alopecia and that they barely noticed. Now, I was being celebrated, not for being a world record smashing athlete at the top of her game, but for my 'bravery' in showing the world my alopecia. Yet not wearing a wig to compete was purely a practical decision. It would have been cumbersome, sweaty, itchy and faintly ridiculous to have a wig on under my helmet for a race and there was little time to put one on afterwards. I didn't take to the podium consciously believing I was being 'brave'.

The media had misunderstood my intentions of making a statement and because of that they were asking me all these questions I simply didn't have the answers to. I couldn't help but feel like a fraud, since the unpalatable truth was that if there was sufficient time to shower, put on make-up and a wig before mounting the podium to have pictures taken, which would then be sent across the globe, I would probably have taken it. At this time I was actually deeply uncomfortable with the idea of being photographed without a wig on, which was what every news outlet seemed to want. Whilst I was comfortable in my cycling gear at the track with no wig, being wig-less for a photoshoot was to me as incongruous as if they had asked me to wear no make-up.

I suddenly found I was being expected to dole out advice to fellow alopecia sufferers and to come up with brilliant, headline-worthy one-liners as a 'message' to anyone who might be experiencing body confidence issues. I'd never thought about those things before, so I wasn't ready to do what was being expected of me. I found myself faced with the task of inventing profound-sounding pearls of wisdom on the spot. Unsurprisingly, I failed utterly.

Additionally, that was the first time there was any public interest in my childhood and initially I found recounting the time when my hair first fell out, aged ten, was quite traumatic. I was being forced to tackle memories and feelings I'd spent a lifetime burying. On top of that, I felt this massive sense of responsibility as a role model to other women who had alopecia, even though I didn't feel I had anything worthwhile to say which might help them deal with the condition. I don't think anyone around me understood how difficult this was for me.

Initially, I had only done the first newspaper interview because they had offered me a fee. At the time, there were only six weeks to go until the Melbourne World Championships and I knew that the other riders were planning to upgrade themselves to business class flights to minimise any negative impact from the long-haul travel in time for the London Olympics. What the newspapers were offering would cover the cost of my upgrade, and as I was currently on half the level of funding my teammates were on, it seemed foolish for me to turn it down.

Somehow, one newspaper piece and photoshoot turned into two and before I knew it, over the course of three days I had also done filming for Channel 5 News, as well as countless phone interviews for local press, radio, and cycling media.

Recently, I looked back over some diary notes I made at the time and I have written about the upset it had caused me when a couple of journalists said, 'Wow, you have a boyfriend! Tell us about him!' I had forgotten how that had made me feel – as though having alopecia meant that I should consider myself fortunate that anyone would ever love me, or want to be seen with me. Now I am more comfortable in my own skin, I think I might interpret the question differently, with genuine curiosity.

I received an overwhelming number of messages via email, Facebook and Twitter from people with alopecia, or parents of children with the condition during those few days. They told me that I had inspired them not to feel ashamed, which made my discomfort worthwhile. One message in particular stood out from the rest – a teenage girl told me she had been bullied at school for having no hair but since seeing me, she had felt more able to stand up for herself and not let the comments of her tormentors get her down. As a consequence, because she was no longer giving the bullies the reaction they wanted, they had begun to leave her alone.

I started to understand that the media furore hadn't been about me at all. I wrote in my diary:

It wasn't about me being special or brave; it was about how it made other people feel. Not just other people with alopecia, but anyone with inhibitions about their body image. I have actually made a difference to other people's lives. Whether it's a small difference or a big difference, it doesn't matter.

I realised, then, that those three torturous days of reliving difficult memories had made a difference.

What I hadn't done during that period, however, was spend any time on my bike. I had been on the form of my life during the Olympic test event, winning two gold medals and setting a new world record. This had left me hungry to replicate a similar sort of performance at the World Championships in Melbourne, the final race before the London Olympics.

Although I approached the Majorca training camp with my mind full of enthusiasm, unfortunately my body decided to say no. A combination of the intensity of the racing in London, having been sick twice, a severe lack of sleep and a jam-packed three days trying to handle all of the media requests had left me running on empty. We had between four and five hours planned on the bike each day, either as long rides or split days of training, and I wasn't going to get anything like the rest I so desperately needed.

I pleaded with Paul, our coach, to let me take it easy. His compromise was that I still had to complete the four or five hours of training every day, but I didn't have to do the intervals the other girls were doing. Unsurprisingly, this didn't suffice. My fatigue became worse until he had to acknowledge I simply wasn't able to join the group for the final day.

That day, I took myself out for an easy ride on my own and pondered how and why everything had gone so wrong. There was the obvious comparison to the other three girls on our squad, and the argument that if they weren't tired then I shouldn't be either. My belief was that we were four totally different types of athlete and it would therefore be beneficial for us to work at a pace which suited us as individuals whilst out in Majorca, before returning to the track as a team. I was upset that some staff had perhaps misinterpreted what had happened with all the media attention over my alopecia, believing that I preferred all this attention to training. Nothing could have been further from the truth. Emotions I'd locked away from times in the past when I had been accused of not being committed to cycling were coming back to haunt me.

Somehow, I made it through to the World Championships, which were being held later than usual, in April. It was a huge inconvenience to have to fly long haul so close to the Olympics and we were all worried about the effect it might have on our performance later in the year. To compensate for this, British Cycling agreed to fly us out there business class. I cannot tell you how much of a difference having a comfortable seat you can sleep in and leg room makes to the quality of a lengthy flight and, consequently, how you feel afterwards.

We flew out to Melbourne ten days before the start of the competition, which was completely unheard of. Usually, we'd arrive just a few days before the race, giving us little time to adjust to the new time zone, hence our coach's instructions last time we were here that we should stay on our feet and keep moving.

Perhaps because we arrived so early, my predominant memory of that trip to Australia was that it was all very relaxed and fun, which is odd when you consider the enormity of the event we were there to participate in. The team dynamic was certainly more calm and stress-free than usual and I put this down primarily to us all being so focussed on the Olympic Games in August. The Olympic test event in London had already been a huge box ticked in terms of performance. It wasn't that the World Championships weren't significant, simply that the Olympics were more important in our eyes.

Although the trip to Melbourne was relaxed in the general sense, a massive rivalry had built up between us and the Australian team following the World Cup. I started to imagine being in the position Australia had been in last time we met in London, i.e. standing by and watching as they smashed our world record. Rumour spread that the Aussies had actually broken our world record in training. The team's social media accounts showed they had posted lots of statuses bragging about how confident they were feeling ahead of the competition. They were on home turf and we were still getting over the jet lag. It began to look like the odds were stacked against us.

I decided to talk to Steve Peters about it. He advised me to expect that Australia would break the record, because that way it couldn't come as a nasty shock. He also said if another team did break our world record, it logically meant the track was running fast. By that reasoning, it meant that we could ride fast on it, too.

As I had predicted, the Aussies did get up and break our world record right before our eyes. Not only that, they rode a hugely impressive time and defeated our previous record by quite a large margin. This was even more impressive to do in a qualifying scenario rather than a final. Quicker times are often recorded in finals not just because a medal is on the line, but because the circulating air created by having another team on the track means you can ride faster for the same power output. Luckily, because of the work I'd done with Steve I was expecting this scenario and my state of mind therefore didn't take quite the tumble it might have done.

As we prepared for our race, you could have heard a pin drop in the velodrome. The thousands of spectators were there to support their home team and remained staunchly silent as we took off. It was such a contrast from the London World Cup a few weeks previously.

It was a tough set of conditions for us to race in, for all kinds of reasons, yet for the second time Australia held the world record for all of about three minutes as we got up and beat the time they had set for us. I was ecstatic! There was little time for celebration though as this was of course just the qualifying round. In just three hours' time we would be racing against the Aussies for the gold medal and coveted rainbow jersey.

We knew that the Australian team would normally start faster than us, yet we decided to stick to the strategy we had devised in training and avoid the pitfall of making emotional, last-minute decisions. We rode our own race and the most distinct memory I have from that race was the change in noise from the crowd. The crowd had been going wild early on in the race, whilst the Aussies were in the lead, but around the halfway point I heard it almost go silent. I decided this must be a good sign! We powered home and were over the moon to win and break the world record again.

Aside from the elation of winning on Aussie soil during Olympic year, I was chuffed about our time of 3:15. Back in 2010, around that dreadful period in which I was recovering from glandular fever and had broken my elbow, we had been told that 3:15 would be a good race time for us to aim for, come 2012. Back then, we were achieving times of around 3:22 and the idea of going so much faster seemed unthinkable. Yet here we were, having hit that target. Not only that, but I'd been tired since we arrived. It struck me that I definitely had more to give.

That week was a great one for the British team, generally. The men's team pursuit beat the Aussies in the final, turning their fortunes around after having lost to them in London a few weeks before. Ben Swift won a world title in the scratch race. Laura Trott won the omnium. Later, she would go on to collect Olympic golds for this event in both London and Rio.

I raced the individual pursuit on Sunday and was placed sixth. My legs weren't really doing what I wanted them to do, although I did ride faster than in the London World Cup. Having failed to secure my place in the final, I was able to join the spectators and cheer the others on from the stands, that evening, having already enjoyed an afternoon trip to the beach.

A fantastic night out followed. The whole of British cycling team went, even though it was only three months before the Olympics. I think we desperately needed to blow off some steam. We all piled into taxis and headed to a nightclub. I hadn't brought a single item of what could be described as 'normal' clothing with me on this trip, so Laura lent me her denim hot pants. They were a size six, whereas I most definitely wasn't. Somehow I managed to struggle into them (which I later jokingly described as my biggest achievement in Melbourne!) although they were cutting me in half. I borrowed flip flops and a tank top from Jess Varnish, one of the girls on the sprint team, and, whilst I was technically the least dressed up of our gang, it turned out I was the most appropriately dressed for the sweltering heat of the club.

Geraint Thomas, who now rides with Team Sky, was buying everybody bottles of champagne. As we toasted, we agreed it had been an incredible week, with most of us performing much better than we had expected. I found the victory in the men's team pursuit particularly heartening as they had had an even longer standing rivalry with Australia.

We flew back on the Monday, having snatched a maximum of two paltry hours' sleep. Luckily, we'd all made the decision to use our own money so that we could fly business class again (British Cycling only paid one way). As I lay back, I couldn't have been gladder I had afforded myself that luxury.

Back home, I had a few days off the bike. In my absence, more requests had come in for me to do photoshoots and interviews about alopecia, but with just a few months to go until the biggest competition of my life, this was a distraction that needed to be managed well.

CHAPTER 19

TEAM GB

I'd never had an agent before, but in the spring of 2012 I was contacted by Gayle Thrush, a formidable Welsh woman who ran her own PR business and worked with some other cyclists, including my friend and British Cycling teammate, multiple Paralympic Champion, Sarah Storey. Gayle was winding down her business so didn't want to become my agent, but she did say she would help me find myself one, whilst assisting me with press management in the meantime.

Gayle had worked with a lot of cyclists in the past and was a phenomenal help during a time when I was so clearly floundering and out of my comfort zone. She handled all of my press requests, instinctively knowing which ones were worthwhile and would boost my profile and which were a waste of time. I also trusted her to be honest. She boosted my confidence by telling me when I looked good and was utterly frank when I didn't. In the latter situation, she had no problem whatsoever in speaking up and demanding a stylist or photographer try something different, something I was too shy to do.

Having Gayle in my corner made everything easier.

That summer, we had a total of three training camps in Majorca. The third took place during a heatwave out there, with the mercury reaching a balmy forty degrees Celsius. I remember one particular afternoon we were completing our second session of the day – capacity efforts along the seafront in the glare of the sunshine. A capacity effort is a simple full-gas effort for a few minutes followed by a long recovery before repeating again. Today was four sets of three-minute efforts. I had a power target to aim for but the effort was mainly about preparing your body to work hard for that length of time. Me being me however, I was obsessed with the power numbers!

My bike was equipped with a power meter to measure my power outputs, measured in watts. On this particular day we learnt that these don't work quite so well in such high temperatures! The heat skews the readings, making them very unreliable. My efforts were reading values around 200 watts, about half of what I would usually be averaging. I had thought I was going well, and at this stage we were just a matter of weeks out from the Olympic Games, and there was part of me wondering if my form might have deserted me.

Eventually Esme Matthew, who was the sports scientist accompanying us on that trip, realised something was awry and put tape over the power meters. She knew the nature of an elite athlete's psychology and that the numbers on our meters still had the ability to put niggling doubts into our minds, even if we knew logically that they weren't working properly. As it turned out, covering the power meters was a good tactic to shake up the routine of our training. Instead I focussed on how much distance I could cover in the three minutes.

We'd been going out early for our rides to try and beat the worst of the heat, but in general, I loved being in that type of weather. I certainly preferred it immeasurably to training in the cold. Whilst some riders moaned about the scorching temperatures I was quite happy with life, chucking bottles of water over myself as we climbed up mountains.

That summer, having conquered the challenges I faced at the last Majorca training camp and bounced back in Melbourne, I was officially named as part of the British Olympic cycling squad, along with Laura, Dani and Wendy. Of course, there were four riders for only three places on the team pursuit, so it was still by no means certain I'd actually get to race. We hadn't been told at this stage who was being lined up as the reserve rider, so this was no time to be complacent or even allow any celebration of selection.

Officially being selected did mean my first experience of a 'kitting out'. All Olympic athletes were invited to Loughborough University to collect all the clothing we would require ahead of the Games. We were given trainers, T-shirts, sweat shirts and hoodies emblazoned with the Team GB logo, in addition to our official cycling kit. Excitingly, we were also offered formalwear for events, as well as something to wear for the opening and closing ceremonies.

As if this wasn't enough, there were also specially branded caps, water bottles, sunscreen and even iPods, all donated by the Team GB sponsors. My eyes were like saucers as I walked around with a personal shopper, trying on all the sizes to ensure everything fitted. The shoppers made note of the sizes we would need and seamstresses were on site to adjust any of the clothes, if needed, so that everything fitted us perfectly.

A lot of the male cyclists had simply supplied their measurements and not attended the kitting out in person, considering it a waste of their time. I had been apprehensive myself – it was a day on my feet, which is inconducive to good recovery – but I'm so glad I went. The experience was incredible and gave me a small realisation of quite how big the London Olympics were going to be.

That was when it really hit home for me: I was on Team GB.

CHAPTER 20

FOUR BECOME THREE

A few weeks before the Games, the Team GB cyclists headed to The Celtic Manor Resort, a five star golf and spa hotel in Newport for a holding camp to ensure we were on peak form by the time the Olympics rolled around. Everyone I had been used to working with during training in Manchester travelled to Wales, including physios, sports scientists and mechanics. Usually, we'd always do our own mechanical work in Manchester, but this time no expense or inconvenience was being spared.

Aside from training, which was fairly heavy during the first week at the Celtic Manor and then tapered back during the second, we didn't have to lift a finger. We had nutritionists to plan all of our meals, which were served in buffet form. I looked forward to the breakfasts the most. They always consisted of a feast, including lashings of porridge, avocado, scrambled eggs, smoked salmon, fresh fruit and Greek yogurt. Lunch and dinner were an equally delicious selection of well-balanced foods, which weren't too greasy or fatty, to keep us in tip-top condition.

Aside from the physical preparation, our other job whilst at Celtic Manor was to test the kit we had received from Team GB. A couple of us weren't happy with the chamois in our cycling shorts, which were different to what we were used to and could almost definitely lead to saddle soreness. We aired our concerns to British Cycling, who were incredibly supportive and arranged for the chamois to be changed. Our shorts were then sent off to a woman named Sally, who meticulously unstitched the chamois and sewed new ones into place for us. I remember thinking it was a goodwill gesture by British Cycling, to take our concerns so seriously and find a solution, even if it meant hours of labour which all had to be done by hand.

Overall, I have great memories of those two weeks in Newport. It was sunny, which instantly ensured I was in good humour. The area around Celtic Manor was great for road rides, encompassing long climbs, rolling terrain as well as flat roads, providing the perfect training variety. It was also just a ten-minute ride in to the velodrome. The only aspect of the place which wasn't completely ideal was that it was itself at the top of a very steep hill, which meant it was always a mission to get home after a training session.

On balance, it felt as though everything was going very well. The coaches had told us that they would select the three of us who would be riding the qualifier of the team pursuit based on a bank of evidence. I assumed they were observing how we were doing at Celtic Manor as well as taking into account our performance over the season so, as ever, there was no specific selection day.

At the Olympics, the team pursuit structure was different to World Cups and World Championships at the time, meaning we would have three rounds of racing rather than two. After the qualifying round all teams are ranked by their time and the first placed team rides against the fourth team and second against third. The winner of each of these races then progresses to the gold medal final.

There was an option to swap riders in and out of the team between each round of racing, meaning that Dani, Laura, Wendy and I couldn't possibly predict with any certainty what would happen. Living with such ambiguity about our future took its toll on all of us, I think.

Personally, this was the most difficult aspect of the Olympic preparation for me. A lot of people talk about the pressure of performing on the big day but I didn't know if I would even get the chance to perform. Good teamwork in our event was essential but the dynamic of not knowing who would race made this a lot more challenging. Dani, Laura and I naturally gelled. The London Olympics being the first Games for all of us this helped us form a natural bond, and we shared a common enthusiasm. Physically, we were all progressing at a rapid rate and with each training session it became obvious we were the fastest three riders, however I never dared become complacent. It was visibly taking its toll on Wendy, who was becoming increasingly hostile, as she began to realise her chances of a gold medal were hanging by a thread. I made an effort to get along with her to ease the tension, but this didn't seem to help matters much.

At this stage, British Cycling had become famous for what are known as 'marginal gains'. These are minute adjustments to your training or lifestyle which might make a difference to how fast you ride. The most important concept behind marginal gains, in my view, is that they are only any use if you have already maximised all the 'major gains'. The major gains are the real game changers, but marginal gains are the cherry on the icing of the cake. If you are already doing all the major things right, marginal gains, although alone may make very little difference, the combination of many small gains can add up to make a difference, which could ultimately be the winning margin of a race in an event which can be decided by tenths of a second.

One of my favourite marginal gain ideas was the special memory foam mattress we had all been given to sleep on. It was lightweight and easily transportable, so we were instructed to use it at home, in the holding camp at the Celtic Manor and then to take it with us to the Olympic Village. The idea was that having the same mattress would minimise any disruption in our sleeping pattern as we moved from place to place as well as of course being comfy.

Another marginal gain was the introduction of 'hot pants'. This time, they weren't at all like the minuscule denim ones I had wrestled myself into on our last night in Melbourne, but ski pants which generated actual heat.

We had learned that the qualifiers for the team pursuit would be on day one, with the first round and finals the following day. What was highly unusual, however, was that there was to be just one hour between the two rounds on the second day. This was well below the usual amount of time you would have to recover, and arguably not enough to complete a normal warm down and then warm up again in time for the final.

We started to refer to the time between rides two and three as the 'golden hour' and to devise various ways we could prepare ourselves for it, the hot pants being one of them. The idea was they kept our muscles warm and supple in the golden hour, thus negating the need to complete a full warm down and warm up. We practised wearing the hot pants in Newport even though the temperature was in the high twenties, which was an experience I can only describe as extremely sweaty. I kept thinking how lovely it would be to have a pair of them in the winter and looking for opportunities to pinch some for keeps.

We were still in Newport when the opening ceremony happened, except for Chris Hoy, who had been voted the flag bearer for Team GB.

The opening ceremony, which was devised by Oscar-winning film director Danny Boyle, was absolutely spectacular. Bradley Wiggins, whom we had all excitedly watched win the Tour de France in July, was given a small part in the festivities. I remember there was some mystery over who was going to be the final torch bearer. I was delighted when I saw the torch being carried to the Olympic flame by six teenagers who were aspiring athletes. It was an exciting yet appropriate twist and a lovely touch.

Just like most of the rest of the country, however, I was watching the opening ceremony on a television screen. It never occurred to me to think this was a missed opportunity. As fun as it would have been to partake in the celebrations, that wasn't what I was going to the Olympics to do. The combination of an early arrival at the Olympic Village, a late night after the ceremony and way too much time on my feet would have played havoc with our carefully devised preparations – I had to have my priorities in place.

Just before we set off for London, the intended line-up for the qualifier, subject to last-minute injuries or illness, was finally revealed to us. As I think we all suspected, given the training evidence, it was to consist of myself, Laura and Dani. That meant of course that Wendy would be in the reserve position.

Understandably, Wendy was terribly upset. I felt for her, because she was currently experiencing the hardest aspect of riding team pursuit. It creates this peculiar dynamic, when you know that four will have to become three, because whilst you are a team and rely on each other, you are also direct competitors.

This system inevitably takes its toll psychologically, since you're experiencing constant cognitive dissonance, simultaneously battling and depending on one another. It's an odd situation to find yourself in and as far as I know, it's unique to team sports. The weirdness of it is magnified in cycling because whereas in, for example, hockey, you might be placed on reserve on the bench, you know that the chances are you'll be swapped into the team at some point during the game. By contrast, in cycling that isn't a certainty or even particularly likely, if everyone is on top form.

Having said that, the blend of skill and personality between Laura, Dani and I worked well as a threesome. Whereas I am quite serious and analytical, Dani is relentlessly optimistic, never letting a setback affect her adversely. Laura is incredibly passionate, an athlete driven more by emotion than by logic. Ahead of the competition, we created a perfect balance of excitement, a need to win and strategic focus.

There was less than a week to go before the race at this point and my biggest fear had been that I would go all the way to the Olympics and not compete. I was by no means in the safe zone just because the coaches had announced their intentions in my favour. One little slip, a twisted ankle or a cold could mean Wendy would be in and I would be out, watching helplessly from the sidelines.

In an effort to avoid befalling any type of calamity, I was studiously avoiding anyone who showed even the slightest signs that they might be coming down with an illness and extended my hand-sanitising routine to even more obsessive levels and was now disinfecting my phone multiple times a day. I kept remembering the way I had felt back at the World Championships in 2011 when I'd missed out on the final. It was such a painful experience.

The same thought was on a loop, repeating itself over and over again in my head: *I cannot go to London and not ride.*

CHAPTER 21

LONDON CALLING

We set off from Celtic Manor in Newport the morning after the opening ceremony, by bus.

Wendy had retreated to her bedroom after being told the previous evening she wouldn't be in the qualifying line-up and no one had seen her all morning. She missed the team photo outside the hotel and didn't emerge until about a minute before the coach was due to set off.

There was definitely an atmosphere on the bus and I kept trying to think of something I could say to Wendy which might soften the blow slightly. Then, I'd remember how I'd felt back in 2011 when I'd been in her situation for the World Championships. I didn't think there was anything anyone could have said to me back then which would have made me feel any less wretched, and whenever anyone did try to say anything to me, it had usually led to tears. I reflected that, with this being the Olympics, it was far worse for Wendy than it was for me. Anything I said might sound patronising or insincere, so I kept my mouth shut, tried to ignore the lingering tenseness and focus on my own performance and the task ahead.

My first thought when I arrived at the newly-built Olympic Village in Stratford, East London, was that it didn't feel like it was in London at all – we could have been absolutely anywhere in the world. There had been a big deal made during our preparatory training of the Games being at home and that putting our team at an advantage. Yet suddenly, in this alien land, it didn't feel like an advantage at all.

I remember the feeling of being very far away from home, which was a strange sensation to have when I was no more than an hour away from my childhood home in Surrey. Perhaps the way I was feeling was more a reflection of how significant it was to be here at the Olympics, how far I'd come since being 'the girl who kept falling off' back at my first training camp, although I didn't register this at the time.

The second thing to hit me was a sensation of being completely overwhelmed by the scale and noise. I remember I'd told Ed Clancy, man one of the men's team pursuit squad and already an Olympic champion from Beijing, when we were on the bus that I was nervous about staying at the village and he had reassured me that I wouldn't 'freak out'. As it happened, whilst his words were reassuring at the time, he was entirely wrong. Freaked out was exactly how I felt. Up until then, I'd only ever experienced cycling-only events. These could be fairly large in scale, but the Olympics was something else entirely. It made me wish I had made an effort to go to Beijing as a spectator, four years earlier. Experiencing another Olympic Games before then might have prepared me for this one a little better.

There was a distinct party atmosphere in the Village, which was so at odds with the more austere environment of Celtic Manor, where everything had been very serious and focussed. Some of the athletes had already competed on day one and therefore finished their events already and were celebrating. I quickly realised that there were also other athletes who had just come along to the Games to enjoy themselves. The Celtic Manor had been sterile by comparison, with everything designed to keep us 100 per cent focussed. Here, distractions were rife. Immediately, I felt like a fish out of water.

When I tell people about the mood of the Olympic Village they're often surprised as there's a perception that we Olympians would all have equal amounts of commitment, looking after ourselves and being in bed by 9pm. Yet I think some athletes were just happy to be there and take part. Fair play to them, but I was under no illusion that I was there to do anything other than win and I had to call on the skills I'd first learned at Fallowfield, not allowing myself to be thrown off-course.

One of the first things I remember about arriving at the Olympic Village is how stunned I was at the size of the food hall. It was absolutely gigantic, encompassing every single style of food you could ever imagine and cuisines from across the globe. I also remember registering a vague, jarring weirdness at seeing McDonald's having such a large presence in a place where elite athletes were eating, before remembering that they were, bizarrely, one of the sponsors of the Games. It was a far cry from the total lockdown on anything remotely unhealthy at Celtic Manor.

The strangest thing of all was that everything was free. Whilst there were various counters set up in the exact same way as your typical fast food restaurant and your order had to be rung through a till, you didn't have to part with any cash. It took me a couple of days before I could get my head around that.

Annoyingly, since the Village was so vast in scale, there was a journey of about half a kilometre between the flats we had been assigned to stay in and the food hall. I know that probably sounds incredibly lazy, but remember it was essential to conserve energy whenever possible and as a cyclist, walking was a big no-no. The week of the Olympic Games is certainly not the time to be adding any extra exertion, even in the form of a ten-minute walk, into your routine. (Interestingly, as soon as my events were over, it was walking I most looked forward to. I'm not a naturally sluggish sort of person in my day-to-day life and I relished the opportunity to go shopping without feeling guilty for spending time on my feet.)

To avoid a delay in us getting breakfast in the morning, our carer, Luc, bought a range of cereals from the supermarket to store in his flat. We became used to taking plastic bottles with us to the food hall at dinner, where we would fill them up with milk and take them back to the apartment to store in the small fridge. We also used to take boiled eggs, since we knew it was so important for us to have protein with every meal. I wasn't sure whether taking food out was technically allowed, so secreting the boiled eggs and milk out of the food hall every evening felt slightly clandestine.

The flats themselves were fairly basic. Wendy and I had single rooms, whilst Dani and Laura shared a twin. There was one bathroom between the four of us. There was very little space to store anything, so I had to rely on my faithful 'floordrobe' (a technical term I had first heard from Andy Tennant, a rider on the men's team pursuit squad, many years before, to describe the organised chaos which ensues when one keeps one's clothes in piles on the floor).

There was a lounge area with some extremely uncomfortable

seating, a small TV, a fridge and a kettle. Team GB had really made an effort to make the flats feel homely, in spite of their basic nature. They had left a few bits and pieces in each of our rooms, including a dressing gown and a mug with the Team GB lion branding and a lovely 'good luck' card. There was also a multiplug, which I was delighted to discover could accommodate my electric toothbrush charger. In fact, I was so chuffed with it that I took it with me when I left and have kept it with me when I travel ever since. (I've since discovered you aren't meant to take anything from the rooms, so I would like to take this opportunity to apologise to whoever from Paralympics GB had my room after me. I owe you a multiplug.)

Team GB also installed air conditioning units for us and even sent a small team ahead of us to thoroughly clean everything and minimise our risk of illness. I appreciated that. My special mattress had been transported from Newport and I placed it on top of the single bed in my room. The foam mattress was, in my humble opinion, one of the best innovations British Cycling had implemented. I heard Bradley Wiggins once say in an interview that he thought they were a 'load of nonsense'. I understood why he said it – after all, the pillow you sleep on isn't going to be the biggest game changer – but for me there was comfort in having the same bedding every night. Whether or not the mattress did all the miraculous things it claimed to, like improve our posture whilst sleeping, it certainly made me feel slightly more at home, something I needed in the alien environs of the Village.

At times I felt lonely, even in the midst of so many people, which I put down to the sensation of being far away from home. When I looked out of the window of my bedroom in the apartment, I could see Canary Wharf. My dad worked there at the time, so whenever I started to feel that disquieting combination of emotions, or like I was out of my depth, I would look out of the window and imagine I could see him in one of the skyscrapers. This simple ritual comforted me.

The velodrome was next door to the Olympic Village, which pleased me. The coaches recommended we take our bikes over, assuring us it would be a very short ride. They were right, but that didn't stop us getting totally lost on the first day. The Village had a few exits with security and it took us a while to find the best one for us to use, which was by using a bridge over the main road and into the velodrome complex.

We had arrived on the afternoon of Saturday, 28 July 2012 and began training the following day (which is, incidentally, my brother's birthday). The weather had turned and we were greeted by pouring rain, although this is, technically, better for track riders since it lowers air pressure and theoretically ensures a faster ride.

That Sunday was the day Lizzie Armitstead was competing in the Olympic road race. I'd been watching it avidly on our TV back at the flat, right until the last second before we left for the velodrome. British Cycling have a 'no phones' policy inside the track, so I'd resigned myself to secretly sneaking away to check for updates on the race via Twitter, feeling like a naughty schoolgirl. Eventually, someone at the velodrome had the great idea to put the race up on the big screen.

I was on the rollers watching Lizzie ride around the roads of Box Hill in Surrey, the very same lanes I had trained on as a teenager. I remember I almost fell off when I saw her cross the finishing line to win a silver medal, behind Dutch legend and standout favourite, Marianne Vos. Whilst Lizzie was a strong contender for that race she was by no means a favourite. The pouring rain had rendered the conditions not ideal for road racing (in my eyes at least, Lizzie tells me she actually quite enjoys riding in the rain. The big weirdo!). I felt completely overcome with emotion when I saw Lizzie and her Yorkshire grit had beaten the odds to get second place. Not only that, Lizzie's was the first medal for Team GB in London 2012, for any sport. Although we had different cycling disciplines, my BFF and I had come together to represent our country in London and after everything we had been through together, that felt significant. It was truly momentous.

We spent a few days on the track preparing for the race. I have never been a particularly great fan of track sessions before a big competition – you don't have the space to yourselves, which effectively advertises your training times to rival nations. As if that wasn't disconcerting enough, you are forced to share the track with athletes who are competing in various disciplines. There will be sprinters flying in for solo efforts, team sprint trios perfecting their start, team pursuiters working on their changes and any number of other random cyclists using the blue line either to warm up or simply to get a feel for the track.

I could never feel comfortable with so many riders around me doing so many different things. Perhaps this is why I found it so difficult being part of a bunch on the road – it's claustrophobic to be in proximity to so many other people with no notion whatsoever of what they are going to do next. I could be riding full gas around the black line, only to come out of the banking and find a coach holding a rider ready for a standing start. In that instance, I'd have just a few seconds to get out of the way whilst simultaneously looking over my shoulder to ensure I wasn't obstructing anyone coming up on the outside. Mixed track sessions, in my view, were very dangerous.

Having said all that, these types of training session are a crucial part of any event. It's essential to get a feel for the unique aspects of the track.

The day before race day we did a one-kilometre effort, which is a third of the total distance of the race, and I felt completely terrible during it and afterwards. I remember worrying about how on earth I would manage another two kilometres in the actual event. However, I made a concentrated effort not to let my worry spiral out of control, calming down by telling myself that if there was any day when feeling bad was a good thing, then today was it. I decided what I needed was a good, hard training effort to wake my legs up a bit more, so hopefully the one-kilometre effort had done the trick.

I'm glad I had that little moment of self-doubt in London, because whenever I have not felt great in the run-up to a race since then, I have used the memory of it to reassure myself that everything will be okay. I guess that gives you an indication, if you didn't know already, of what was going to happen next.

We were to race on the second day of competition for track cycling. On the first day, the men had won the team sprint. This was a surprising turn of events in many ways, because at the time they weren't the world champions. The women's team had huddled around our tiny television in our apartment and watched them win, providing a running commentary on their performance and cheering them on with rapidly growing excitement.

On the same day, Vicky Pendelton and Jess Varnish were disqualified from the women's team sprint, for what was deemed to be an illegal changeover. I remember feeling torn in two, emotionally – my heart was breaking for Vicky and Jess, yet I couldn't get over the male team having already won a gold before we'd even taken to the track. That was quite the starting point, from our perspective. We decided it would be best to focus on the positives and to try and imbibe and internalise some of the highs from the men's victory in the hope that it would rub off.

Our qualifying race took place on 3 August 2012, which was a Friday. We weren't racing until the afternoon, so in the morning I did a protracted warm up known as 'turbo activation' to wake my legs up and get ready for the challenge ahead. This consisted of three ten-minute blocks of effort – referred to as zone one, zone two and zone three – followed by some short sprints.

Warming up properly is a really important part of my race routine. I know from first-hand experience that were I to laze around in the morning before a race I'd be feeling lethargic by the afternoon. Getting myself moving not only optimises the blood flow to my legs, it improves my mindset.

Even though there was a tiny part of me that had been questioning whether I would succeed in light of the previous day, as I went through my pre-race ritual that morning, I felt really good. My legs had the right balance between being not too fresh, but neither too fatigued. I felt I could connect properly with the pedals whilst still reaching my peak speed. I had the sensation of being full of power and I was raring to go.

Perhaps because of this, I wasn't nervous in the slightest ahead of the qualifier. I'd spent a lot of time working with Steve Peters during the few weeks at the Celtic Manor in the run-up to the Games. He'd taught me to anchor myself to positive feelings, like the fact that I was confident in both my own ability and that of my team, and to dismiss the creeping doubts which were questioning whether our best would be good enough.

Everything was coming together and the conditions for the race were as close to perfection as was humanly possible. I was at the pinnacle of my abilities, both physically and mentally, and the home crowd was cheering thunderously.

We rode a fantastic race, qualifying a whole four seconds faster than the next team and breaking the previous world record. This was a staggering result, since each team rides the qualifying round individually, meaning there is no other team on the track to create circulating air. Under normal circumstances, qualifying times are always slower.

I still think to this day that qualifying race was the strongest I have ever felt in a team pursuit. The elation and adrenaline of finally being at the Olympics, combined with all my physical preparation, meant I was on the form of my life. It was a brilliant team performance and we were all buzzing. Now, in theory, all we had to do was repeat this extraordinary performance the following day. Twice. Easy peasy.

At least that was what I told myself as we entered what history would call 'Super Saturday'.

CHAPTER 22

SUPER SATURDAY

If you weren't living under a rock during the summer of 2012, you'll probably already know that 4 August 2012 came to be known as 'Super Saturday' in the British media.

As host nation, we won a staggering number of Olympic medals on that day. Yet the optimistic nickname 4 August 2012 would be given could not have been more at odds with how I was feeling that morning when I woke up in my apartment in the Village. I was, quite suddenly, nervous as hell. My mood wasn't improved when one of our coaches, Shane Sutton, decided it was time to give us a 'pep talk'. Looking back, I'm pretty sure what he said was motivated by believing that our stupendous victory the day before might have left us complacent and therefore primed for a fall. This is the only explanation I can fathom for him choosing to say things like 'You beat everyone by a lot yesterday, but they'll be a lot quicker today.'

Needless to say, Shane's talk didn't have the desired effect on the bundle of nerves that was me, that day. The enormity of the task ahead actually made me feel queasy to the extent where after lunch I had to dash to the toilet, whereupon I immediately threw up. Unlike the day before, I wasn't able to dismiss the small, creeping doubts circling in my mind so easily. I kept thinking, *What if I'm not as good?*, and such misgivings just refused to dislodge from my already overwrought brain.

The semi-final was against Canada, who had come fourth in the qualifier. Just as Shane had predicted, they raised their game considerably from the previous round, but we still beat them by a comfortable margin. This victory ended up being the perfect tonic to soothe my jangled nerves. I realised it was ridiculous to think we could have 'lost it' in the past twenty-four hours and approached the final with renewed confidence.

With just one hour to go until the final, Shane asked us how we were. I verified that I was feeling good and that our performance in the semis had shaken out any lingering wobbles I had been experiencing earlier in the day. At this point, it was confirmed that it would be the same team consisting of myself, Laura Trott and Dani King who would ride again in the final. Wendy Houvenaghel was facing every team pursuiter's worst nightmare: she wouldn't have the chance to participate in any of the rounds.

When she heard the news, Wendy gave me a hug, wished me luck and immediately marched out of the velodrome. By the time we got back to our apartment that evening, she had gone. I didn't understand the significance of it at the time, although I did think it was slightly odd when she completely ignored Laura and Dani, who were stood next to me. Later, Wendy would claim she had been treated unfairly by British Cycling and would describe us as 'juvenile' in an interview.

After Wendy walked out it was just the three of us, in our hot pants, waiting to ride the most important race of our lives. Now that the enormity of being included in all three rounds of racing had sunk in, I realised my mentality had completely changed. Up until that point, my main concern had been doing everything I could to ensure I was included in the team. When I found out that I would definitely be racing in the final, I experienced a huge wave of relief. Now the fear of sitting out had been assuaged, I could start to think about winning. The prospect made me very happy indeed and I felt so excited to race now – I couldn't wait.

It was during the final that we obtained our sixth world record in a row that year. Laura, Dani and I were on the form of our lives, achieving a time of three minutes and fourteen seconds exactly and beating our rivals, America, by a clear six seconds. Considering how unobtainable three minutes and fifteen seconds had seemed to us just a few short months ago, this was a stupendous result. I'd say this was a near-perfect ride, with all of us on great form and all pulling our turns, as planned.

We were ahead of the Americans from the very start of the race. Each lap, the gap between us got bigger. In retrospect, I always think this must have made the final a pretty boring race to watch. It was obvious from the beginning that we were going to win, but that didn't stop the crowd from erupting in sheer joy when it happened.

The applause inside the velodrome was so thunderous, I couldn't hear myself think, let alone what the coaches and the mechanics might have been saying to me. I *pun alert* lapped up the crowd support, circling the velodrome a further five times, drinking in the applause and the adulation. Spectators were sticking out their hands so that I could high five them as I passed by. At some point, someone handed me a Union Jack flag.

I was fortunate enough to have lots of family members there

to watch, including my Auntie Linda and my cousins, Claire and David, who had bought tickets via America due to the lack of tickets available in the UK, as well as my parents and my brother, Erick, but they were all in different places around the stadium. I remember scouring the spectators, trying to find Dan. As I approached the fence I saw him and he enveloped me in a massive hug and someone took a photo. There are lots of lovely photos taken from those moments (including one of me, Dani and Laura, having dismounted our bikes and standing side by side, beaming in triumph, which ended up being made into a commemorative stamp), but I think that one is my favourite.

The victory laps and posing for photos were over swiftly. Then, without *another pun alert* ceremony, we were taken off the track and ushered into a small room beneath the velodrome to get ready for the podium. There were a matter of minutes to take our cycling shoes off and put our trainers on and before I knew it, the gold medal was being placed round my neck. I was in such a daze from the high of winning, I can't even remember who was presenting the medals. My first conscious thought was how heavy the medal felt around my neck.

We were each given a bouquet of flowers and I must have passed mine to someone, although I cannot for the life of me remember who (or indeed why) and they disappeared without trace. I regret not holding onto my flowers. Laura and Dani got their bunches pressed afterwards, as a memento, which I would have liked to do.

After the podium, it was straight to dope control. There was less than half an hour between winning the race and being in a small, stark room, squatting over a plastic pot. I think it's safe to say the reality of the aftermath of getting an Olympic gold is nowhere near as glamorous as some people might imagine.

After completing the drugs test, Dani and I were whisked off in a car to the part of the Village where the BBC had set up a makeshift studio. As part of our agreement with Team GB, we were obliged to do what is called 'managing victory', a euphemistic way of referring to the rounds of media interviews you are taken to after winning a race. Laura was riding the omnium in two days' time, so was exempt from the managing victory duties, but I was grateful to have Dani with me.

Dani is a very easy person to be around. Her chat game is second to none and she is always ready and willing to talk through any problems. I suppose you might say she was the 'agony aunt' of our group. It's little wonder that she has legions of friends all over the UK and indeed across the world.

Both Laura and Dani are extremely extrovert. If I had met them at school, I'm pretty certain we would never have been friends. Yet in the types of situations we found ourselves in at the Olympics, they were the perfect companions, not least because I had to assert myself around them in order to be heard. This, in turn, taught me to be more confident.

Still dressed in our podium jackets and cycle gear, Dani and I went straight to the BBC camp, which was a weird-looking, transparent container with a view of the Olympic Park, accessed via a ladder. When we arrived, the make-up artist immediately began applying some pressed powder to try and counteract the shine from how much we had been sweating during the race. We were also advised to switch off our phones, which were constantly vibrating with the swathes of congratulatory text messages, voicemails and social media notifications.

I can't remember anything I said during that interview, or the ones that followed for other media outlets – I was too high on a combination of adrenaline and joy to really be present in my own body. On occasions such as these, you always tend to be asked how it feels to win, but at the best of times it is incredibly difficult to quantify the excitement and elation in words which will adequately convey what it's like. I suspect I probably didn't make much sense, I was just saying random platitudes whenever a microphone was shoved in my face. Luckily, no one asked me anything remotely controversial which I wouldn't have been able to process, or answer diplomatically enough, at the time.

The one feeling I remember clearly is that I didn't feel relief at winning. Other Olympic champions, especially those who had started out as the favourites as we ourselves had done, often describe winning as a feeling of relief. However, I had already felt that emotion at an hour to go when it was confirmed I would be in the team. The feeling of winning was one of elation and amazement and something I still to this day struggle to put into words. I think it will take many years to sink in quite what we achieved that day.

This was also the day Jessica Ennis, Mo Farah and Greg Rutherford won their gold medals, plus there were another two golds in rowing in the men's coxless four and the women's lightweight double sculls (hence 'Super Saturday').

Team GB had hired a large area in the Westfield Stratford City shopping centre, which they called 'Team GB House'. It was a designated place where you could convene and spend time with your friends and family after events. By the time I had arrived my phone's battery had given up the ghost under the strain of so many congratulatory messages and was totally flat, so I wasn't sure who would be there. I was delighted to see Dan and his twin sister, Natalie, as well as his older sister, Keeley. Both Dan's sisters had bought themselves Team GB tops so they really looked the part. Erick and my parents were also there and they all gave a huge cheer as I walked in.

Dan ran forward to hug me and Natalie managed to capture that moment in another gorgeous photo, which I've since had put onto canvas and put on my wall at home. (Incidentally, that canvas is the only indication you'd get, if you visited my house, of my career as a cyclist.)

Dan was staying at my parents' house in Surrey that evening and his sisters were staying with their Auntie Sue, up in Milton Keynes. So whilst it was fantastic to see everyone and to have the opportunity to celebrate, my time with them felt all too brief when they had to leave in order to get the last trains out of London.

After my family left, the first thing I did was head to the food hall to eat a McDonald's with Dani. Those golden arches had been taunting me all week, but of course my pre-race training regime didn't allow me to indulge. As I ordered my chicken nuggets, the hall was fairly empty. The quiet, after the roar of the crowds and the enthusiastic cheering of my family at Team GB House, was absolutely deafening.

As I chomped on my hard-earned, greasy treats, I couldn't help but think they were a bit of a let-down. Whatever I had imagined I might be doing on the evening of winning my first Olympic gold medal, it wasn't eating cheap fast food. It was a surreal, confusing moment.

I also had an abrupt and disturbing realisation: for a long time, the calendar in my head had only gone up to 4 August. Everything up until that point had been building up to the Olympic team pursuit and now it was over, leaving me with one nagging concern.

What next?

CHAPTER 23

FAME

Whilst the question I'd been asking myself – 'What next?' – had been a fairly philosophical one, the more practical answer was a 6am start the day after the final, to appear on *BBC Breakfast*.

As I mentioned before, Laura and Dani had been sharing a twin room in our apartment in the Olympic Village but, in an effort not to disturb Laura ahead of the omnium, Dani had dragged her mattress into my room the night before. It was very cramped, both of us sharing my tiny single room, with our medals locked in the bedside cabinet. The next morning, the first thing I did was unlock the cabinet and look at my medal, in an effort to assure myself the preceding day hadn't been a glorious dream.

We had instructions to turn up to the makeshift BBC studio without any make-up on, because there would be an opportunity for us to be made up professionally once we arrived. Ever the obedient one, I had followed those instructions, whilst Dani went rogue and did her own make-up before we left.

When we arrived, the studio was incredibly busy, with several athletes and pundits queueing up for their scheduled appearances, one after the other. There was a backlog of people waiting to have their face and hair done and my natural shyness meant I didn't speak up and demand to skip the queue, even when I realised there were only a few minutes until we were due on air.

That was how I ended up on TV in front of millions of people with a few make-up items having been hurriedly applied to my face in the space of approximately sixty seconds. Although it wasn't my biggest concern at the time (I had just won a gold medal, after all), I do remember being distinctly unimpressed as I would never normally leave the house without my eyeliner on!

What followed was a whirlwind morning, as we were taken from studio to studio, including one for the local BBC news station in London, which was situated on the top floor of a block of flats near Stratford. The place was like a sauna, with the combination of studio lights and the fierce August sunshine streaming in through the window.

After we had done the rounds and were freed from our media obligations, Dani and I decided the best way to celebrate our win would be to do a spot of shopping. The Olympic Park was right next to one of the capital's biggest shopping centres (confusingly called Westfield although it is situated in the East of the city).

A representative from Team GB had been assigned to look after us and we expressed our wish to go. Mysteriously, he wasn't at all keen on the idea of us going to Westfield but we were insistent, failing to see why this would be a problem. The rep advised us to be careful and not to take our medals, which, when they weren't in the bedside cabinet overnight, had been around our necks the entire time since the win. We were taken to Team GB House, where there were safe lockers for us to leave them. I remember being worried my medal would get mixed up with Dani's, so we left a small piece of paper on one of them in order that we could decipher which was which when we returned.

We were given a police escort to go with us to the shopping centre, which seemed at first like an unnecessarily paranoid gesture. That was until we turned up. As we walked into the doors of Westfield we were what can only be described as totally mobbed. Crowds of people surrounded and enveloped us, asking for autographs and selfies and even handing us their babies, which, as much as I didn't particularly mind, struck me as a bizarre thing to do (what if I dropped him or her?).

Our progress as we attempted to traverse the shopping centre floor was incredibly slow. We attempted to sign as many autographs and pose for as many selfies as possible, although it would have been impossible to meet every demand. The first shop we came to was high street fashion chain Oasis, which we darted into, grateful for the respite.

I'd reconciled myself to the idea we weren't going to get into any other shops under these circumstances, so set about choosing a couple of outfits in Oasis. I gathered up anything that caught my fancy, unconcerned by how much it was costing me. The enduring high from our win took away any worries about bills, or indeed anything which wasn't happening in that very moment.

The police officer we had been assigned followed us the whole time. As we chatted he told us that his name was Alex and he was, coincidentally, a friend of Gayle Thrush, my agent. Alex had been great at controlling the crowds and clearly had a lot of experience in that area. The Westfield shoppers hadn't been at all aggressive, but it was overwhelming to be approached by a crowd of that magnitude, particularly because it was the last thing we expected.

There had been a lot of people asking if they could see our medals. We told them we didn't have them with us, but we could tell they didn't really believe us. Imagine if someone came up to you in the street and demanded to see the most treasured possession you had, then eyed you suspiciously when you told them you didn't have it on you, right then. If you think it would be slightly intimidating, you would be right – that's exactly how it felt. Whilst I don't think anyone was prepared to wrestle us to the ground and strip-search us, we were definitely given the right advice by Team GB when they told us not to take our medals out.

Perhaps it was naive of me, but I genuinely didn't think anyone would know who I was outside of the velodrome. Fortunately, the kind of intense attention we'd received at Westfield only lasted for a couple of weeks after the Olympics. After that, things died down and I only got recognised occasionally. Yet having that transitory experience has allowed me to empathise with people who get mobbed all the time – I'm not sure I would be able to handle it.

At some point during the afternoon, Dani and I went back to the track with the intention of watching some of the other cycling events. The passes we had been given allowed us unlimited access to the velodrome, but not to see any of the other sports. Our recent win hadn't changed that. It's certainly not the case, as some people believe, that if you have a gold medal, you can meander into any part of the Olympics you please.

Going back to the scene of our win meant yet more attention from the public. I suppose it was quite silly in retrospect that we had imagined we'd be able to slip in unobserved and watch from the stands, undisturbed.

Initially, it had been quite difficult for us to find a seat. The disruption we caused as we entered meant we caught the attention of a few people who recognised us. After that, there was no going back. I quickly learned that if one person approaches you and asks for a selfie, a herd will inevitably follow. We were constantly being asked for pictures and autographs, which meant we couldn't focus on what was happening on the track.

If I'd thought the press scrutiny I'd faced after the London World Cup and all the interest in my alopecia was overwhelming, that was nothing in comparison to the glare of the spotlight that was shone on me after the Olympics. I wouldn't say I was bothered by it, having addressed any lingering feelings of discomfort earlier that year, but it did take me by surprise.

Being a world champion, I'd assumed I'd experienced everything the world of professional sport had to offer. Again, I found myself wishing I had gone to Beijing. Being in another country, the British medal-winning athletes wouldn't have got quite the same amount of attention, but at least it might have given me a flavour.

In addition to never having experienced an Olympics before, Steve Peters had kept saying to me in the run-up, 'It's just another race'. He frequently reminded me that the cyclists I would be competing against in the Olympic team pursuit were the same ones I had taken on (and beaten) in other competitions. This had become my mantra. In teaching me to think in this way, Steve had encouraged me to play the Olympics down in my head and thus to stop me freaking out and sabotaging my own performance. It was an excellent strategy in helping me to prepare for the race itself, but it hadn't done anything to prepare me for what would happen afterwards.

After the frantic hullabaloo that followed our victory, I reflected on how many people must have been watching the cycling on the day we won who would never watch professional bike racing usually. I remember in the run-up to the Olympics there had been some negativity about how much the Games were going to cost. Newspapers were incredulous about the amount of public money being allocated for building the Olympic Village, when they felt it would be better spent on public services. Comedians were also doing a lot of material predicting that the Games were going to be a washout. I suppose it's a facet of the British mentality, to manage our expectations, but the cumulative effect of all that pessimism was that there had been a part of me that had assumed the Games wouldn't be at all popular.

Perhaps it's the case that no one was able to accurately predict just how much the British public would get behind the London Olympics and how much it would transform the whole attitude of the nation. That was another reason why my sudden fame and notoriety was so unforeseen.

Before the Olympics, it was incredibly rare for me to have conversations with anyone outside the world of cycling about what I do. I remember one atypical occasion, which happened when I was in the lift at Celtic Manor (remember, a cyclist never takes the stairs), wearing all of my Team GB Lycra. A man and his wife, also in the lift, asked me what I did and without thinking that they might not know what it meant, I said 'team pursuit' – I didn't want to patronise them by saying 'cycling' if they were already fans of the sport.

A few months later, they tweeted to tell me that they'd returned to their hotel room and googled 'team pursuit' having absolutely no idea what it was. They were so intrigued by what the internet threw up, they eventually ended up getting into cycling themselves. The woman, Deborah, now regularly competes in triathlons and always tweets to let me know how she is doing. This year, she is training for an Iron Man competition. She maintains to this day that it's all down to meeting me in that lift. I guess that was the first time I realised it was possible to have that sort of impact on someone's life.

It's a powerful thing, being in the public eye, and the cumulative impact of what had happened after the London World Cup and my subsequent labelling in the press as the 'poster girl' for alopecia after the Olympics meant I was beginning to realise that.

And so the press interest in me, my childhood and my condition began again. This time, though, I was prepared.

CHAPTER 24

BREAKING

That week, I did an interview with Lizzie Armitstead in which we talked about our friendship. We had a photoshoot together, which was far more fun than the ones I had done alone (although Lizzie got to wear a much nicer outfit, which made me jealous). In general, it was more comfortable for me knowing that I wouldn't be the entire focus of the interview and that it would be shared between the two of us.

Lizzie spoke some wonderful words about me and what I mean to her during that interview, which of course I reciprocated. I explained how she has always believed in me, even during those times when I have doubted myself. She has all these handy little mantras, which she doles out when you need them, like 'keep the faith' and 'don't let the hiccups get you down'. She's like my own, highly motivational Jiminy Cricket.

Again, the press hailed me as 'brave' for standing on a podium without my wig on. Whilst I still didn't think of it as a conscious decision or statement, previous experience had taught me that the gesture had meant a lot to some of the people who had seen it, so I let it slide.

My dad bought me a gift to congratulate me on my win – a large, framed print of the London tube map, with the names of all the medal winners where the stations should be. It was designed by an artist who only made a few, limited edition copies. The cyclists took the central line – Chris Hoy is Stratford, where the Games were held, presumably because he was the flag bearer. Dani King is Queensway and I am Lancaster Gate. Of course, Wimbledon is Andy Murray. I've always found going on the Tube a really exciting experience, ever since I was a little girl, so it was the best present I'd ever had.

After our win at the velodrome I went to stay at my parents' house in Cheam. This was just a Tube and a train ride away from the Olympic Village, meaning that I could return for some of the events if I wanted to. Dan was desperate to see me since we'd only snatched a few hours together after the final and kept asking me to come home. I went there for a day but ultimately the allure of the fun surrounding the Olympics was too strong and so I returned to the Village. Dan visited whenever he could.

I was flooded with invites to VIP parties and press events. Dani and I threw ourselves enthusiastically onto the scene, going to exclusive clubs like Mahiki and China White and never paying for transport or drinks.

Those few days were terrific fun. The biggest obstacle I had to contend with were blisters. After spending so much time studiously avoiding doing any walking, I was now constantly on my feet. Blisters were erupting on every available surface of my poor trotters. Even the soles of my feet were covered in them. I remember one night Dani persuaded me to swap shoes with her, since she was wearing heels and I was in flats and she'd reached the stage where her 'balls were burning' (we've all been there!). I agreed, before promptly realising I was going to find it impossible to walk in her shoes, either. Somehow, I ended up walking home barefoot, carrying Dani's shoes (I'm still not sure how that happened) whilst passers-by pointed and laughed at me. Even this wasn't enough to dampen my jubilant mood.

That was, until something terrible happened.

I had joined the spectators to watch the Olympic BMX racing. I'd done incredibly well to sneak in there, since our passes were only for the velodrome, but Dani and I had somehow blagged it through the cunning use of 'walking confidently'.

As the event finished, I glanced down at my phone and saw that I had ten missed calls from Dan. As I wondered what could be wrong, the phone leapt into life again and this time I answered his call. But the voice at the other end of the line wasn't Dan's: it was a paramedic's. He told me Dan had been involved in a road traffic accident, that he couldn't speak to me himself because he was in an ambulance, on gas, being taken into hospital.

After the elation following our Olympic win, this news brought me back down to earth with an almighty bang. The paramedic told me Dan was being taken to St Helier, which happens to be the hospital I was born in. He had been riding on his motorbike when a van had pulled out in front of him. He'd been unable to stop in time and had crashed into its side.

Dan had multiple fractures in his right leg and his right foot was a total mess. This was all the detail I was given, other than to get to the hospital asap. Of course, in situations such as these your brain always jumps to the worst possible scenario. I'm told this is a survival technique to prepare yourself mentally should the worst happen, although in reality it's mostly bloody annoying.

I convinced myself Dan must be dying – I was panicking,

gulping for air, tears streaming down my face. Then I called the one person I could think of in my fug of despair – Steve Peters. He talked me down from my emotional ledge, instructed me to pack a bag and take a train to Sutton. By the time I got there I was sufficiently possessed of myself to jump in a taxi to St Helier.

When I arrived, the nurses recognised me and began chatting animatedly about my gold medal. I didn't want to appear rude, but I was in no mood for celebration and told them I just wanted to know about Dan. Eventually, I found his bed.

As it turned out, Dan was as okay as it was possible for him to be under the circumstances, having sustained broken bones, although he did need to have surgery and to stay in hospital for over a week. By the time I arrived he'd been given lots of morphine to help him cope with the pain and was high as a kite. He had apparently been bragging to the nurses about me.

In his drugged-up-state all Dan could say was, 'Show the nurses your medal!', whilst I was still trying to ascertain what on earth was going on. It was a long time before I could get enough sense from anyone to know that he was going to be fine.

At the same time as all this was going on, my parents had travelled to Holland to watch my brother Erick race in the European Road Championships and he had a really bad crash, shattering his collarbone in multiple places. Mum and Dad would need to drive him home, where he too would eventually end up in St Helier.

I spent the remaining few days of the Olympics by Dan's bedside, but I couldn't help but feel the timing could have been better (if, indeed, there is such a thing as a good time for something like that to happen). The Olympic competition was still on at this point. I'd been given a special gold card which allowed me access to some of the swankiest events happening throughout the country. I was having to cancel personal appearances and the perfectionist in me was worried I'd somehow get a reputation for being unreliable, even though I'd explained the exceptional circumstances. But none of this really mattered, as deep down all I really cared about was the health of my family.

One thing was for sure, after the high of my first ever Olympic gold, Dan and Erick's accidents had brought me crashing back to earth with a bang.

CHAPTER 25

LEGACY

There is little that could have tempted me to leave Dan's bedside during those few days and I'd already reconciled myself to the idea that I was going to miss the Olympic closing ceremony. Yet Dan, being the wonderful bloke he is, was really insistent I shouldn't miss it. He was feeling a lot stronger by that stage and predicted, rightly, that I'd always regret it if I didn't go.

I eventually relented, promising to send him loads of photos. As I approached the Olympic stadium, dressed in the special garments which had been issued by Team GB (red chinos and a white top embellished with sequins), I couldn't help but feel sad it was all over.

The ceremony itself was a blur of colour and noise. It was beautifully done, but my mind was elsewhere, worrying about Dan. I don't remember much specifically about it, other than my excitement when The Spice Girls appeared (I've always been a huge fan) and making the most of the opportunity to get as many photos as possible.

Most of the athletes had made plans to return home to their

families, who had come to collect them the day after the ceremony. British Cycling had also arranged a coach to take anyone who wanted back to Manchester, but I needed to stay at my parents' home and near St Helier hospital. With my parents still en route back from Holland with Erick, and Dan lying in a hospital bed, I had no one to collect me from the Olympic Village.

After all the hard work, the excitement, the elation and the adoration, it ultimately came to me standing on my own on the outskirts of the Village with seven large bags (my kit bags, plus many extras as I had also done a fair bit of shopping by this point) and a travel mattress, wondering how on earth I was going to get out of there. Thankfully, Doug Dailey, who was the logistics manager for British Cycling, came to the rescue and offered to drive me to Cheam himself.

Life was pretty hectic after that. Erick returned to the UK and was also admitted to St Helier hospital, where he too would require surgery. He and Dan actually ended up in beds next to each other on the same ward! It was a surreal situation, and I spent lots of time visiting the hospital, ensuring neither Erick nor Dan spent too much time alone (and making a gigantic donation to St Helier's parking fund in the process). When Dan came out of hospital it was an incredibly difficult time for us both. He couldn't walk unaided and needed huge amounts of rest. Piles of invitations were arriving through the letterbox of my parents' house (where we were both staying for the time being), asking me to attend movie premieres, West End shows and VIP events, but it just seemed so unfair to go without Dan.

Obviously, partying and living the life of a celebrity isn't why anyone gets into cycling, but I admit it did strike me as a shame I couldn't revel in the opportunities life was throwing at me at this unique time of my life for a while.

As Dan recovered, life slowly returned to normal. I did a couple of TV interviews about alopecia, growing more confident in my ability to talk about the condition as well as my relationship with it. The Paralympics were approaching and my agent, Gayle Thrush, had arranged for me to do some work as a pundit.

Now Dan was well enough for me to leave him, I began working each day with Channel 4 at the Olympic Park for their coverage of the track cycling. I enjoyed myself immensely, especially as I have quite a few friends who are on the Paralympic squad, including one of my best friends, Sarah Storey, who won an incredible total of four Paralympic golds that week!

The public had really got behind the Paralympics and it was receiving record viewing figures. As a pundit I was being recognised whilst out and about even more than before. To me it was still a strange feeling, being approached and complimented by strangers.

During this time, the postbox in Cheam village was painted gold. This was a brilliant idea by the Royal Mail to honour the gold medallists at the home Games and had begun straight after the event. Since my birthplace was listed as Carshalton, someone had taken the initiative to paint the postbox gold in that town and considered the job a good'un. It was my dad who had rung Royal Mail HQ and requested the box in Cheam be painted instead. The postbox in Carshalton was promptly returned to its original red.

The gold postbox in Cheam stands on the route walked by pupils at Nonsuch to get to school. There is a plaque stating who it is in honour of and I like to think sometimes the girls may look at it and remind themselves that you can achieve amazing things if you're not afraid to take opportunities and to persevere in the face of challenges.

Dani, Laura and I were also put on a special commemorative stamp (I bought a large batch, which I still use today whenever I send a letter to my nan). The three of us had become close in the build-up to London but now the aftermath was pulling us in different directions. It was the first Olympic Games any of us had competed in and none of us was quite prepared for the realities of it. That allowed us to bond, as we supported each other. The trust and understanding we had built up by being honest and showing each other our vulnerabilities had been one of the factors which had allowed us to win our race. Whilst it isn't always comfortable to put your trust in another person, it definitely pays off when it counts.

The slogan which had been used throughout the London Olympics was 'Inspire a generation' and a great deal of emphasis was placed on the legacy of the event. I went back to my old cycling club – Sutton Cycling Club – in Surrey, taking my medal with me to show off to the kids, and was delighted to discover that since the Olympics the number of girls who were members had quadrupled. I don't think I realised up until that point that the effect of the Games could be so immediate and direct – parents had literally taken their daughters along to the club the week after seeing our race on the television.

I really enjoyed hearing those sorts of stories and knowing that I had in some way had a positive impact on other people's lives. I especially revelled in the knowledge that more girls were being encouraged into sport. There are some terrifying statistics floating around about the number of teenage girls who stop doing sports they enjoy around about thirteen or fourteen because they are worried about things they consider 'unfeminine', like gaining muscle and sweating. To me it seems such a shame that beauty standards should stop young women from participating in something which can have so many benefits for their health and their confidence.

After the Paralympics there was a parade day in central London, with a float for each sport. I was given instructions to meet everyone from Team GB and Paralympics GB at Guildhall, near Bank, in the East part of Central London. Even after everything I'd experienced at the Olympic Village, I still found it difficult to believe my eyes when I showed up and saw hoards of people who had turned up to support us.

As we passed through the streets, I spotted three or four people holding banners with my name on it and one that said 'I went to Cuddington Croft'. It was incredibly touching, to be able to revel in that kind of direct connection with other people. I've never had another experience, even to this day, which has quite been able to rival the post-London parade. There was such an outpouring of appreciation for what we athletes had achieved for our country.

CHAPTER 26

STAGE FRIGHT

B y the winter of 2012, Dan had recovered sufficiently from his accident to be able to walk on his injured leg, just about. Whilst there were piles of invitations flooding in that we still weren't able to attend, we did manage to go to the Beatles Musical, *Let It Be*, together in the West End.

We were surprised when we showed up at the theatre and there was a red carpet there. We had, perhaps foolishly considering we had been given our tickets for free, assumed it was just another night for the production and we would be able to slip in unobtrusively. I realised that, whilst the outfit I'd selected was ideal for sitting on my arse for two hours in the dark, it probably wasn't one I'd ideally like to see reproduced in the papers the next day. Until that point, I had pretty much spent my entire life living in a tracksuit – picking out formal dresses wasn't my forte. The experience taught me to be more conscious about what I wore on any public occasion.

I also did the BBC's *A Question of Sport* that winter and can say with some authority that my performance was absolutely abysmal. I can only put my stage fright down to the presence of the live studio audience. As I walked on set, I was shocked by how many people had shown up. Dan's dad, Kev, and his sisters had come to watch, although Dan himself still wasn't well enough to travel.

Again, I was dressed wrong and I knew it. We'd been instructed not to wear anything with a pattern, or in black or white. This ruled out the vast majority of my wardrobe. After a fruitless hour spent scrutinising and dismissing every item of clothing I owned, I simply wore a black and white ensemble and reconciled myself to everyone being pissed off with me.

The very first question I was asked was to name a Dutch cyclist, Teun Mulder, from looking at his picture. Everyone in the cycling world was aware of him – he'd recently been awarded a bronze medal at London 2012 in the keiren, a sprinter's event where riders are paced behind a motorbike for the opening laps before unleashing their sprint for the line, and it had attracted a lot of attention because it was a joint bronze. Two riders had crossed the line at the exact same moment and it had been concluded there was absolutely no way to separate them from the photo finish. This was highly unusual.

In short, I should have been able to answer the question easily enough but of course my brain simply refused to be on my side. I kept trying to remember the name of the rider, I knew I knew it, but my mind was completely blank. The camera was focussed on me for what felt like half an hour whilst our team captain, Matt Dawson, urged me on – 'Come on, Jo! Think! You MUST know this!' In the end, I was forced to concede defeat and say that I didn't know.

That was my very first experience of stage fright. Before then,

I could never understand it when people said their knowledge simply deserted them in a pressured situation, like an exam, but now I totally got it. Even though I managed to get the rest of my questions right, I was crippled by feelings of embarrassment.

When I watched the show back, a combination of the way it had been edited and the fact that pauses seem a lot longer when you're on set than they do as a viewer meant that excruciating moment lasted only a few seconds. I breathed a sigh of relief – there had been an irrational part of me that thought perhaps the entire half hour would have been dedicated to me trying to remember that first question.

I was also present when Bradley Wiggins won Sports Personality of the Year, beating an unprecedented four other cyclists who had made it onto the shortlist. The sports personality event had a red carpet, something I still wasn't used to at all. Really, you need to be trained in order to have the skills to deal with the red carpet experience. I see actresses, musicians and models taking it in their stride and now I know what it's like out there, I have more admiration for them.

As I 'glided' along the carpet (trying not to stumble in my heels – have you ever tried to 'walk elegantly' once you have become aware of the need to do so?) one of the paparazzi called 'Joanna, over here!' As soon as he made the rest aware of my presence, they all began yelling at me, trying to get me to look directly into their camera lens. The cacophony of flashes was blinding. I couldn't see who was calling my name and tried to turn a little this way and that, hand on my hip, like I'd seen other people do in this situation. In retrospect I probably looked a little bit like a rabbit in the headlights.

I did feel slightly hard done by that Dani, Laura and I weren't given the Team of the Year gong at the sports personality event.

We had, after all, set six new world records and remained unbeaten throughout the year. That kind of performance had been unheard of up until that point. It was decided, in defence to the spirit of the Games, to give the award to the whole of Team GB and Paralympics GB – all the athletes who had taken part across the various disciplines were included. Perhaps it's sour grapes but that struck me as a bit of a cop out. I suppose with it being such an amazing year for sport in the UK they wanted to find a way of recognising everyone.

The media had started to take our sporting success for granted. That's the problem with having been so dominant in such a high-profile event – the public become complacent, assuming your victory is a sure thing. I heard comments like, 'You could put your house on these girls winning!' It has only been in subsequent years when we haven't dominated the event in the same way that I think we've actually had more recognition of the significance of our achievements back in 2012.

Not only did this irk me for reasons of wanting all the graft we had put in to be acknowledged – after all, we hadn't got to this point using just talent and some fairy dust – it also meant that when we suffered our first failure, no one was prepared.

CHAPTER 27

WIGGLE HONDA

B ut I'm getting ahead of myself. It would be another two and a half years before the GB women's team pursuit squad would endure a humiliating thrashing at the hands of another team. In the meantime, we all had the difficult decision of deciding what we would do in the immediate aftermath of the London Games. It was now winter, which would traditionally mean a return to the track, but after so much track racing during the summer I began to feel like I needed some respite.

I say it was a 'difficult' decision – for Laura Trott and Dani King the answer seemed to be obvious. They wanted to carry on working together as a unit and winning on the track. In fact, Laura was quoted in the press around that time as saying something along the lines of 'Why would you want to leave a winning team?'

I knew that comment had been directed at me. After our unprecedented victory, she and Dani just couldn't understand why I wouldn't want to capitalise on our success and jump straight back into team pursuit. Yet I felt strongly, instinctively, that I needed to try something different, at least for a while. After all, there is only so long I can bear having every tenth of a second relentlessly analysed and scrutinised before I need to come up for a little air.

I joined a road team called Wiggle Honda, whilst a younger rider called Elinor Barker took my place on the team pursuit with Dani and Laura. That previous autumn I'd met a road cyclist called Rochelle Gilmore and she had put forward the idea of a women's professional road cycling team with an ethos of operating as professionally as many men's equivalents.

At that time, there wasn't much that you could call 'professional' about many women's road racing teams. Not all but many were run on a shoestring budget, with women's road racing receiving little to no TV coverage and therefore attracting much less media attention and therefore less sponsorship than the men's side of the sport. This was something which often becomes a vicious circle in women's sport. Rochelle was keen to change that and this appealed to me, since I'd had a thing about injecting more equality into cycling ever since my own foray into the sport.

I signed a contract with Wiggle Honda and spent the winter preparing for an entirely different sort of racing by doing road miles. After having devoted most of my winters to going round and round in circles at the velodrome, this felt like a treat. I got satisfaction from the notion that I was building up road miles, whilst at the same time I didn't have to do the same sort of intense intervals I associated with track racing. Laura and Dani also signed with the team but still had their ambitions on the track for the winter.

I first met the rest of the Wiggle Honda team in January 2013, at a launch event in London. I knew very few of the riders there but most of them knew me after my performance during the Olympics. There were five Brits in total (Elinor Barker and Amy Roberts were the other two), joining cyclists from Australia, New Zealand, Italy and Japan. I remember feeling extremely nervous about meeting everyone. Despite the huge boost in confidence the win at London had given me professionally, I had yet to completely conquer my social shyness.

My first race was in late February, what is known as a 'cobbled classic', a famous race in Belgium called Omloop Het Nieuwsblad. The day that we happened to ride the race, it was minus two degrees, although mercifully it wasn't wet or icy. I remember wrapping myself up in layer after layer to combat the cold, but being able to do nothing to protect my face, which stung horribly in the wind. I had just flown in from a training camp in Lanzarote a couple of days before and was nicely acclimatised to a temperature of around twenty-five degrees, so this sharp contrast was a shock to my system.

The roads in this particular race are incredibly narrow, making it even more fundamental that you are able to force your way to the front of the bunch early on. I seemed to be in the worst position at all the crucial moments, so was doomed from the beginning. For all these reasons, I ended up receiving a 'DNF', which stands for 'Did Not Finish' and is a badge of shame for any cyclist.

In the interests of accuracy I should say that actually I did finish, just not within the specified time limit (which unfortunately still means receiving the dreaded DNF). All I can really remember is that by the time I reached the finish line I was shuddering with cold to the extent that my cheeks felt frozen and I couldn't form coherent sentences. My dad was there to meet me and I wanted to ask him to get me a hot chocolate to help me warm up, but all I could muster was 'h-h-hot'. Understandably, he had no idea what I was talking about.

As it happened, that year the track world championships were early, falling in February, the same week as Het Nieuwsbald. I returned from Belgium to Manchester and worked with the BBC as a pundit on the last day of racing from their studio in Salford. Elinor Barker, Laura Trott and Dani King won the team pursuit and it was at that moment I knew with absolute certainty I'd made the right decision to take a break. I didn't feel even a twinge of jealousy or longing, I was simply happy for the three of them and their achievement.

I'd also begun to carve something of a niche for myself as a pundit. It suited me to reflect on other people's performances and in turn, judging by social media comments, I was getting a good response from the viewing public. Where my propensity for being 'nice' had been perceived as a disadvantage as an elite sportsperson, in the world of TV it had become something audiences were relating to. The public don't tend to warm to arrogance, which is a quality many of the athletes who considered themselves psychologically 'stronger' than me had in spades, and instead my objectivity as well as knowledge and insight were going down well.

During the winter I'd mainly self-coached, a freedom I relished, but in the spring of 2013 I'd been assigned a new coach called Chris Newton. He immediately recognised that whilst I excelled at maintaining a steady pace on the bike, I wasn't so good when it came to change of pace in races. To remedy this, he had me undertaking many interval sessions, varying in duration and intensity, but very few steady state efforts. These intervals really helped me to tackle the weakness in my skill set which he had identified. I enjoyed the hard work and the new challenge of mixing my training up with different sessions. There is little

Winning a Commonwealth gold medal in the individual 3000m Pursuit final in 2014.

The big day – my wedding to Dan.

© Chelsea Shoesmith Photography

Joanna & Dan Shand's Wedding Day

11th July 2015

'Achievement unlocked: Married – 50 Gamer Points'

© *Chelsea Shoesmith Photography*

Above left: Crammed into a lift in Rio with poor Greg Rutherford, who had to fit in around our bikes. Sorry, Greg! We later decided to begin taking the stairs, after hearing stories of athletes who'd been stuck in broken lifts before their events. As cyclists normally avoid walking at all costs, this was a significant decision!

Above right: With Ciara, such an incredible friend during the rocky road to Rio, in the Athletes' Village.

Below: The dreaded Rio dining room. You can see, it was fairly empty here!

Above: Elinor, Katie, Laura and I take the gold in the 2016 Women's Team Pursuit final, with our third world record of the week. Somehow the pressure was less than in London, and we felt empowered to leave everything on the track.

Below: GB's Golden Girls!

Above left: Punditry work with Clare Balding and Chris Hoy! Dashing around between TV sets and radio interviews that day was a workout in itself.

Below left: Dance class at Club la Santa, wearing my Alopecia UK buff!

Below right: When this photo was shown at a British Cycling gala dinner, another rider made an unpleasant comment about it, which totally took the wind out of my sails. I think things would be different now, and I'm so proud of the moment that picture captures.

Above: Some well-deserved relaxation with Dan at Club la Santa.

Below left: My career medal haul. I posted this on social media when I announced my retirement, and was touched by the responses I got.

Below right: Retirement means I get to spend a lot more time with my cat. Priorities!

Whatever the future holds for us now, it's bound to be exciting.

point in focussing only on the things you enjoy as an athlete, or are already accomplished in. As the saying goes, train your weaknesses, race your strengths.

I'd entered a ten-mile time trial one weekend as part of my training. Chris had instructed me to ride the race as I would normally – take my number off, have a quick fifteen-minute break and ride the entire thing again. That meant two efforts of twenty-plus minutes at full gas for me. I remember thinking it would feel a little strange to go back and do the entire thing again, and I think all the other competitors thought exactly the same, but this was the kind of creative thinking Chris excelled at.

That summer, my main target was to train to win the National Time Trial Championships, which were taking place in Glasgow in June 2013. I'd always fancied having a pop at that competition, but in my previous incarnation as a track rider time simply didn't allow for me to prepare for it properly.

Time trialling is a fairly simple discipline to understand – the aim is to ride from A to B as fast as possible, with few thoughts of tactics and team dynamics. Riders race alone, set off at one-minute intervals, and the rider with the fastest time to complete the course wins. Some riders refer to it as a boring discipline, a lonely race on your own, just you and your bike against the clock, with none of the 'fun' elements of attacking and jostling for position in the bunch. However, I always thought the opposite. A time trial requires complete concentration throughout. There are so many things to focus on, such as your heart rate, cadence and speed, which will be shown on a small bike computer on your handlebars (I didn't race with power output this year), as well as maintaining complete focus on the course and holding a tucked aerodynamic position on your bike. You need to know when the next hill is coming up or the next headwind section in order to distribute your effort, as well as where the corners are and how sharp they are so you can take the correct line and not lose any speed unnecessarily.

That year, the National Time Trial would be twenty-three miles in distance, which would take the best part of an hour. I'd been working on my endurance and increasing my threshold, having spent so long on the track focussing on increasing peak power and speed. Now, the trick was to reach and maintain an effort at threshold, which until this season had been relatively neglected. This is, fortunately, a very trainable area and all the work I had done with Chris had brought me on in leaps and bounds.

I drove to Glasgow with Dan the weekend before the event, which was on a Thursday. Dan, who had a job as a Finance Officer at a school, had to work on Monday morning and so he flew back, giving me Monday to Wednesday to get to know the intricacies of the course – the corners, inclines and descents which might have a bearing on my performance on the day.

I was spending a lot of time resting, too, tapering my training down on my own terms ahead of the race. This was a new experience for me. As a team pursuiter, I had very little say on my taper into a competition as training efforts had to be done as a team. There had been times when I had desperately wanted to rest but everyone else had been keen to do another training effort, meaning I had to relent. And conversely, there had been times when I wanted to put more effort in my legs but the others hadn't been keen. This is partly what makes the team pursuit even more of a fascinating event. The challenge of getting a team of girls, all with different physiology, to perform optimally on one given day was an incredible challenge that required not just a great deal of planning but also flexibility to adjust training plans as the competition approached.

The National Time Trial was therefore an interesting experiment for me, having the complete freedom to try out exactly what I wanted to do in the days leading up, moment by moment.

The race course had quite a few corners and I'll be honest, I wasn't known for my cornering ability. When race day rolled around the Thursday after my arrival, it was the first time I had felt genuine nerves since the Olympics the previous summer. In a strange way, those jitters were welcome. I'd done a few big races since London and felt nothing at all. No butterflies in my tummy, which worryingly meant no adrenaline rush. There was a part of me that wondered whether I'd lost the ability to feel nervous (on the bike, that is – obviously I could feel an abundance of nerves during televised gameshows). Nerves are actually a key part of the process of performing at your highest level and conquering them had become part of my pre-race ritual; I was glad they were back.

Dan surprised me by booking the day off work and getting a flight back to Glasgow. He'd been coming to all my weekend races all season and we had built up a routine of him helping me to get my warm up timed to perfection and my bike ready to go, so I was immensely grateful he was there.

I'd taken the unusual decision not to race with a power output measurement on my bike despite always training with one. I trained at this time with a Power Tap wheel whilst out on the road to record my data, but this wasn't suitable for racing on, and I had taken the decision not to invest in a crank based power meter for the race. This was partly due to the cost, but as I had a bike computer which measured my speed, cadence and my heart rate, I decided that as long as these were where I wanted them to be, my power output wasn't essential. A lot of people were surprised by this, since it's not the conventional way of doing things. I sweared by training with power, but when it came to racing I'd adopted the mantra of focussing on speed, as the fastest rider was ultimately the race winner, and it turned out that had been a good strategy.

Reader, I won.

I crossed the finish line forty seconds ahead of Lizzie Armitstead, who came second. My team manager, Simon Cope, and mechanic, Ernie Feargrieve, who were both in the following car, said I'd been unrecognisable from the rider they knew before in terms of the way I was riding and cornering. Switching things up training-wise and the addition of a road racing programme had paid off.

Dan, who was more used to road racing, had helped me with time trials and negotiating corners when I was preparing for the race. In that respect, my win felt like a team effort – something we had accomplished as a couple.

Afterwards, Dan said Glasgow was, and still is, the time when he was most proud of me. After self-defining as a track rider for so long, I'd undeniably found my road legs.

During the summer of 2013 I'd worked on a new discipline, tried a new training programme with Chris and most importantly, I'd given myself some breathing space from the scrutiny of the velodrome. The combination of these things, I believed, would allow me to come back to the track even stronger. Unfortunately, it wasn't quite that simple!

CHAPTER 28

CHARLIE

Some people describe the moment they knew they were destined to marry their partner as being a sudden realisation, like a thunderbolt. Whilst I find that quite a romantic notion, it was never like that with Dan and me. From the very beginning (or, almost the beginning, depending on whether you believe Dan or my version of the first time we met), I had felt comfortable around him. Ever since we'd gradually kind of melted together, until I couldn't imagine life without him.

In the winter of 2009 I had begun looking for a house. I'd been renting in Wilmslow, South Manchester, and Dan had been dividing his time between my flat and his dad's house, which was in Littleborough, north-east of the city. I'd always felt that by renting, I might as well be chucking my money up in the air and that I'd rather be investing in a mortgage. When the time came for me to start viewing houses, Dan came with me and we found a small house in Middleton in the borough of Rochdale, not far from the rest of his family. In April 2010 he came to live with me.

We stayed in that house for the next seven years (as I write this, we have literally only just moved). The property was teeny tiny, with only two small bedrooms and a pocket handkerchief-sized garden, but I was proud of it and what it represented. I got really excited looking at home brochures for soft furnishings and finishing touches.

The first argument Dan and I ever had was about the fireplace in that house. He felt very strongly that it should be taken out, arguing that it just wasn't practical in a room so small. I wasn't so sure. It wasn't the sort of dispute that spelled disaster for our relationship. In fact, I don't think we've ever had that sort of barney – one that betrays a fundamental difference in values. We mostly argue about small, unimportant things. Dan is very tidy, for example, whereas I find that the floor is generally quite a good place to keep things (the floordrobe, of course).

Living with Dan in my own place, as well as having a ready-made support network in the form of his family nearby, made me feel serene and settled. As someone whose job typically involves a lot of travel, I enjoyed that feeling.

When Dan proposed, (more on that later), I didn't hesitate in saying yes. It just made sense that we would make everything official; we already felt like a little family. Whilst I know a lot of people who despised the stress of planning their weddings, for me it was a convenient way to redirect my focus away from training when I needed some downtime.

In 2014 we got our cat, Charlie. I'd just won two world titles at the 2014 track World Championships in Cali and had struck a deal with Dan that if I won the team pursuit we'd buy unlimited cinema passes, and if I won the individual pursuit, we'd get a pet. As funding was based on the annual World Championships, it made sense that financial decisions also coincided with the results. Charlie was just seven weeks old when we brought him home, a precocious little ginger and white Tom with a penchant for strutting about like he owned the place. I was completely obsessed with him (which only served to fuel his already-rapidly growing ego).

Just before the Women's Tour in 2015 we bought Charlie a cat flap, so he could come and go as he pleased. Whilst I was away at the race, Dan installed the cat flap and Charlie left and simply didn't come back. I didn't know this at the time, but this is something he is wont to do quite often.

After forty-eight hours, I was absolutely distraught. I printed out 300 flyers and handed them out to our neighbours and local businesses, as well as ringing all the local vets in case the worst had happened. I even rang the local paper and put 'missing' posts on my social media.

I was turning up for training, but my mind was elsewhere: any time I wasn't outside roaming the streets looking for Charlie was wasted time to me. Occasionally, someone from the team would say something like 'I heard about your cat' and that was enough to make me burst into tears.

Amazingly, no one told me to pull myself together. Ed Clancy, now a triple Olympic champion on the men's squad, who also has a beloved cat, sent me a message saying, 'Hi Jo. I heard your cat has gone for a little wander. It happens all the time and that's why we love cats, because they do what they want. He will be back soon'. Another friend, Ottilie Quince, told me her cat had once gone missing for fourteen days. She said sometimes they go for long walks. I know she was trying to reassure me, but after that fourteen days became my 'cut-off point' in my head. I had two weeks for Charlie to turn up and if he didn't, I decided, the chances of him ever coming back were extremely thin. The thought was devastating.

Ultimately, Charlie was just being a cat. I realise that, logically.

Yet I'd formed such a strong bond with him that I couldn't focus on anything else until he was safely at home. This, of course, included my impending wedding. In fact, there was a small part of me that wondered whether I could go through with the marriage at all if he didn't come home. Now that sounds incredibly melodramatic, but it was how I felt at the time.

After Charlie had been MIA for eight whole days, I went away to Lincoln for a race, and I would be away for another four days. That cat flap had a setting on it which meant I could allow him to enter but not exit again. Clinging to my last scraps of hope, I put out food and water for him. Everyone had learned not to try and talk to me about the cat situation by that stage and I was being grimly stoic about the whole thing.

When I came back from Lincoln and approached my front door, I could hear a meowing coming from inside the house. I hadn't dare to dream he might have returned whilst we'd been away, but sure enough, Charlie was sat in the window, bold as you like, as though he hadn't just gone on a twelve-day adventure and frightened the living daylights out of me. He was slightly thinner than he had been when he left, but otherwise appeared fine. I immediately burst into tears and began frantically whatsapping everyone to let them know he was home.

My theory is that Charlie got stuck in someone's garage. Even now, he is always poking his nose into other people's properties. He will still occasionally disappear for a couple of days and every time it feels as though I am holding my breath until he returns. Even my friend Lizzie Armitstead, who is terrified of animals, acknowledges how important he is to me. She messaged me when he went missing, acknowledging that whilst she wasn't a cat fan, she knew how much he meant to me and was hoping for his safe return. That meant a lot.

CHARLIE

Anyone who follows me on Instagram will already be familiar with Charlie and his cheeky antics. Despite having had him for three years now, I'm no less obsessed with him than I was when he was a kitten and I'm always taking photos. He fervently believes he is Lord of the Manor in our house and, in fairness, he is probably right.

CHAPTER 29

OUCH!

There wasn't much time to celebrate my triumph at Glasgow as following the road race on the Sunday, I had to travel straight back to Manchester to have my tonsils out. Throughout the years of my career I'd been plagued with constant illnesses, colds and sore throats, including multiple bouts of tonsillitis, so the British Cycling doctor, Richard Freeman, had advised me the best thing would be to have my tonsils removed.

I had a small chunk of downtime after the Nationals, which seemed a logical window in which to have the procedure. So, whilst other riders went off to exotic places on holiday, I made my way to hospital.

I had assumed the minor operation wouldn't be that bad, yet the aftermath was a hundred times worse than I could ever have imagined. Luckily, I was covered by British Cycling's insurance policy, so I was able to go to a private hospital in Lancashire. The place was much like a hotel, set in beautiful grounds, and I had my own private room for the night following the surgery.

Upon being discharged I spent ten days taking strong painkillers to try and combat the excruciating pain. Many people couldn't understand how a sore throat could be so painful, but it really was. Despite having broken a few bones in my life and even knocking my teeth out back in 2010, this was by far the most pain I had ever experienced. Eventually, my GP recognised that I had contracted an infection and prescribed me some antibiotics.

I'd been advised to eat a combination of foods which would soothe my throat, like ice cream as well as foods with a crunchy texture, which would help with the scarring. It was incredibly painful to force anything down my gullet and I had to squeeze something each and every time I swallowed. In the end, I consumed so much ice cream, which was the only food to have a soothing effect – I did gain a fair amount of fat.

Recovering from the tonsillectomy meant two weeks off the bike. I'd only planned a week away, but a fortnight is enough to lose a significant amount of fitness. Added to that, I'd been tapering in the lead up to the National Championships in Glasgow, so in reality, the time when I hadn't been training had been nearer a month.

I had, foolishly in retrospect, agreed to a stage race in Germany – the Thüringen Rundfahrt Der Frauen – three weeks after the tonsil surgery. Even under normal circumstances, this is an incredibly difficult race. It lasts for seven days with many lengthy stages over one hundred kilometres.

We stayed in the same hotel every night, which minimised time spent travelling and packing. The excursion was well organised, but I simply wasn't fit or healthy enough to be there. It really was a grim week, suffering just to finish each day.

I couldn't physically swallow enough water to hydrate myself for the race, with my throat still worryingly sore, yet somehow

I managed to struggle through. At the time I was reading the autobiography of Rob Hayles, a British rider who had won track cycling medals in both the Sydney and Athens Olympics. He spoke in his book about times he had struggled in road races and I think relating to his experiences helped me find the strength to carry on.

After a stage race, you need a fair bit of recovery time. However, I spent another ten days not training properly because I was knackered. It struck me as a shame I was feeling this way, which was in sharp contrast to how fit I'd been just a few weeks before at the National Championships. I was still over race weight from the ice cream, unfit from the inconsistency of training and I still had a sore throat. I think it's fair to say I was feeling rather wretched, at the time.

The next event on my calendar was Ride London. It had been organised by the same people who arrange the London Marathon and was a post-Olympic legacy event. The race took place on a Saturday, coinciding with one year since the London Olympics, and the roads in the centre of London had been closed for a mass participation family event and a women's circuit race. On the Sunday there was also to be a mass participation one hundred-mile ride and men's road race, taking in my old favourite climb, Box Hill. I was, and still am, disappointed that the women's race was a simple circuit race whilst the men got a full road race, but the event was due to be broadcast live on TV, which is unfortunately still rare for women's road racing, so it was a step forward and I can't deny a spectacular setting.

Again, for Wiggle Honda, the race was a really big deal. The circuit finished on The Mall in front of Buckingham Palace and I was keen to get stuck in and race aggressively. On the second to last corner, however, there was an enormous crash in front of me. On live TV, in front of thousands of viewers, I went over my handlebars, hit my head and broke my collarbone.

Afterwards, as I lay on the floor, I drifted in and out of consciousness. I wasn't aware of much, apart from being in huge amounts of pain. At one point, someone put their hand on my shoulder and I screamed out in agony. Weirdly, the paramedic who was sent to the scene was my cousin, Ian – I was concussed after hitting my head and assumed I was hallucinating.

I was given gas and air, which I didn't like at all. Then I lost all the sensation in my hands, feet and legs. In my confused state, I remember simply lying on the floor, shouting at anyone who would listen that I couldn't feel my legs. After that, I passed out.

Ian and his team took me to a hospital in Central London, where I was given an X-ray. I had to stand for this procedure and that was difficult. My head was pounding and I was swaying from side to side. Straight afterwards, I collapsed back into the wheelchair. Whilst lying in my bed in A&E, I worried the hospital staff when they saw my resting heart rate was only thirty-seven beats per minute – well below average. I managed to explain through the fug of a migraine that for an endurance athlete that's actually quite normal. Still, they were keen to keep me in overnight for observation. I knew the following day the roads would still be closed for the mass participation event and I was keen to get out of there and get home.

At 3am, I announced I was discharging myself. I focussed hard on walking in a straight line through my concussion, like a drunk person trying to convince a copper they weren't driving under the influence. I had been told they wouldn't be able to do the surgery on my collarbone for another week and my parents' house wasn't too far away. If I could just get there, I reasoned, I could rest. This may sound irresponsible, and I would urge anyone to take a head injury very seriously, but I knew I would feel better at home and would still have people to look after me.

Dan came to collect me and we were just in time to beat the road closures and made it back to Cheam. British Cycling arranged for me to have my surgery done in Manchester by a well-known surgeon who had worked with many other cyclists. He was actually away on holiday at the time but when he returned it was a painful journey up the motorway a few days later, with my bones badly displaced and a constant feeling as if they were going to break the skin.

I needed a metal plate as well as six pins to reconstruct my collarbone. This procedure was carried out five days after the crash and immediately made me feel a lot better. I had been in a lot of pain before (although still admittedly not as much as with my tonsils, a few weeks prior), but now everything felt back in place and I could rest more comfortably. I was warned that I shouldn't ride a bike for another six weeks. If I had another crash whilst the bone was still fusing together, it could get a lot worse, I was told.

This was a problem, since four weeks from the date of the surgery was the last qualifying event for the track World Cup series that winter and I *had* to do it. As a solution, I got involved with a company called Wattbike, who have since become one of my best sponsors.

A Wattbike is an indoor trainer, a bit like a static exercise bike, but far more high tech. It will show you your pedalling technique and power output as well as plenty of other data and is completely adjustable. The features of the bike meant that I could raise the handlebars really high, out of the usual aerodynamic position, and place my arm, which was in a sling, on a pillow and still pedal – I got to training.

I was doing intense interval sessions on the Wattbike, short in length, as instructed by my coach, Chris. I put a mirror in front of me to check I was sitting up straight, since any inadvertent leaning to one side or the other hurt my back.

I get asked a lot about overcoming setbacks and how to stay motivated. For me a setback like this only serves to motivate me even more. The additional motivation comes from a combination of frustration that training has been missed and therefore a newfound determination to attack sessions even harder once able to; also, a desire to prove people wrong. There will always be those who see an injury and say that person won't be back to their best anytime soon, and that always fuels my desire even more. I also think victories are even sweeter when they come after a setback as the memories of overcoming the adversity and the risk of not even competing at all are so freshly etched on my mind.

Eventually, my arm came out of the sling, and I enquired about venturing onto the track. Strictly speaking, I wasn't supposed to be riding a track bike at all during this period, but compared to being on the road with cars and hazards, I considered it relatively risk-free.

Just over a year since I'd competed in London, it was time to return to the velodrome. I'd taken a battering, both psychologically and physically, over the preceding weeks and I knew British Cycling had taken on yet more girls who were keen to do team pursuit in the meantime.

And so it was with no small amount of trepidation that I returned to the track.

CHAPTER 30

THAT EXTRA MILE

The biggest obstacle I faced upon my return to track racing was being able to do a standing start with a broken collarbone. Despite this, the times I was achieving were, objectively, fairly promising.

I was told to qualify for the World Cups I'd need to be in the top ten riders in the International Belgian Open in Ghent, a UCI class 2 race. It never occurred to me to think I might not be able to manage this. That's not to say, however, that I wasn't feeling the pressure: this was the last qualifying event it was possible to take part in and I hadn't planned to spend quite so long away from training.

After practising doing some standing starts on a very low gear, I was just about capable of getting my bike out of the start gate by the time we headed to Belgium. It was a very low-key event and I was the only girl on the trip. For me, being the only female was bizarre. I was used to the camaraderie that came from being part of a team on trips such as this, but none of the other girls needed to collect any more points at this stage.

Don't ask me how, but despite all the obstacles and to everyone's surprise (not least of all mine), I won the race. I did a time of 3.36 over a three-kilometre individual pursuit, which was pretty respectable when you consider it was only four weeks after the surgery on my collarbone. There was no doubt that I'd had a huge setback, but through grit, determination and, yes, probably a dash of stupidity, I had pulled through.

Two weeks later (six weeks since my surgery), I raced the team time trial at the road World Championships. This was a new event for Wiggle Honda and Rochelle Gilmore was keen for me, as the national time trial champion, to take part. I would be part of a team of six, racing forty kilometres from Pistoia to Florence, Italy. The course wasn't too technical but, despite that, I didn't feel at all comfortable on the bike – it was too soon really, having spent nearly all my time on the Wattbike and track bike for the previous six weeks. And there is a big difference to getting in the aero position (tucked in and low down on tri-bars) for just three kilometres compared to the forty we had in Italy.

We ended up coming in sixth. Whilst I did everything I could for the team, ultimately as a squad we hadn't spent enough time together. I was still below par, but I did love the opportunity to race at the road World Championships. That night it was a flight straight back to Manchester and time to focus entirely on the next track season. I was now full of renewed enthusiasm for track racing, following my extended break, and my win in Ghent had left me hungry for more.

The first competition was taking place at Apeldoorn, a velodrome I hadn't had a particularly good relationship with, historically. We also had a new addition to our team, Katie

Archibald. Our coach said that, since this was the European championships, all five of us – myself, Laura Trott, Dani King, Elinor Barker and Katie – would be used at some point during the events.

It was Dani's turn to sit out during the team qualifier and she was devastated. Our coach, Chris, tried to calm her by telling her she was a definite shoe-in for the final. Even though perhaps I should have known at that point, it still came a shock to me to discover that Dani's inclusion in the final would mean that I was sitting out.

I was angry about this, especially since I had ridden in the 'man one' position in the qualifier and been told it had been as close to a 'perfect' race as it was possible to achieve. Chris's reasoning was that I had nailed the first round and there was no need for me to repeat the performance, since he had seen what I could do. Instead he wanted to use the opportunity to try something different.

Once again, I found myself sitting out of an important race whilst in Appeldorn. I remember remarking to Shane Sutton, British Cycling's Technical Director, how I was beginning to get superstitious about that particular venue being bad luck for me, saying 'this bloody velodrome' through gritted teeth and crossed arms.

A tad despondent, I flew back from Holland with only two weeks until the Manchester World Cup. This was a big deal to me and it would involve a home crowd. This time, Katie Archibald was representing Scotland in the individual events so we were back to just four girls, which meant we were all guaranteed a place on the team for all the rounds.

The biggest challenge in Manchester was to put in a fast time and there was a lot of talk about just how fast could we go. The velodrome there is known as being a fast track, unlike Apeldoorn, meaning that everyone's performances were likely to be impressive. Of course we wanted to come out on top.

We qualified for the final and were up against Canada. We ended up putting in a time of 4.19 over the distance of four kilometres and nearly caught our opponents. I'm very proud to say that this was the first time ever a team of women had broken the four minutes twenty seconds barrier. As well as giving us a boost, achieving this sent a message to the world.

This was the first World Cup where women's teams raced over four kilometres, with four riders, and boy, did we rock at it!

CHAPTER 31

ALTITUDE

The following day in Manchester I won the individual pursuit, meaning two, new, shiny gold medals to add to my collection. I have a lot of medals, but these ones still have a particular sentimental value for me. They represent the moment I realised that my broken collarbone wasn't going to ruin my entire season; they signify a triumph over adversity.

Our next event was in December 2013, in Mexico, in a city called Aguascalientes, which is Spanish for 'hot water'. The competition took place nearly 2,000 metres above sea level. The air would be extremely thin that high up, which made it ideal for riding a fast time, but a challenge as far as breathing was concerned.

We used altitude tents to sleep in during the run-up to the competition to help us prepare. The tents were airtight and attached to a pump, which would supply a little less oxygen than normal overnight, meaning we were breathing equivalent levels for around eight hours every day. However, the pumps were so noisy that it made sleeping pretty much impossible. I'd invariably turn the wretched thing off after about two hours and try to make up the time by sitting in the tent during the day and reading. This was about as fun as it sounds.

The first day in Mexico was what I can only describe as horrendous. We went on a group ride with the men's squad and they were all riding so fast, I remember feeling like my lungs were about to collapse as I tried to keep up. On one of the days in the run-up to the race I felt quite unwell, with a constant headache. I understand that this was due to the altitude, although fortunately for me it didn't actually involve being sick. That was until almost everyone on the team ended up catching a stomach bug (fun!).

By the time race day rolled around we were all feeling more or less okay. The team was myself, Dani King, Katie Archibald and Elinor Barker and we surprised ourselves by qualifying a few tenths of a second quicker than the world record we'd set in Manchester. In the final we rode even quicker again – a time of four minutes sixteen seconds – another new world record!

In just a few weeks we had shaved an entire ten seconds off the time we were riding in training. We were progressing at such a brisk rate, and I remember feeling stronger than I had in a long while and optimistic about the forthcoming World Championships in February 2014, in Colombia. I was back in the 'man one' position and now trialling a new idea of doing a lap and three-quarter start, as opposed to the standard lap and a quarter, giving me an extra half-lap of work early on, but settling the team well for the rest of the ride. At the time this longer starting turn was almost unheard of, but it seemed to be working well.

The velodrome in Colombia was just under 1,000 metres in altitude which, although not as high, made me think it might feel similar to the one in Aguascalientes where I'd felt so good. I'd done a couple of training camps in Majorca in the interim and everything was going well.

That was until two weeks before we were due to race, when my immune system failed me yet again and I caught a chest infection. Chris, my coach, decided the best strategy was for me to have total rest to conquer the bug. That meant four days off the bike. In retrospect this was entirely the right decision, but at the time I wasn't happy in the slightest.

I was hugely stressed out, cursing my body for letting me down at such a crucial time. I tried to temper my jangled nerves by telling myself there was no magic wand which would make me better and that working myself up into a state would only impede my recovery. This was another one of life's uncontrollables and I was just going to have to accept that.

I eventually made it to Colombia, now nervous about the altitude but relishing the heat and humidity which should make my lungs burn far less than they had in the cold Manchester velodrome. The track there was very oval in shape, meaning the corners were tight and this would make the wheel difficult to follow. As if that wasn't enough, the track has a roof but no sides around it, meaning the added distraction of winds blowing onto the track.

We had to ride using different wheels, a front five-spoked wheel as opposed to a disc wheel, since the front discs we were used to would be too difficult to control under these conditions. On one of the days leading up to the race the track flooded, with the wind blowing heavy rains in through the exposed sides. We waded through inches of water and saw a solitary caretaker trying to deal with the situation using an inadequate-looking mop. I remember thinking grumpily, as I doused myself in copious quantities of mosquito repellent. that it was a very odd place to hold a World Championship. The Cali velodrome had a completely different atmosphere to any other velodrome I had raced in. It felt far less clinical and there was more of a festival vibe about the place. This meant I was able to just laugh at the seemingly ridiculous situation we found ourselves in for the most important race of the season.

Having said this, during our first training session I thought, *OMG, I absolutely cannot race on this stupid track*! I struggled to control the bike around the tight bends and hated the feeling of changing wind direction, which is completely unheard of in a normal velodrome, where we would notice if there was a change as slight as a door being opened. I was trying desperately not to panic, sensing this could be the race where everything fell apart.

Fortunately, we had a few days before the race to get used to the velodrome, plus the humidity was good for my chest. By the time the competition rolled around I felt comfortable enough with the track to be able to push the lion's share of my fears to one side and focus on the task in hand.

We qualified fastest in the team pursuit by just over two seconds. Again, we had five riders, meaning one of us would have to miss out during each round. I was worried it would be me, again, but I ended up racing in both, and surprised myself with how good my legs felt.

We won the final, but there was a technical hitch during the last lap. Katie was on the front and I was behind, but unbeknownst to me, we had split and Laura and Elinor, who were next in line, were frantically chasing to catch up with us. Unfortunately, however fast the first two riders are, it is the third rider whose time determines the result given to the entire team.

Of course, Katie and I had no idea this had happened, we were far too focussed on what was ahead of us, and in the eyeballs-out effort of the last lap, there is no way to effectively communicate. After the race, the coaches ushered us off the track straight away. I remember thinking something catastrophic must have happened for them to react in this way, it seemed a very odd way to react to a gold medal-winning ride!

A few journalists came over to interview us whilst we were warming down on the rollers. One or two of them said something along the lines of 'Ooh, that last lap...?' whilst looking at me meaningfully. I had absolutely no idea what they were talking about and could only assume it had been a very close race against the Canadian girls.

It was only when we watched the race back that we were able to see what had happened. There was no need to be disappointed, as we had still won the race, and these things happen when you are pushed to the limit, but I felt indignant that we had been removed from the track so quickly for what was ultimately a very small mistake (and one which didn't even cost us the race, at that). It wasn't the end of the world.

Some of the staff, however, seemed embarrassed by our performance. We'd been so dominant up until that point, but then in this race had been losing for the first two kilometres of the 4K race until we'd clawed it back in the later stages.

That night I shared a room with Elinor and attempted to comfort her as she was upset. I told her I thought the coaches had overreacted, and she had done totally the right thing in the situation. But I didn't have time to dwell on things because the next day I was competing in the individual pursuit. I liked the fact that the length of time between team and individual pursuits was exactly the same as it had been in Manchester when I'd performed so well – it felt like a good omen.

I qualified second fastest, meaning I'd get to ride for gold against an American cyclist called Sarah Hammer. Sarah is a multiple World Champion and Olympic medallist as well as being the current world record holder for this particular event. She hadn't ridden in the team pursuit the previous day, meaning she was in an advantaged position, being fresher for the race.

People around me kept saying, 'Whatever happens, you're guaranteed a medal', but for me it wasn't about that. In a ride-off situation like that, with gold and silver up for grabs, it is all about the win. Chris Newton was the only person who shared my attitude, telling me 'We are here to get the gold.'

During the final, I started faster than Sarah and was quicker than her by a second in the first lap. Whilst this might seem on the surface to be a positive thing, it wasn't. I had started faster than my schedule and that usually spells disaster for the rest of the race. Pursuiting is all about the art of pacing yourself, and I had seemingly forgotten that for lap one. After six laps, Chris began walking the line to show me if I was winning or losing. Seeing I was winning at six laps to go, my thought was, *I've not come this far to lose this now.*

I managed to hold my pace until the end, beating Sarah by just over one second, meaning we had both ridden at pretty much the same pace throughout the race except for that first lap. My time was also a new personal best by one tenth of a second. When I realised this I put my hand over my mouth in shock – I simply couldn't believe that this was the result under such less-than-ideal conditions. From an outside perspective, my reaction must have seemed like a strange way to celebrate.

Whilst it was a brilliant week for me, it wasn't for British Cycling in general. We only won the two gold medals (the ones that had been awarded to me and our team pursuit team), as well as a handful of silvers and bronzes. When the British press approached me for interviews afterwards, they were asking me why the team had failed to perform. It was my first experience of being asked questions like that.

After the endless victories of London 2012, there had been an assumption by the media that we were going to win everything. I felt frustrated by that, like British athletes were being taken for granted. I responded feistily, asking why they weren't choosing to focus on what we *had* won, as opposed to what we hadn't. This was my best ever World Championships yet the results were spun in a negative light.

Despite all the disasters, in many respects Colombia was a fantastic place to compete. The people were super-friendly and the crowds cheered loudly.

If only they would rebuild that sodding velodrome!

CHAPTER 32

'FLUKE'?

I switched to a new agent after the World Championships. I had been with a woman called Jane, whose knowledge wasn't specific to the cycling world. Sarah Storey, a friend of mine from the Paralympic team, introduced me to her agent, a guy called Gab Stone. I was also talking to another agent for a while, but Gab was incredibly persuasive and adamant I should choose him. At the time, whilst it registered that Gab was being a little over the top, I took it as a sign that he must be incredibly enthusiastic about representing me and relented. This was, I would discover, a mistake.

I continued to ride with Wiggle Honda, but my main priority was to train for the Commonwealth Games that summer of 2014, where I would be focussing on the individual pursuit. After the World Championships, some people had made comments about my performance being a fluke. Although to anyone who had followed my season, my wins at the Belgian Open and the Manchester World Cup would have been good indicators as to my pursuiting form. Whether those remarks were made out of jealousy or with the intention of putting me off my stride I do not know, but I was determined to prove them wrong. Whilst the Commonwealth Games didn't receive the same attention as the Olympics, in my mind they became just as important, as my only opportunity to compete in an individual event at a multi-sport Games.

The day we travelled by coach to Glasgow for the competition it was absolutely tipping it down with rain. I remember reflecting drearily that this fitted in with my stereotypical view of Scotland and I fully expected the weather to be like that for the entire trip. To my delight, however, the next day the sun began to shine, raising the temperature to twenty-five degrees. In the sunshine the city looked friendlier and less imposing.

Our accommodation was just a couple of minutes' ride from the velodrome. Whilst it had a proper roof and walls, it was very similar in its dimensions to the track in Cali, Colombia. This wasn't my favourite shape to ride on, but I felt like having performed well in Colombia might give me an advantage over the other riders, who would probably have preferred a bowl-shaped track.

I was sharing a room with Vicky Williamson, who was in the sprint squad. I liked her a lot. She managed to strike a perfect balance between being relaxed and fun to be around and motivating me when I needed it. It helped of course that she was from a different discipline, so there was no unfriendly competition cracking in the air between us.

Despite this, I knew I was going to face a lot of tough competition. Everyone had been concentrating far more on the individual pursuit, unlike at the World Championships, because in this competition there was no team pursuit event to draw focus. The Aussie girls, in particular, took the event very seriously – it was a big deal in their country.

I was in the last round of the qualifying heats and rode a new personal best of 3 minutes 29.038 seconds, which made me fastest qualifier. I can't remember exactly why, but I was kicking myself that I hadn't managed 3:28. I guess that's part and parcel of having a perfectionist's personality – you hardly ever take a moment just to smell the roses, or to self-congratulate.

When I returned that evening for the final I started more slowly than my opponent, but stuck to my schedule and worked away at the lead lap by lap and eventually won the race by a huge margin of 3.8 seconds. I shared the podium with two girls from Australia, Annette Edmondson and Amy Cure, with Katie Archibald taking fourth.

I was absolutely over the moon! This was just as big as winning the Olympics to me, although I know no one else will ever see it that way. I also felt like I'd done what I'd come out to do and proven my recent wins weren't, in fact, a fluke. I'd also proved myself as an individual, which is something I'd always wanted to do since knowing I wouldn't have this opportunity at an Olympic Games. To do the World Championships and Commonwealth Games double in the same year was incredible and at this time I now held titles at Olympic, World, Commonwealth and European level concurrently.

A couple of days later, I was due to race the time trial. In 2013 I was officially the best in the UK at this, but by 2014 I had developed a weird injury in my left leg which meant it started to become numb if I rode a hard effort for more than ten minutes. To this day I am affected by this bizarre affliction and, as a result, I knew I wouldn't be able to put in the sort of performance that had won me the national title a year ago. I was pleased, however, to see my English teammate, Emma Pooley, who was due to retire from cycle racing after this competition, take the silver medal.

I stayed in Glasgow until the very last cycling event, which was the road race. I was in reserve for this, but wasn't required so instead, I did a bit of commentary for BBC radio and was over the moon when Lizzie won. She had been through a recent stint of just being pipped at the post and getting silver, so for her to win the gold marked the end of that phase and was a huge moment for her.

Lizzie and I enjoyed the closing ceremony together. The event was similar in scope to the Olympic closing ceremony and had an Australian theme, since that was where the Commonwealth Games were going next.

During 2013, Dan had been working in London, whereas I had been up in Manchester since I broke my collarbone that summer. I missed him terribly as I rattled around my house which, despite being tiny, felt empty without him in it. I started looking for jobs for him in Manchester and eventually found one for a Finance Officer role at a fairly local secondary school with just twenty-four hours left for applications. He applied at lightning speed, got the position and came to live with me from January 2014. That year was by far the best year of my career and I think in general I was just a lot happier with life now Dan and I were living together again and this reflected in my performances on the bike.

Dan planned a two-week holiday to Venice following the Commonwealth Games. To take this much time away from training was rare for me, but since he worked in a school the summer presented a good opportunity for this sort of vacation. He took care of all the planning and decided to make a road trip of it, by driving to Italy, through the Austrian Alps on the way there and the French Alps on the way back.

Just before we left, I had to do an event at the Excel in London for a sponsor. I was chatting to a woman there and when I told her I was going to Venice she asked if I thought I'd get engaged there, since the place had a reputation for being somewhere people proposed. I told her that, whilst we had been together for five years, Dan had always been very vocal about not wanting to get married.

Little did I know that his anti-marriage protestations were a 'Chandler from *Friends*' style ploy...

CHAPTER 33

MY 'MONICA' MOMENT

Dan had always told me he 'didn't see the point' in getting married. For that reason, after we'd been together for a few years and friends started asking if there were wedding bells on the horizon, I always brushed off their comments. This didn't bother me and I liked him for being him, and how he wasn't worried about conforming to social rules. It was consequently a genuinely massive shock when he got down on one knee and asked me to be his wife on holiday in Venice, in August 2014.

Throughout the trip, true to his frugal nature Dan had been booking relatively cheap hotels. When we arrived in Venice, I was therefore pleasantly surprised to see that the hotel was a definite notch up from the places we had been staying before. He had obviously put in a lot of effort to find such a lovely temporary dwelling for us.

One night, we were going out for a meal and Dan kept making comments about wanting it to be special and how we should both get dressed up. Although I remember thinking it was a little odd to pick this one night in particular, I still didn't twig.

Dan took *forever* to get ready that evening. I remember sitting on the bed in the hotel room getting increasingly annoyed because I was hungry and he was still in the bathroom. To this day, I have no idea what he was doing in there (and I don't particularly want to know, if I'm completely honest!).

As we stepped out into the hallway, Dan said, 'Hang on, I've forgotten something,' and dived back into the room. Five minutes later, I was still standing about like a lemon so I went into the room to see what the hold-up was. Dan was kneeling on the floor, brandishing a diamond ring.

My heart literally stopped in that second, a combination of shock, disbelief and delight. He said, 'Joanna, will you marry me?' and it took me thirty seconds before I could summon up a reply, but there was never any possibility of me saying no.

After he slid the ring onto my finger, my natural curiosity took over. I wanted to know everything. Had he asked my parents? (Yes.) Where had he got the ring? How had he managed to hide it from me? (The ring had been in the car all along and I'm a trusting fool who didn't see all the signs!)

The ring was a princess-cut diamond on a gold band. Later, when I showed it to my friends and teammates, some people made negative comments about it being gold. There's a feeling in some quarters that yellow gold is a little passé. Yet Dan had deliberately picked that colour because I'd won gold medals. He knew me well enough to know I'd have positive associations with it. Besides, I love that it's different from the fashionable white gold and platinum rings you see absolutely everywhere.

It turned out that Dan, along with his sisters, were huge fans of the sitcom *Friends*, and this had given him the idea of pretending not to be into marriage to throw me off the scent, just like Chandler does in the show. It was therefore completely appropriate that I felt exactly like Monica in the moments after his proposal – the part where she is out on the balcony screaming, 'I'm ENGAGED!'

There was another reason, besides his fake reluctance, which made it so surprising when Dan asked me to be his bride. There was a part of me which had bought into the idea that women with alopecia didn't get their happily ever after. Growing up, other girls around me had begun planning their weddings before they started their periods, but I told myself not to dream about that, assuming I would ultimately be disappointed. I remember once Lizzie Armitstead tried to draw me into a conversation about our respective fantasy weddings and I'd been dismissive, thinking it was dangerous to indulge in that train of thought. On the outside I probably appeared a little rude and grouchy on the topic of marriage, but it was a defence mechanism against being hurt, emotionally.

After we were engaged, my reluctance to talk about marriage completely dissipated and I wanted to tell everyone. The first people to get the news were my parents and Lizzie, via WhatsApp. We sent a postcard from Venice to Dan's Mum and Dad with the cryptic message 'got lots to tell you'. I was dying to get home so I could break the news to everyone else in person and then put it on social media.

I didn't know anyone else who had got engaged, at the time. Sarah Storey is twelve years older than me and already married but apart from her, I would be the first out of my social group to tie the knot. In fact, I'd only ever been to one wedding as a guest, myself.

My biggest concern in terms of planning was 'when?'. When

would I ever find time to do it? Should I wait until after the Rio Olympics in 2016? How would wedding planning fit around my training schedule? In the end, I decided I just had to bite the bullet and that I would somehow find whatever time was necessary.

Dan was keen to have the ceremony sooner rather than later, whereas for me having it during the summer was a non-negotiable. It therefore seemed like fate when my favourite out of the venues I had been looking at had a cancellation in the summer of 2015. The date was a Saturday and Dan's birthday (meaning he'd never have any excuse to forget our anniversary). I booked it in October, with less than ten months to go.

After all the challenges I'd faced to date, the one I now had to contend with was juggling the challenges of training, now less than two years to go until the Olympics, around wedding planning.

CHAPTER 34

SORE LOSER

I threw myself into wedding planning with buckets of energy and enthusiasm. I enjoyed the opportunity to have something to focus on other than training, for once.

I knew I didn't want a church wedding – it seemed hypocritical to me since I wasn't a regular church-goer. I liked the idea of having the entire thing outdoors (and thereby throwing myself at the mercy of the British weather, which can be unpredictable even during the summer months). In general, it appealed to me to try and be a little quirky and less traditional.

I found a farm with barns which hosted weddings. Of course, my biggest priority was that there was room on the land to host a bouncy castle, after so many years of missing out on one for my birthday. In general, I wanted the vibe of the day to be relaxed and fun. I had a notion of wanting the food to be Italian themed, as a tribute to Dan proposing to me in Venice.

I knew straight away I wanted Lizzie Armitstead to be my maid of honour. After all, without her, Dan and I might never have got together. More than that, Lizzie's friendship had boosted my confidence to the extent that I truly believed I could be happy. It's important to take that sort of belief into a long-term relationship.

I asked Dan's sisters, Keeley and Natalie, to be bridesmaids. I was so excited at the prospect of having new sisters and wanted them to feel part of the day. I also asked Sarah Storey. As it turned out, Sarah was a veritable mine of useful information on the topic of weddings. She was fundamental in helping me plan, and took complete care of the hen do.

I bought stacks of wedding magazines and got myself a pinterest account and launched myself fully into the planning alongside my mum, who was equally excited. Whilst I wouldn't say I morphed into your typical bridezilla, I did find it difficult to have conversations about anything else in the lead-up to my nuptials.

But it wasn't just my marriage which was taking my focus away from cycling. My triumph in Glasgow marked the first point in my career where I genuinely felt like I'd ticked all the boxes and won everything I'd ever had an ambition to. I was simultaneously a reigning Olympic, World, Commonwealth and European Champion. For the first time in my career, there were no 'firsts' left – any medals I gained from now on would be about defending a title I'd already won.

I knew I definitely wanted to go to the Rio Olympics, but the motivation felt different. This time I wanted, rather than needed, to get the gold. Back before London, when I'd needed to win, there had been no question in my mind as to why I was putting myself through every super-hard training session, every early start, every time my training schedule meant missing out on family time or social occasions. Now that need had been replaced by want, I found I had a little voice in my head which said, *You don't have to do this, you know*, whenever things got tough.

Between September 2014 and the World Championships of 2015 was a really difficult season for me. It had taken me a while to get back to fitness after a long period of training inconsistently, in addition to my two-week holiday in Venice.

When I came back to training in September I couldn't help but feel I was on the back foot and I knew I had to work hard to prove myself. Dani King had left the squad and we had a new girl called Ciara Horne. Ciara became a really close friend. Being new to the team, she also felt like she had some catching up to do and we helped to motivate one another. Ciara is also similar in age to me, just under a year younger. The other riders are all three to six years younger than me so it was nice to have someone a little closer and our similar music tastes made us great roommates.

Since I wasn't on top form that winter, the coaches began putting me in man four, as opposed to the man one position in the run-up to the Worlds. I'd never really felt man four was my forte. As if that wasn't enough, I kept getting ill. As we got closer to the competition I came down with a cold and chesty cough, in addition to a painful ear infection so bad that to this day, I still can't hear as well in one ear as in the other.

We had switched coaches from Chris Newton back to Paul Manning. The doctor had confirmed I was poorly and said he didn't think it was a good idea for me to continue training that week in light of my state of health. I told Paul, who went on to tell me that this would make it 'difficult' to select me for the Worlds. I felt if I took the team doctor's advice and rested, I would miss out on selection for the Worlds, and would therefore also have my funding halved. UK Sport funding was awarded annually based on World Championship performances alone. I was on the top level of funding but a non-selection for the Worlds would see me drop to the bottom level that very next month. I therefore struggled through the efforts, determined not to miss out.

My instinct was to rest, recover and get back into training when I felt 100 per cent, but with the days until we travelled numbered, and the pressure of gaining selection, I felt like I had no choice but to continue to train through the illness, whilst also taking a short course of antibiotics. It was a battle to balance the challenges of proving myself to get selected versus doing what was right to have optimum form on race day.

By the time race day rolled around, I felt healthy enough to race but in general very rundown and far from the form I would have liked. My training sessions had felt compromised due to being unwell – it was all I could do to drag myself through them, rather than work hard and focus on good-quality efforts. But this was the situation, there was nothing more I could do now, and I just had to give everything I had on the day.

In the qualifying rounds we missed out on first place by just one tenth of a second. The Aussies won, achieving a time of four minutes eighteen, which was staggering for sea level. We were gutted, since a new rule that winter meant we would race for three rounds rather than the usual two rounds of racing. In the extra middle round, the fastest team rides against the fourth-fastest team and the second against the third team. There was a feeling that by just missing out on that first place in qualifying we would now have a far tougher ride on our hands.

As a team we all probably cracked a little bit psychologically at that point. We weren't used to losing so this was unfamiliar territory. In reality, our performance was very far from being the end of the world, but that's how it felt at the time.

Steve Peters hadn't worked with us since 2013 as he had moved on to British Athletics among other things, and we hadn't been given a replacement psychiatrist or psychologist, for reasons I don't know! We literally didn't have anyone to go to during that time, when the pressure felt like it was too much. I had felt that was a mistake on the part of British Cycling, since preparing yourself mentally is just as important as physical preparation in my eyes.

The following day we came back to the velodrome to race the third-place team. Although we won, I knew I wasn't performing well. I would have been more than happy to sit out and to be replaced by Ciara at that point.

For the final, the plan we had developed during training was changed at the last minute. The coaches had realised that it was endurance which was my main problem and decided I should take up man one position. They instructed me to get everyone up to speed and duck out by the second turn, leaving the other three girls to finish it off.

Although that race was the fastest we had ever ridden at sea level, the Aussies beat us by three whole seconds. They rode a time of four minutes thirteen, which, if I'm honest, I'm not sure I could have matched even at optimum health. Those sorts of times were completely unheard of and we just had take our hats off to them and congratulate them on their race. They were the better team on the day.

We got a silver medal. It was the first time the other three girls had ever lost a team pursuit. The mood at the camp was low. I tried to cheer everyone up by pointing out that the Australian team had achieved a time no one expected, and that we still did well, but to little avail.

As I took to the podium, I attempted to accept defeat gracefully and plaster on a smile. I remember looking at the Australian team singing their national anthem and thinking, *Enjoy it while it lasts*. Afterwards, I said as much to the media too.

After that, the mood in the camp deteriorated even more. During the debrief meeting, Paul singled me out and made me feel like it was all my fault that we had lost. He told me I hadn't committed fully and that my teammates deserved an apology from me.

I stood my ground, arguing that I'd given it everything I had in difficult circumstances, to the point where I'd even completed training sessions, against mine and the doctor's judgement, to appease the team. I also pointed out that even if I had been healthy there was no way we would have achieved a time of four minutes thirteen. The Aussies' performance had moved the goalposts, creating a much faster world record than had ever been seen before.

The following day I had to defend my title in the individual pursuit. I think some people assumed I wouldn't take to the start in this event, after my below-par performances in the team pursuit, but I was determined to start rather than just walk away. There were also mutterings of perhaps I had been saving myself for the individual pursuit and simply taking it easy in the team pursuit.

In reality, that couldn't have been further from the truth. In any case, it's pretty much impossible to go easy in a team pursuit – you have to keep up with the other girls. I was frustrated that the general consensus seemed to be that I'd deliberately sabotaged the team pursuit, which would have been a stupid move, especially just over a year out from the Olympics and also as the team pursuit is the event our funding level is based on. My performance in the individual pursuit would count for nothing in terms of my lottery funding, but I made the decision to still ride the individual pursuit regardless. I wanted to at least have a shot at defending my title. Even if I lost, I wanted to go out fighting.

I qualified fourth fastest and raced off for the bronze. I lost the final and didn't medal, having absolutely nothing left in my legs. Whilst of course I was disappointed, in some respects it was a good thing that my performance in the individual pursuit mirrored what I'd done in the team pursuit, at least it proved I hadn't been tactically saving my energy in a quest for personal glory.

I'd already arranged my flight back the following morning and I couldn't have been happier to get out of there. The atmosphere was terrible, with no other British rider winning a gold medal all week.

There was just over a year to go until Rio and we had failed to gain any titles. The media were slating us, highlighting our 'terrible' performance (as though silver is catastrophic) and claiming that we weren't ready to represent our country at the Olympics.

Whilst we were all disappointed, again I was frustrated by the media response. Our training programme was based totally around peaking every four years for the Olympics. Other teams around the world do it differently, but our programme is based almost exclusively on our Olympic performance. I felt the media were being harsh, yet again, exaggerating the flaws in our performance to try and generate headlines.

If I had thought the previous year was a bad one for media response, it was nothing compared to this, I reflected gloomily.

CHAPTER 35

BATTLING THE FREEZE

I slumped away from Paris on a massive low. As if trying to deal with our defeat and the mood amongst the team wasn't enough of a headache, when I got back to Manchester I had to deal with the problem of my agent, Gab Stone.

Gab hadn't paid me for an entire year. I'd been chasing my share of the money for my various media appearances and sponsorship commitments, but he'd always fobbed me off. At first, I'd trusted that there was a legitimate delay but after a few months I'd started to grow suspicious.

It was Sarah Storey who eventually uncovered the truth. Gab had a gambling addiction problem and had spent all of our money. She'd actually discovered this whilst I'd been away in France but had waited until I returned home to break the full story to me, not wanting to distract me from my performance on the track, although I'd been aware something was very wrong.

I spent the next few days making some very angry phone calls and composing some strongly worded emails in an attempt to get my money back. To this day, I still haven't managed to recoup all of it.

I don't think it's unnecessarily hyperbolic to say that week was the worst of my life. The press were slating our performance at the Worlds, with a couple of articles singling me out as being responsible for the downfall of the entire team. Added to that, with just a few months to go until my wedding, I had discovered that my agent had stolen a year's worth of commercial income.

Eventually, I plucked up the courage to arrange a meeting with Shane. I was incredibly nervous, not knowing whether he was going to throw me off the team there and then. I'd seen him on TV essentially saying what the rest of the media had been suggesting, that it hadn't been a good week for me. At that point, I texted him saying we needed to talk.

I've always trusted Shane to be open with me. The first thing he said to me when I arrived at the meeting was, 'Sit back and relax. You're not going anywhere, Jo.' This was an immense relief and immediately put me at my ease.

I'd made a list of everything that had gone wrong in the run-up to the World Championships. Shane was surprised by a lot of it – he hadn't been aware I'd been ill and been on antibiotics, or that I'd had to do the training efforts against doctor's orders.

I asked Shane what he was doing stuck in an office when he would be much better at trackside, where he could be aware of everything that was happening. He was very responsive to everything I said.

As my confidence blossomed, I told him I was categorically not going to finish my career on a loss at the World Championships. All I wanted was to go to Rio and win the gold. Shane called Paul in at that point, which was incredibly awkward. Paul was told that he should not have applied pressure for me to train when I was unwell and I was incredibly grateful to Shane for making that point.

Paul changed, after that. Up until that point, I had felt he was angry with me, but afterwards, I sensed he understood that I hadn't tried to become ill – in fact I'd done everything I could to avoid it. Shane told Paul to trust me, since I had a good record of planning my training well and performing on the big day when it mattered. In all subsequent times after this meeting, if I was struggling with illness I was given space to recover.

Over time, Paul and I re-established trust and he began to value my opinion more. By the time I got to Rio I was twenty-seven years old, which seemed to make me more prone to injury than I had been during my younger years. It was therefore imperative I had a coach who would listen to me and understand that, whilst there were five of us training for the event, one size would not fit all.

During the summer of 2015 I had started working with a sports scientist and strength and conditioning coach called Joe Hewitt, as well as a physiologist called Len Parker Simpson. Joe and Len's philosophy revolved around me doing more gym work to build muscle, which meant that road training had to take a back seat.

I'd done virtually no gym work in 2013 and 2014, despite it being a winning formula before London, but I now embraced the gym work again with newfound motivation. They had me using the leg press and leg extension machines to build up my muscles. I also did a little work on my upper body and core. There are some photos of me taken around that time with huge muscles in my arms. For some reason, my arms toned up really well. In fact, if anyone in the gym commented on my 'guns' I used to get really annoyed, since the whole purpose of me being there was to try and work on my legs.

The hard work paid off – by incorporating a regular gym routine I found that I was able to develop my peak power and peak speed again.

After our defeat at the Worlds, we were also given a new sports psychologist to replace Steve Peters, in the form of Ruth Anderson. I felt sorry for her, in a way, since she came in during a real low point for the team and at a time when I had a need to offload all my tensions and frustrations. Yet talking to her was as cathartic as it was needed.

The new influx of support gave me a timely boost. By then I'd left Wiggle Honda and was riding for a new team called Pearl Izumi Sports Tours International. The team was run by Sarah Storey and her husband, Barney, and I was much happier there.

At Wiggle Honda I had always felt too many demands were being placed on me – that I was being pulled in several different directions all at once, and I just wasn't happy. It had made finding a balance in my life difficult. Sarah, on the other hand, was a British Cycling rider and knew how important my training commitments with them were, so she ran a very different ship. I parted with Rochelle on good terms, but I do remember it was a relief to start the beginning of a significant new chapter.

As a further pick-me-up, I'd had a nice little result in April 2015. The race, known as the 'Tour of the Reservoir', took place in Northumbria and it had snowed on the day. It was the coldest I can ever remember being, even worse than 2013's Omloop Het Nieuwsblad, and I couldn't feel my hands or feet for most of the race. Paul came out to watch and Dan was driving the following car for our team, as Barney Storey was away at a different event.

I won that race, in conditions I was widely known for despising. As I crossed the finish line and was wrapped in a silver blanket to protect me from the snow and winds, I knew categorically that I had made a very public statement: I wasn't wimping out, I had grit and determination.

It was all go for Rio.

CHAPTER 36

A SILVER SIXPENCE
IN HER SHOE

Outside of all my efforts to bounce back from our defeat in Paris, my other focus during this time was planning for my wedding.

True to my (slightly) food-obsessed form, the first thing I thought to arrange was the wedding breakfast. I was determined I didn't want anything too traditional. Instead, we went for sharing platters with Italian flavours, comprising mozzarella and Parma ham, because we had got engaged in Italy. Dan and I also settled on a fairground theme for the day, to reflect the fact that our first date had been at the fairgrounds (or kermesses) in Belgium.

As the big day, which had been arranged for July 2015, got closer, I competed in a road race with my team called the Aviva Women's Tour. The race was run by a company called Sweetspot and one of their main focuses was to provide equality between men and women's racing, endeavouring to give an equal amount of publicity and prize money to each event.

I was a keen advocate of Sweetspot and what they were trying to achieve and had been vocal in my support for them. They had faced some opposition from fans, but on the day of the race crowds turned up in their droves to watch, silencing the critics' protestations that no one was interested in women's cycling. However I'd woken up that morning with one red, bloodshot eyeball. I'd got some grit in my eye the day before and was initially distraught that I'd done some serious damage. I was given the okay to race but to make matters worse, I was stung by a wasp out on the road, which it turns out I'm allergic to.

My left arm swelled to twice its original size and was boiling hot to the touch. I was taken out of the race and taken straight to a doctor, who proceeded to put me on two types of antibiotics. I was kicking myself (mentally, I was in enough physical pain already!), feeling as though I was quitting, even though leaving the race was the logical thing to do.

My eye was also looking worse each day and having had that checked out by an expert and being given some eye drops, I was still terrified it wouldn't be cleared up in time for my wedding in just a couple of weeks' time. And so it was that I spent the days leading up to my big day with a red zombie eyeball, a ridiculously swollen arm and, if you remember from the earlier chapter about Charlie, a beloved missing feline.

Although it was never said to me, I got the impression some people were unimpressed with me for arranging my wedding to be before the Rio Olympics in 2016. Other riders had planned their day for after Rio, whereas I'd felt I wanted to get it done, so that I could fully focus on training afterwards. I didn't relish the prospect of still being in the planning stages during the actual Games. I was confident July 2015, over a year out from Rio, was a good time for me so I endeavoured to ignore the mutterings around me.

My biggest fear in the lead-up to my wedding was that it would rain. Dan and I had planned an outdoor ceremony (as well as, of course, the bouncy castle). It was very much an outdoor event and depended on clement weather conditions.

On the morning itself I was incredibly nervous. Not about marrying Dan, which was a no-brainer as far as I was concerned, but about the prospect of doing it in front of more than one hundred guests. Being a naturally shy person, I was apprehensive about being the centre of attention. I suddenly regretted inviting so many people. I'd written my own vows and was frantically making last-minute alterations, crossing things out because I was embarrassed by the sheer volume of them.

The night before, Lizzie Armitstead and I had stayed at a local hotel. We woke up to find my fears had been realised – it was raining. As we drove to the venue I kept thinking about Steve Peters and his uncontrollables. There was, after all, nothing I could do about the sky.

For the first time, I would be wearing a wig made of real human hair. I wanted to be like other brides who had their hair specially styled for their big day and the synthetic wigs I had been wearing up until that point weren't styleable. The wig had been made especially for me by Aderans Hair Centre and moulded to my head; the snug fit meant that it wouldn't rub and itch or irritate me whilst I was busy living the happiest day of my life.

I employed a hair and make-up artist on the day, who teased my hair into a half-up, half-down 'do'. It was my very first experience of having my hair done and a huge novelty for me.

I wore two pairs of false eyelashes – one to replace the real eyelashes I had lost to alopecia and the other set to look like false eyelashes. When I posted pictures of myself to social media after the wedding, a few of my followers questioned why I had done that, saying I didn't need the wig or fake lashes, but I wanted to experience the usual things other brides take for granted. It's not at all unusual for women without alopecia to wear false eyelashes for their wedding and I didn't see why I should miss out.

I never questioned whether or not to wear a wig on the day, although Dan was kind enough to make a point of saying he thinks I'm beautiful either way and would support me whatever I decided.

I wanted our day to reflect who we were as a couple, as well as to be a unique event all our guests would remember. We put up lashings of home-made bunting, as well as pictures of everyone who was going to be attending. We made sure they were all well fed, with a pic'n'mix stand and canapés. Fortunately, it stopped raining by late morning meaning we could still go ahead with the outdoor ceremony and that everyone could enjoy the fairground theme. To everyone's surprise I made my entrance in a gorgeous red 1960s Corvette, driven by Dan's step-dad, Gary, who is also the proud owner of this American classic car.

Thirty extra guests came for the evening celebrations, when we had a hog roast. Dan always says that was his favourite part. Personally I had been indulging in the cake and pic'n'mix and was so full, I never actually got any!

People kept reminding me to eat, which might be sound advice for other brides but was a ridiculous thing to say to me as I've never skipped a meal in my life. I'd filled up on porridge as well as a cooked breakfast in addition to munching on sandwiches along with Buck's Fizz as I got ready before the ceremony.

Both my dad and Dan made a speech and we had arranged for Lizzie Armitstead to speak as maid of honour, rather than the best man. Dan said, 'It was Joanna's beaming smile and her kindness that drew me to her. I will make it my mission to make sure Joanna is the most loved and supported wife the world has ever seen.' I don't think there was a dry eye in the house.

Music for the ceremony was provided by a string quartet, who played modern songs. I walked down the aisle to 'A Thousand Years' by Christina Perri. The first dance was by far the worst bit – for us. I had put on my to-do list to have some lessons together in the run-up. Of course I had been far too busy. Saskia from the venue, who was in charge of ensuring the day ran smoothly, kept approaching Dan and I to tell us it was first dance time and we kept finding reasons to put it off. Eventually he and I shuffled about to 'Iris' by the Goo Goo Dolls.

I'd instructed my bridesmaids to get on the dance floor and start throwing shapes after a couple of minutes of the first dance. For the rest of the evening, as the DJ played nineties dance music, I was on the dance floor. In fact, I was so absorbed in the music that I was often one of only three people dancing (along with our friends, Scottie and Naomi) because Dan was busy devouring ungodly quantities of hog roast.

My dress had been the very first one I had tried on in the shop which I'd initially visited with Sarah Storey the previous October and had since returned to with my mum and other bridesmaids. I immediately knew it was 'The One'. It was in a princess style, with a full skirt and delicate capped lace sleeves. The bodice was covered in pearls and crystals and had a lace back. I chose not to have a veil because the back of my dress was so pretty, it would have been a shame to cover it up.

My 'borrowed' item was from Sarah, who lent me her tiara. 'Something old' was a pearl necklace, which both my nan and my mum had worn on their wedding days. My wig was new, so that was covered and there was a small piece of blue on the garter I was wearing.

Someone, and I still don't know to this day who it was, had glued a sixpence to the bottom of my shoe. Apparently, this is traditional since the 'something old, something new, something borrowed, something blue' rhyme has an extra, forgotten line 'and a silver sixpence in her shoe', which has been lost through the ages. I asked everyone I spoke to during the day who had done it, but they all denied it was them, and I still don't know who it was to this day.

We didn't have enough time for a proper honeymoon straight after the wedding, so we postponed it until after Rio. Instead, we had a 'mini moon' in North Wales, in a village called Betws-y-Coed, during the first week of August. We visited an outside activity centre which had a high ropes course between the tree tops, so I was in my element.

People always ask 'What's married life like?' It seems to be a sort of default thing you say to new brides. It took me a while to get used to calling Dan 'my husband', especially since I hadn't had that long to acclimatise to saying 'my fiancé', but I can honestly say, other than that, everything was the same. We'd been living together for a while and I was still training for Rio. I decided to change my name to Joanna Rowsell Shand, with no hyphen, inspired by our physiologist Len Parker Simpson (who was always very particular about the lack of hyphen in his own surname).

I had exactly one week off the bike and then it was time to get my head down and train in the last twelve months before the Olympic Games.

I was glad I had my wedding when I did, since I was able to take the attitude of thinking, *Okay, I'm married. Time for this, now.*

CHAPTER 37

SEESAW

That year, 2015, the European Championships were in Grenchen, Switzerland. Whilst in my mind it would be a test of how well our new summer training regime had served us, the coaches kept reminding us that it wasn't about performing in Switzerland, but in Rio.

We didn't feel there was a great deal of threatening competition for us at the Europeans, which gave us freedom to experiment with the line-up between rounds. After some deliberation, it was decided that Ciara Horne would miss out on the final, which she was understandably less than happy about. After we won, there was some confusion as to whether all five of us would be able to appear on the podium, and I felt quite strongly that we should go up as a five. Eventually, it was confirmed that we could and that is one of my favourite photos of the whole road to Rio.

The men's team had had six alternating riders and there was a powerful picture of all eleven of us, which British Cycling put together, beaming in our blue and yellow European Champion jerseys.

Almost immediately after our victory in Switzerland, we had to head off to Colombia for a World Cup in early November. I wasn't delighted by the prospect of the long-haul flight, plus I was apprehensive about the velodrome, despite having won there in 2014. Elinor Barker was also feeling very unwell with respiratory problems, which, in addition to having contend with the strong winds and tight corners of the velodrome, meant we only walked away with a bronze.

Still, under the circumstances, with Elinor in hospital and Laura Trott resting at the hotel ahead of the omnium (meaning the final against China was just the three of us – myself, Katie Archibald and Ciara – versus their four riders) that bronze felt like a win.

We returned to Manchester with a bit of time before the next major competition, in January 2016. We did road rides with some threshold work, as well as track and gym sessions. All of the training was incredibly intense and I had to keep visiting the physio in order to be physically able to keep on top of it all.

I experienced a number of little setbacks during this time – minor injuries and other tiny failings in my twenty-seven-year-old body, which made it harder to train. I certainly felt a long way from the twenty-three-year-old who had won the gold in London. My mind was determined to push myself to the limits but my body kept saying no.

I was frustrated at one point when it seemed like I was spending more time with the physio than I was on the bike. Usually, I loved these training periods where my only job was to knuckle down and work hard, but this time I was finding it challenging (and not in the good sense).

Before I knew it, it was 2016 and officially Olympic year. I remember seeing a lot of very negative pieces in the press, saying that the Village was not up to scratch and that the venues would not be ready in time. Although there had been similar stories flying around before London and everything had turned out fine, it still played on my mind. In addition, there was a lot of publicity about the Zika virus, a virus passed on by mosquitos which can have consequences for unborn babies if contracted by a pregnant woman, and which had already caused a few of the higher profile golfers to pull out of the Games.

I didn't have too much time to worry, however, as there were major competitions to focus on before Rio. We had welcomed Emily Nelson into our squad, after Katie Archibald had a crash and injured her knee just before Christmas.

There was a World Cup in Hong Kong, which presented not only the opportunity to gain the qualification points we needed for Rio, but also a chance to put into action what we had practised in training since Colombia. We had mainly been focussing on speed work and this was our opportunity to see if the training was paying off.

I was immediately fascinated by Hong Kong, which was a sprawling concrete jungle, vibrating with energy. Once again, my jet lag was terrible and I don't think I slept for a spell of more than two hours throughout the entire trip. Becky James and Jess Varnish, who were on the sprint programme, forced me to try coffee for the first time during this trip, insisting that I needed the caffeine to stay awake. I ordered a milky latte and put several sugars in it to mask the taste. Desperate times call for desperate measures! Up until this point I must have been the only cyclist not to be a coffee drinker.

We raced a time of four minutes nineteen in the qualification round, which was decent not only for the phase of training we were in, but also taking into account we were at sea level. That race marked the first time since the Glasgow Commonwealth Games where I had felt like myself again. For a year and a half I had been, at least to my mind, just barely hanging in there, with illness and injury always seeming to strike at the wrong time.

Having qualified fastest, we competed in the semis against China and won a straightforward victory. We wanted to experiment so were instructed to start fast, in a bigger gear than usual, and whilst I was in my element, relishing the chance to get our team up to speed during the first two laps, that big effort cost me a lot. By the time the final rolled around, my legs felt like jelly.

Laura Trott was sitting out during the final to focus on the omnium and this made room for Emily Nelson, who the coaches thought could do with gaining the experience. Emily did well, but I was struggling. She had completed her turns and pulled out as instructed, but my legs were finished and the last few laps seemed to last a lifetime.

I managed to drag myself over the finish line, but we lost to Canada by a couple of tenths of a second. The defeat was disappointing and I couldn't help but feel it was a long way to come to try an experiment and ultimately lose. But overall I was seeing glimmers of my previous form coming through, although that only currently extended to two rounds of racing and not all three.

We weren't due to fly back until the following evening, so on our final day, GB road racer and sprinter Mark Cavendish treated us all to a traditional Hong Kong dinner. There was crispy duck, pancakes, various dumplings, plus a whole load of unidentifiable things I didn't want described to me. I tucked in enthusiastically, pleased there was now only one more competition to go between us and the Olympics.

We had a couple of easy training days before heading off to Majorca for a camp. My solar-powered self saw my threshold, capacity and peak power efforts all improving as we trained in the sunshine. I was enjoying myself and looking forward to the World Championships in early March, which would be on home turf in London.

Some riders wanted to train on the final day in Majorca, whereas I was of the opinion that it would be better to rest. It was important, especially for me, not to weaken my immune system ahead of the flight home and a hard session wouldn't allow me to do that.

I was ultimately overruled and went out on the bike, but I wasn't happy. I'd told myself it would be okay because I didn't have to push myself too hard if I didn't want to, but when you're training in a group there is an obligation to at least keep up, so it didn't really pan out that way. I should have listened to my instinct here and my years of experience, but instead I went with the flow.

Annoyingly, and somewhat predictably, by Monday I could sense that I was coming down with an illness. I can't attribute it certainly to that final training ride, but I realised I hadn't listened to my body enough and was now rundown and susceptible to illness. I had a sore throat and the glands in my neck were so swollen I could barely swallow. I was absolutely dreading telling Paul, fearing my coach's reaction would be much the same as when I had fallen ill in the run-up to Paris.

Fortunately, when I did pluck up the courage to talk to him, whilst he wasn't exactly thrilled by the news, he was sympathetic. The doctor advised me to rest and Paul was supportive although

I couldn't help but fret, internally. Here I was again, in the run-up to the Worlds, under the weather.

After a few days the doctor reassured me I was no longer contagious and I went back to the track. I'd stayed away up until that point since I'd always found it really irritating and inconsiderate when other riders 'pushed through' illness and came to the velodrome with germs. For the first few training sessions I felt groggy, but over time I gradually started to see an improvement.

I focussed on simply taking one day at a time and in the few days before travelling down to London, I was feeling strong again. Perhaps the extended rest following the big training camp had done me good. In general we worked so hard in training, and I don't think I ever really had quite enough rest to adapt from the work, and at some point my body said no and I got ill. Everyone is different and this is yet another challenge of working towards a team event.

The atmosphere at the London World Championships immediately took me back to the 2012 Olympics. I remember looking at the velodrome and exclaiming, 'I love this track!' It was the very opposite of the velodrome in Colombia – bowl-shaped and smooth.

Our strategy in the build-up to London had been to give me longer and longer turns whilst also still starting in the man one position. The accepted philosophy is that the less changeovers you have during a race, the better, and my form in training was improving rapidly. I wasn't 100 per cent confident about the race structure, but the evidence was showing I was in a good enough physical condition and we wouldn't learn anything without trying something new.

Come race day, our carefully orchestrated strategy didn't unfold as we had planned. We had observed that the track was running quite fast during training, but were still absolutely stunned when the American team rode a time of four minutes sixteen in the qualifiers. The previous fastest time anyone else had ever done in a qualification round was a whole two seconds slower than that, so this performance blew our minds. We had been aiming for four minutes seventeen and now knew this wouldn't be good enough to qualify fastest.

Still, if we executed our plan we would qualify second and still have the chance to race for gold. That was my reasoning, anyway. Unfortunately, not everyone in the team felt the same way and it's fair to say we all responded differently to the shock of the Americans' time and we didn't have enough communication between us. I learnt a lot on this day about how different people respond to these sort of situations. As a result when we took to the start line, we probably each had a different game plan in mind, which always spells disaster in a team pursuit.

Throughout the race we oscillated at an inconsistent speed which breaks rule number one of team pursuiting and doesn't do your legs any favours as accelerations and decelerations are far more costly than a constant pace.

By my third turn I felt as though I had hit a brick wall. I got my turn done as best I could, swung up and down the track and tucked in at the back with four laps to go. I remember thinking, *I just need to hold on.* My legs were locking up but I focussed on the wheel in front of me and nothing else. At one point, I recall registering that the race felt easier than it had up until now. I looked up and saw that the rider in front of me, Ciara Horne, had lost contact with the first two riders, Laura Trott and Elinor Barker, who had accelerated away, leaving a large gap. The effort it takes to close a gap like that is monumental, and of course the time is taken by the third rider. I shouted to Ciara to swing up, thinking I could chase back to them.

Paul was frantically making signals with his arms at this point. It was clear to Laura and Elinor that something had gone awry, but his gestures weren't precise enough to communicate exactly what. I tried to chase back to them but they just extended their lead over us so I swung up, letting Ciara through again to chase. She put in a huge effort to minimise our losses and we finished with a time of four minutes twenty-one, a pitiful four seconds slower than our projection and enough for a fifth place. This eliminated any opportunity of us riding for gold the next day. We could, however, win bronze by racing off against the eighth-place team.

This was my first ever experience of being at a World Championships with zero potential to win on the second day. It was an alien feeling as with every bike race I've ever ridden, no matter what the event, there is always a chance of winning. You have to be in it to win it and we were now in a situation where we couldn't be in it. My next thought, in the midst of the crushing disappointment, was, *It's not all over, we can come back fighting*. It became crucial for us all to change our mindset and start telling ourselves that a bronze medal represented a win, at that stage.

I slumped back to the hotel and checked my phone. That's when I saw a text from my dad. It said, '*Never mind. Come back fighting tomorrow x ps Don't go on Twitter.*'

CHAPTER 38

BACKLASH

'L ACK OF COMPOSURE COSTS GB WOMEN RACE IN TEAM PURSUIT,' screamed the newspaper headline, the next day.

London, being a home World Championship, had garnered a great deal of media attention and what had been directed at us was, it is fair to say, very far from complimentary. To make matters worse, the public agreed and I was being bombarded with comments on social media like 'The rest of the world have raised their game and you haven't. Shocking'.

I tried to take my dad's advice and stay away from Twitter, but it was difficult to resist taking the odd sneaky peek when I knew that people were talking about us. I've never been very good at switching off from social media. I know other athletes who delete their apps ahead of a major competition, considering them too much of a distraction, whereas I found it kept me grounded to know there were other things going on. Plus, at that stage, I'd had very limited experience of trolls.

The comments from the public struck me as being incredibly

unfair. They were used to seeing a very polished performance and aren't privy to all the work that goes into those few minutes behind the scenes. Most of them can't imagine what it's like to ride a team pursuit, which made me wonder what gave them the right to pass judgement.

People were saying we clearly didn't have what it takes to win at the Olympics in just a few months' time and this fired me up to prove them wrong. I knew, deep down, that whilst we'd had a disappointing performance, they were way off the mark.

The team set about analysing the previous day's race, alongside a graph showing the speeds of each individual racer. We decided it would be wise to spread out the effort more evenly, with the data showing who had good legs and could take on more laps on the front. Looking back now, the girls and I laugh at that race. We think it's funny to watch it back and do a running commentary of what we were all thinking at each stage ('oh sh*t!' comes up quite a lot). Yet, at the time, it was all very serious and focussed.

The semi-finals were against China and we won comfortably, riding a new National record of four minutes sixteen, finally beating our time from altitude at Aguascalientes over two years ago. Our performance was quite reserved, since we knew we couldn't afford to take any risks and mess up, but it looked polished from the outside and allowed us to qualify for the bronze.

In the final we were up against New Zealand, who had been riding really well with times of around four minutes eighteen. In theory we should have been two seconds faster than them, but we knew that teams could save a little something to pull out of the bag in a final. There was no room for us to be complacent.

When we rode another time of four sixteen and beat the New Zealand girls by a clear three seconds, we celebrated our bronze as though it was a gold. I was so proud of our team for coming back from the disappointment the previous day. We had never been in that situation before and with the added pressure of the media and questions being raised about the upcoming Olympic Games, we were able to show the world the kind of performance we were capable of. We all rode really well technically and distributed the effort well physically. It was also particularly pleasing for me to see Ciara Horne win her first ever World Championship medal. Our victory was compounded when America won by four minutes sixteen point eight seconds, three tenths of a second slower than the time we had ridden. As much as I acknowledged America were riding extremely strongly, I knew it was all to play for in Rio.

It's funny how some medals mean more than others and that's not necessarily determined by their colour – in Paris, we had been so miserable following our silver but here we were ecstatic over a bronze.

After that, Laura won the omnium, Jonathan Dibben won the points race, Jason Kenny won the sprint and Mark Cavendish and Bradley Wiggins won the Madison. It was a promising week for British Cycling and by the end of it the media had all but forgotten about our mishap in the qualifiers. We were all feeling optimistic about Rio.

The planets aligned and Dan was able to come down to London for my week off, following the Championships. We even managed to have a night out at Mahiki – a nightclub in Mayfair – which is virtually unheard of in the run-up to an Olympic Games, but echoed similar celebrations we had in Melbourne four years ago. We also visited the Harry Potter Studios. I'm a huge fan and was as excited as most of the children there.

I went around the studio squealing in amazement. My favourite part was seeing the to-scale-model of Hogwarts which they had used for the outside shots, which was pretty spectacular. I just about resisted the urge to buy a wand in the gift shop!

Back in Manchester, I was going heavy on gym work, doing up to three sessions every week, as well as road and track sessions. I only had one day off a week and two training sessions most days. Eating the quantities of protein which had been recommended to me was a task which completely took over my life. I had to eat thirty grams, which is the equivalent of about five eggs, six times per day, in order to build and maintain muscle mass.

The only opportunity for a bit of downtime was at Lizzie Armitstead's hen do, which took place in Leeds in mid-April 2016. Lizzie was due to marry Philip Deignan, an Irish professional cyclist, who raced for Team Sky, in September 2016, and she had a small hen do for close family and friends from her hometown of Otley.

The hen do happened to coincide with me getting back from a training camp in Valencia and I was completely exhausted the entire time. I was like a zombie, always on the lookout for a seat I could sit in and constantly thinking about my protein intake. I remember Lizzie's sister Kate saying to me, 'Wow, you look tired, Jo!'

We did clay pigeon shooting in the morning, followed by a life drawing class. After that, the other girls went on a night out but I headed to Lizzie's parents' house to sleep. I knew that Lizzie, being a fellow professional athlete, would understand.

Training continued throughout April but British Cycling found itself in the headlines for all the wrong reasons. The big news was Jess Varnish had been removed from the World Class Programme and, amidst accusations of bullying and sexism, Shane Sutton resigned. The topic of 'a culture of fear' kept coming up too, resulting in many more questions about athlete welfare.

(At the time of writing, investigations into these allegations and cycling culture are ongoing, and whilst the claim that Shane used 'inappropriate and discriminatory language' has been upheld, other claims have not.) During this time it was important for me to keep focussed on the job in hand but I actually became quite fearful of the media. Stories were being leaked and no one knew who was leaking them. I didn't want to give any interviews myself as I was worried my words could be twisted to create a sensationalised headline, although when giving interviews about other subjects, I found all the questions came back to these topics. I had mixed emotions – I knew I would miss Shane, who I found to be one of the best motivators in the world and I had always trusted him to be honest with me, but I also felt sympathy for Jess and couldn't disagree that the timing of her removal from the programme was odd. After an Olympic Games is a natural time for reviews so to remove someone with just a few months to go with no warning was highly unorthodox.

My whole career there had always contained that element of fear about not being good enough for selection each time a major competition came around, but this was the first time I began to wonder about my place on the programme itself, as questions emerged around the wording of our contracts and whether a review period was mandatory before a rider was removed. In general, though, I was good at staying focussed on my training with little distraction, just with a new fear of answering my phone to a private number in case it was a journalist trying to catch me out, until May when things took a turn for the worst.

It all started on a Friday. We were right in the middle of a hard training block and I was feeling tired, although not unusually so. That morning was a road session involving a thirty-minute effort during which I surprised myself by producing a new personal best power output for thirty minutes. In the afternoon we had some interval training down at the track, which included a five-minute full-gas effort. Again I surprised myself to sneak another personal best, which was particularly unexpected after the morning session, before completing the rest of the interval session. I was feeling quite pleased with myself!

Afterwards, I noticed that I had a stiff neck. Our physio, Hannah, agreed that my neck felt tight and massaged it for me, although she couldn't find anything specifically wrong. The massage didn't particularly help and afterwards it still hurt to turn my head from side to side. I thought perhaps I had slept on it funny.

I was due to complete a hard road ride on the Saturday with a variety of different intervals, followed by a rest day on Sunday before travelling to Valencia for a training camp on the Monday. I woke up on the Saturday feeling completely exhausted. This doesn't sound particularly surprising, especially after the tough day the day before, but I should have been able to complete the week. My neck also felt even worse. I didn't feel it would be safe to ride on the road as I would struggle to look over my shoulder and see if cars were coming, so I decided to take the day off as rest.

I felt incredibly guilty that I was taking this rest day, even though my body was screaming at me that I needed rest. I kept telling myself I would get the training done on Sunday instead but a part of me was sceptical my neck would make a recovery by then.

I sat on the sofa and found I couldn't even watch the TV properly, because I couldn't move my head. Then I started to develop a fever. I assumed I was coming down with yet another bug and not for the first time, cursed my weak immune system.

Throughout the course of that day, it became clear that the

entire weekend would be a write-off, but I told myself the most important thing was to ensure I was well enough to make it to Valencia on the Monday. I awoke Sunday to find my neck had swollen, width-wise, giving me the appearance of the Incredible Hulk, and now I couldn't move it at all. My temperature had reached thirty-nine degrees. Dan was frantically Googling my symptoms and was concerned that meningitis could be a risk, although I didn't have a rash.

He kept bringing up frozen items from the freezer to the bedroom, like bags of peas, for me to put on my head and bring my temperature down. It was a good idea, but I didn't feel as though I was hot at all. In fact, I was shivering violently from cold. I spent the day slipping in and out of consciousness.

I contacted the doctor and he instructed me to come and see him at the velodrome on the Monday morning. By this stage, my whole body was in unbearable amounts of pain to the extent that I found it impossible to keep my legs still as I lay in bed, meaning I was writhing around. Going to the toilet was a mission – I needed Dan to help me get to the loo each time because I was so weak, although by now I was becoming dehydrated so this wasn't a trip I had to make often.

My first thought was the conversation in which I'd have to tell our coaches I might not be able to fly to Valencia. These worries circled round and round in my head as I somehow made it through Sunday night, wrapped in a blanket and shuddering with cold and pain.

Dan drove me to the velodrome on the Monday, since by that point I wasn't even able to tilt my head to look in the mirrors on my car. Every time we went over a speed bump I groaned in agony. He held me up as I put all of my focus and energy into getting one foot in front of the other and making it to the doctor's office.

The first thing the doctor did was take a blood sample. As a professional athlete, this was something I was completely used to as part of drug testing procedures and normally they don't bother me in the slightest. Yet, this time the needle pricking my skin felt unbearable. I was suddenly incredibly light-headed and had to ask the doctor to stop.

My blood pressure was dangerously low. I lay down on the floor of the doctor's office, the world spinning around me, feeling a mixture of panic and confusion.

It was then that everyone sprang into action, realising they needed to get me to a hospital.

CHAPTER 39

VULNERABILITY

I tried to leave the doctor's office, with Richard supporting me as I struggled to walk, but I collapsed again on the corridor floor. After seeing me collapse, Dan sprinted down to reception and asked Diane, the lady who works there, to get a wheelchair for me. Whilst she was searching for the chair, he fetched his car and drove it right up to the door of the velodrome. I had to be wheeled out to the car and, after much ado trying to get me into the bloody thing, I was taken to Manchester Royal Infirmary.

I don't remember much of what happened, other than being put on a bed with wheels and taken to another part of the hospital, where I was subjected to endless blood tests. Dan sent a WhatsApp message from my phone explaining to the other girls that I wouldn't be coming to Valencia and why, and I presume Richard rang Paul to explain the situation.

It was, without exaggeration, the worst physical pain I have ever been in. It exceeded even the tonsil surgery and the subsequent infection I'd picked up in 2013. I was admitted to hospital and given intravenous antibiotics; I was also placed on a drip because I was severely dehydrated. The nurse described the medication they were giving me as 'like bleach'.

The blood tests showed my CRP, or C-reactive protein, was 140. In a healthy person it would be between 0–3 and anything over 100 indicates a worryingly high level of infection. Later that day, my reading went up to 190.

I was tested for glandular fever, flu, mumps, rubella and meningitis and they all came back negative. Meanwhile, ever focussed on the Olympics, I fretted about being in hospital, an environment fraught with germs, so close to the Games. It's safe to say I wasn't thinking particularly logically at this point – I certainly wasn't in a fit state to be arguing with anyone.

Dan had to leave overnight, under hospital regulations. This was a problem for me as I couldn't get to the toilet by myself and had to suffer the indignity of calling the nurse every time I needed to go (I was now on a drip so more hydrated). They kept telling me to eat and drink, and Dan had instructed them to ensure I ate plenty of protein so that all my hard-earned muscle wouldn't wither away. During his visits, Dan was bringing me high-protein yogurts and protein gels. He also brought me gingerbread men and Maltesers, foods which I would usually devour with gusto, but I had no appetite and they were left untouched. Dan said, 'Wow, you really are ill!'

The first night in the hospital was a blur. At one point I have a vague memory of having a nurse and a doctor standing over my bed and fighting with them, trying to keep my blanket on me. I was insisting I was cold but they were trying to bring my temperature down and I ultimately lost the tug of war – too weak to hold onto the covers.

During the following day the pain was still all-consuming. I was doing anything I could to try and distract myself. There was a very basic game I had on my phone which involved matching pairs of coloured dots and I used that simply to give me something to look at. My brain was so befuddled, even this was a struggle and the physical effort of holding my phone was tiring.

By Tuesday, my CRP reading was still high, even though the doctors had done every test they could think of and they had all come back negative. It was a frightening situation to find yourself in, knowing you are ill but the medical experts are not able to give you a name for it. They now thought perhaps it was a viral infection rather than bacterial, so I was given no more antibiotics. I remember genuinely thinking I wouldn't recover. My temperature was fluctuating but still hitting over thirty-nine degrees and I remember asking at one point to be put in a coma. This idea was purely based on the pain I was in and wanting it to stop, not any medical knowledge, and my requests were met with shakes of the head from the nurses and a reminder that the next paracetamol dose would be soon.

On Wednesday morning my first thought upon waking was that I felt cold, but in a good way. I could feel the gentle caress of the breeze as it came in through the open window. My neck was less swollen.

I began talking to the other women on the ward but they looked at me like I was a crazy fantasist when I told them what I did for a living. With my grey skin, sheen of sweat from even the simplest tasks and my shaking limbs I couldn't have looked further away from a professional athlete. I could tell by the looks on their faces that they thought I was lying but they smiled and nodded politely.

The doctors inspected me and declared that I was well enough to go home, but I would need constant observation due to my dangerously low blood pressure making me still feel very faint. The very first thing I did after being discharged was to go straight to the velodrome to see Richard.

Richard advised me to continue to rest and said he had never seen an athlete so unwell before and that unfortunately I wouldn't be going to Valencia to join the others any time soon. I can't say I was devastated as my main concerns now weren't training for the Olympics, but simply getting healthy again. At this point I couldn't even imagine riding a bike.

Upon consultation with a physician at the hospital, we agreed I would need more rest until my CRP levels were back down to a normal level and we could then plan a gentle reintroduction to training. The next day Dan took me to my parents' house to recover as he wouldn't be able to look after me each day.

After eight days of total rest I went on a one-hour bike ride, on a lovely sunny day, around the gentle slopes of Shropshire. Normally, that would have been a recovery session for me, but I was absolutely exhausted afterwards. I had a two-hour nap that afternoon. The next day, I did another hour-long ride, which forced me to take a day off after that. I was shocked at how much this unnamed illness had taken out of me.

Usually, once you're back on the bike following an illness like a cold you start to see quick improvements, but this time I was so fatigued constantly I couldn't even consider the amount of training I'd usually be doing so close to the Olympics. I could barely function properly as an adult, even off the bike. My first concern had to be my health as a human, rather than as an athlete, I realised.

Paul was being extremely understanding at this point and wasn't putting any pressure on me to come back and train with the team. After they returned from Valencia he gave me another two weeks away from team duties and said to train by myself, doing whatever I felt I could.

I came back to my first training session at the track and everyone was being incredibly optimistic, telling me that I would probably find that the rest had done me good (as I had found in the past) and I may surprise myself. But their positivity was misplaced – the only thing that was surprising was how terrible I was. My usual gear for a standing start felt huge and I could barely get the bike off the start line. I tried to do a flying lap and couldn't get anywhere near the speeds I'd been achieving just a few weeks before. My personal bests felt a million miles away.

I had support from Richard, Joe, Len, Paul, our nutritionist Kath, and Ruth to help get me back to full strength. Ruth commented that I didn't seem to be stressing too much and appeared quite calm about the whole thing. After everything that had happened, I'd resigned myself to the uncontrollable nature of my illness and my recovery from it. I was simply trying to take one day at a time. The process of getting myself to a point where I could train properly was frustratingly slow, yet I could see, little by little, day by day, I was making incremental progress.

I knew I could only do what my body was capable of. I had to listen to myself, not do too much too soon and just soldier on.

Before I knew it, it was time to go to Valencia again. I was nervous, convincing myself that I was somehow cursed and that something else would go wrong in the lead-up. I lived for these warm weather training camps and I was trying even harder than usual to avoid germs, constantly on ultra-high-alert.

I felt vulnerable when we arrived in the sunny climes of Spain and told myself not to be greedy and go in too hard, too soon. Gradually, I started to see my old form coming back. I had good days and bad days, sometimes thinking, *It's all over*, and at others telling myself it was impossible to have lost all of the fitness I'd had before my illness.

By July, I was almost fully recovered. We had a few days off from training, during which we were sent to the NEC to get our Team GB kit. It was a completely different experience from the last time. Before London, going around all the various stalls and selecting clothing had seemed like the definition of 'fun', now it simply felt like unnecessary time to be spending on my feet. I still appreciated the effort that had gone into the experience and enjoyed the day, but was far more aware of my need for recovery.

Everyone had to get vaccinations ahead of Rio, for hepatitis, typhoid and yellow fever. When I went to the doctor for mine he told me that he was concerned my immune system wouldn't cope, following this bad illness. When I had first been diagnosed with alopecia my childhood doctor had told my parents it was an autoimmune disease and for that reason he would advise against me having vaccinations. I hadn't had my meningitis injection or my BCG at school, for example, on medical advice. Since then subsequent doctors had disagreed and said I would be fine to have vaccinations, but as it happened I hadn't been anywhere in the world that would require one.

In the end, after much deliberation I decided to run the risk of going to Rio unvaccinated. This was amidst all the other publicity around the Zika virus and stories about the toilets not being finished properly in the Olympic Village.

Before travelling to Rio we made the journey to Newport in South Wales to stay at Celtic Manor once again for our final two-week holding camp before the Games. This was set to be a real treat again, staying in five-star accommodation with wonderful food, brilliant training roads and the Newport velodrome close by. I was riding stronger by the day and was finally seeing the fruits of my labours by posting some fast times on the track again. Team efforts were generally going well but naturally everyone was having up-and-down days as the week went on.

At the start of our second week in Newport the plan was to complete a full dress rehearsal, in our Olympic kit, with the full warm-up procedure we would do on race day. This was a great chance to test a full four-kilometre effort and I was quietly confident we could post a fast time in training. It was therefore highly unfortunate that the day we were due to complete this effort, I came down with a bout of food poisoning.

Only one other person in the hotel reported themselves to be ill. This was typical of me and my track record of getting ill at crucial times. If it was going around, I would get it. I will spare you the full details but I initially had a high temperature, which led to a little worry on the part of the doctor that I was perhaps having a relapse of the illness from May. Fortunately, I was able to make a quick recovery but it did mean missing the remaining track sessions that week. Paul was supportive and once again we were back to re-writing my training plan.

During that week the full dress rehearsal four kilometre effort still went ahead without me and the girls smashed it – not just setting a new personal best, but also an unofficial world record. This was an incredible boost of confidence for the team and of course I was pleased for them, but we now had a situation where four girls had ridden quicker than anyone else in the world had ever ridden and I would need to prove myself if I wanted to get back in the team.

After a decade-long career I was becoming accustomed to situations like this, and once again Ruth praised me for my approach on this occasion. I realised stressing wouldn't make matters better and I simply needed to rest and let my body recover. There would be more training sessions before the race so I would have more chances to prove myself.

I think I was also helped here by the fact I'd already won in London and now, although I still wanted to win, I didn't need to do so. The difference was subtle but it meant a more professional and less emotional approach by me to the worries of non-selection. The final training session in Newport actually went extremely well and I proved myself to be strong enough to be part of the line-up, but we would still have the situation of five girls for four spots in the team. My health was the most important thing and the travel to Rio and keeping myself healthy out there would be my focus.

And so it was that I boarded the plane to Brazil, stocked up with antiseptic hand gels and instructions about not going anywhere near tap water, all the while experiencing extremely high levels of anxiety.

CHAPTER 40

LET THE GAMES BEGIN

Just before we flew out to Rio, something happened to upset the balance and cause a huge distraction from my world, which at that point purely focussed on riding round in circles. The *MailOnline* had run a story, reporting that Lizzie Armitstead had three strikes on the 'whereabouts system'.

The whereabouts system was the bane of my life as an athlete, which I had been on since 1 January 2007, aged eighteen. It's a computerised system, which all athletes have to fill in three months in advance, stating where we will be every single day and night, so that the random drugs testing team can always find us. The compulsory fields are an overnight accommodation address and a one-hour testing slot address every day, in addition to as much detail of your training locations as possible. If your plans change during the three months, you are able to log in to make alterations or text in any last-minute changes. It sounds simple, but there are always times when you have no internet, your phone doesn't have any signal and you're immersed in a last-minute emergency where it all becomes a gigantic headache and mistakes are easily made.

If, for whatever reason, you aren't where the drugs testers expect to be then you get a 'strike' and three strikes counts as a violation of the anti-doping rules.

For one of Lizzie's strikes, she had been staying at a hotel in Sweden. She had filled in the whereabouts system as she was supposed to and was where she had said she would be. However, when the drugs tester turned up at the hotel, the receptionist wouldn't give the number of Lizzie's room. Obviously, no one knows a drugs test is going to happen ahead of time, so Lizzie was sleeping soundly upstairs, oblivious to all that was happening.

Lizzie had prepared her defence and had gone to the Court of Arbitration for Sport and had this strike rescinded. It was deemed by the judge to be the fault of the tester, since she had done everything she was supposed to do. Hence, Lizzie was able to return to cycling and compete in the Rio Olympics and, at that time, was technically on two strikes as opposed to three.

All this had been done privately but unfortunately, in keeping with the current issues surrounding British Cycling, the story had been leaked to the media.

The *Mail* broke the story just before we were due to fly out to Rio. They released it onto their website late in the evening. By breakfast the following morning at the holding camp at Celtic Manor, everyone had already heard about the story. When I walked in, the room fell silent, presumably because everyone knew Lizzie was my friend and they couldn't say anything negative about her in front of me. Although the silence was eerie, I was glad of it – I was hurting so badly for her and would have been even angrier if someone else had said something against her.

That day the track squad made the journey to Heathrow, where we would stay the night before our flight to Brazil the following morning. Lizzie flew in to Heathrow to join us as she was also on our flight. We were sharing a room and her mobile was ringing all evening and she spent the night preparing a statement to release the following day.

I felt desperately sorry for Lizzie. The media were treating her as though she was guilty, when actually what had happened had been an administrative error. Many athletes find themselves receiving strikes which no one ever hears about. I'm sure many more have made mistakes but got lucky as no one was looking to test them on that specific day and therefore they have not received a strike.

It was difficult for me to see the impact the incident had on Lizzie, who was understandably incredibly hurt and upset. She went on to place fifth in the road race in Rio. Under the circumstances she pulled off a fantastic performance and I was very proud of her.

One topic the British press *had* reported accurately was the state of the Olympic Village in Rio – it wasn't very nice at all. The five of us on the team pursuit squad plus the two sprint girls were sharing an apartment. I was sharing a room with Ciara Horne and on the first evening the light randomly came on in the middle of the night. I couldn't work out how this had happened as the light switch was nowhere near the bed. The following day I realised there was a light switch in the bathroom, which seemed to work the light in our room! I used a permanent marker pen to draw a cross on this switch the following day to make sure no one used it again. The water which came out of the shower smelled absolutely foul, to the extent that I actually didn't feel like I was getting any cleaner when I washed in it. We had been advised not to drink the tap water and also not to wash up with the water, which, trust me, is a pain when you're trying to wash up a protein shaker without the pressure of water coming out of a tap.

The food hall was also really disappointing. The quality of the meals was very poor, oscillating between completely tasteless and far too spicy. One night, I cut into a chicken breast to find that it was raw. We were told not to have the salad or the seafood, which would have been washed in potentially unsafe water, to try and avoid any risk of illness.

In the end the carers cooked porridge oats with milk in the rice cookers in their apartment for breakfast and I relied on sports nutrition products I'd brought with me to supplement the safe-looking plain pasta I ate for every meal from the food hall. At this point I felt like I was just trying to get myself to race day without getting ill. A healthy balanced diet was long forgotten.

There were also issues with the laundry system. The idea was that we were issued with wash bags that had a barcode which could be scanned and then our accreditation could be scanned. This should have meant we could hand in our laundry bags then go to collect them the following day, having been washed. In reality, however, the system failed. Laura Trott and I went to collect our kit only for our accreditations to be scanned and then be told they had no laundry matching our names! We persuaded them to let us into the laundry area and we had to go searching through all the wash bags from many nations to find our stuff. Every time we came across a bag with Team GB kit we would think we'd found ours, but of course Team GB was huge so there were a lot of people with kit that looked exactly the same. As you would imagine, it took absolutely ages but we did eventually find our kit.

My first thought about the velodrome in Rio was that it was designed with long straights and tight bankings, although not to the extent of Cali in Colombia. When we had been training in Newport directly before flying out to Brazil the temperatures in the velodrome had reached nearly thirty degrees, but here the velodrome was air-conditioned, meaning the temperature inside was only twenty-one degrees. To a track cyclist, this is freezing! We like it the hotter the better as it lends itself to faster times and also less risk of the dreaded pursuiter's cough, which is common when doing hard efforts in cooler climes. This temperature change meant that initially our times were slower than they had been back home, which led to questions of whether to change gearing or the projected pace we had spent so long perfecting.

As ever, the biggest challenge was knowing that of the five riders who had come out for the Games, only four of us would be competing for each round, and each round the team could be changed up until one hour to go. Interestingly, I didn't fear not being in the team in Rio in the same way I did in London four years ago, even though it was the same situation. I think having already won an Olympic gold medal meant everything about Rio was a bonus for me: I wanted to win but I didn't *need* to win. A subtle difference but a significant one, which did mean that I was a lot more relaxed than four years ago.

A few days before race day it was decided that Ciara would sit out the qualifiers.

I felt for Ciara – she had done everything right, trained by the book and made all the progress she was supposed to, and yet still she found herself missing out. This is one of the toughest things about elite sport – all the hard work can result in nothing and that's completely out of your control. Although she always behaved with the utmost professionalism, it was clear that Ciara was disappointed and I couldn't blame her.

We set a new world record during the qualifying round, riding a time of four minutes thirteen seconds and qualifying fastest, meaning we would race against fourth-placed Canada in the next round. This time we officially beat the previous record, which had been held by Australia for the last eighteen months, but it wasn't a complete surprise being similar to the time the girls had ridden in training in Newport.

America, who were our biggest competition and the current World Champions, had ridden just one second slower than us. They had gone last, which can be an advantage in that it means you can see what times the other teams do and potentially pace your ride so you do just enough to progress to the next round without expending any unnecessary energy. There is quite an art to pursuiting and this is easier said than done, but it didn't stop me thinking that perhaps the Americans had been merely pacing themselves and would have a lot more to give in the subsequent rounds.

That day, the men's team sprint won gold. They'd come sixth at the World Championships in March so to some may have been perceived as the underdogs of the competition. Becky James also won silver in the keirin. She had had many setbacks, from illness to injury, over the previous two years so to see her triumph was a huge boost. Their results filled me with confidence that as a team we had got our preparation right and it was all going to come together for the rest of us.

A new challenge in Rio was that we had a day off between qualifier and final. This was virtually unheard of and involved an entire day spent back at the Olympic Village, just waiting.

We had spent a long time analysing what would be the best thing for us to do that day ever since the Olympic programme was announced. The key was to keep the legs activated – too little riding and our bodies could go into recovery mode, but too much riding and we could increase our fatigue ahead of the finals. I opted for two sessions on the turbo, one in the morning and the other in the afternoon, mirroring the times of the races the following day. I did a combination of some zone three blocks as well as some short sprints, which were similar to my normal warm-up routine.

At some point I noticed I had a sore throat and thought, *Oh God, not again!*, but mercifully it never developed beyond a sniffle.

I was keen to keep my mind off the impending finals as much as possible. It would have been easy for me to work myself up into a bag of jangling nerves, double-guessing and questioning whether I'd done too much or too little riding that day, whether my legs hurt the 'right' or the 'wrong' amount; whether my throat would get worse too. Whether our opponents had more to give. Whether I'd even be in the line-up.

In an effort to distract myself, I listened to Beyonce's *Lemonade*, which had just come out at the time. In particular, the lyrics of the song '6 Inch' resonated with me, for reasons I think are probably obvious: '*She fights for the power, keeping time / She grinds day and night*'.

To this day, I can't listen to that album without it reminding me of how I was feeling that day in Rio.

CHAPTER 41

HER NAME IS RIO

And then it was race day.

The semi-finals were against Canada. On paper, it seemed as though we would be able to beat them without too much of a problem, but again I had that lingering worry that our opponents might not have given 100 per cent the day before, so we hadn't truly seen what they were capable of.

I put forward my opinion to our coach, Paul, that Ciara Horne should be swapped into the team for this round. Not only did I believe it was the right thing to do morally, I also knew the finals against the Americans would be incredibly challenging and if one of us sat out the semis, we would be fresher for the final battle.

Paul overruled me. He knew as I did that Ciara was well up to the required standard and there was no reason to think she wasn't capable of participating in the semis. His philosophy, however, was 'if it ain't broke, don't fix it' and for that reason he thought we should stick with the original team.

Ciara was very upset when it became clear that she wouldn't be riding. It was her first Olympic Games and I cannot even begin to imagine how it must have felt for her, watching from the sidelines. My instinct was to comfort her, but I also knew I had to focus entirely on the forthcoming race. Once again she was extremely professional.

We beat Canada, despite my not feeling particularly good during that round. It quickly became clear I hadn't done enough during the course of my rest day – I'd misjudged the delicate balance required. America, as predicted, beat Australia in their round, riding a time of four minutes twelve seconds and setting a new world record in the process. We had ridden two tenths of a second faster during our semi-finals, breaking the world record again and stealing it back from the US. It was our best performance as a team to date.

Between rounds, I was mostly sat on the floor considering being sick. It's quite normal to vomit after putting in the amount of effort required to perform at that level. At one point, Katie piped up and said the semis had been 'about 80 per cent', for her, in terms of the effort she had put in. I wanted to laugh. Katie's performance had been so strong, to an extent it had been what had carried us through the semis. *If she was planning to go 100 per cent for the final*, I reflected, *it would be bloody hard to hang onto her wheel!*

I wanted to ride a bigger gear for the final. I'd been saying all week that I felt I was capable of riding a bigger gear but was told by Paul it was important to conserve my energy and save my legs. Now it was the last race and I had nothing to lose.

I rode that huge gear out of the start gate. I felt powerful as I brought the team up to speed. We ended up riding a time of four minutes ten seconds. As we tore around the track I remember thinking over and over, *Thank God I have this higher gear*. I felt I was pedalling at the same speed I had been for the semis, but the gear allowed me to ride that little bit faster. I came into man one position for the third time, gave it everything I had before swinging out with three laps to go. At that point I could see that, barring an unexpected disaster, we were going to win.

The original time we had always projected to achieve in Rio was 4:10. When I first heard it, it had seemed completely ludicrous to even dream we could ride that fast, but now we had done it. In addition to the gold and of course creating our third new world record of the week, it was that time which brought us joy. There were quite a few victory laps after that race.

Afterwards, we were taken to the media mix zone and I was interviewed by Jill Douglas for the BBC. I was flying high as a kite, elated not only by our performance but by how we had managed to turn things around since our disastrous race in March.

We had to change into our podium tracksuits, a new tradition which had been instigated after London. I just about had enough time to re-do my eyeliner before it was podium time. The whole process, from winning the race to being presented with a medal, passes by in the blink of an eye. There were a few photos, including one of all five of us (including Ciara) and then it was straight off to dope control.

Minutes later, I was in the bowels of the velodrome attempting to pee in a pot. By the time I'd finished, the venue was completely deserted save for the doctor and my agent, Jess Henig, who was sitting alone amidst thousands of empty seats.

Jess and I weren't sure what to do. Elinor Barker and Katie Archibald had gone back to Team GB house, but my phone was once again out of juice and I had no way of contacting them to find out where it was. In the end, we decided to get on a bus back to the Village. The bus brought us to the back end, which was the opposite side to where the taxi rank was.

Jess needed a taxi to get back to her hotel and I wasn't going to let her walk around the perimeter of the Village alone, at night. I asked one of the guards if she could come in to the Village so that I could escort her through. I was told no, since Jess wasn't accredited, but I kept debating with them, trying to explain our situation.

At some point the guard clocked that I had something around my neck, under my tracksuit top, and she asked what it was. I showed her the gold medal and at that stage she stopped arguing and simply waved us through: the medal changed everything. I remember feeling very surprised – a gold medal shouldn't have granted me any special privileges in terms of security at all. In retrospect, I would have preferred to have lost that debate, or at least to have had a guard escort us both, safe in the knowledge that correct security procedures were being followed.

After Jess got in her taxi, I went to the pretty-much silent food hall and sat by myself eating cold pizza. Just as with the London McDonald's, I'd been looking forward to pizza all week, but when it came to it, it was disappointing. Once again, I reflected what a strange comedown this was.

People assume that if you win an Olympic gold you're automatically treated like a celebrity thereafter, with hoards of fans and immediate invitations to glamorous, all-night parties. Yet both my Olympic victories had ended with me in a canteen eating slightly lacklustre fast food.

It's a difficult thing to get your mind around, going from being under the scrutiny of millions of pairs of eyes, the roar of the crowd and the elation of the win to being all alone. In some ways I had run the full gamut of human experience in less than an hour. It was an exhausting thing to go through, yet I was still buzzing from the adrenaline of it all. I headed back to our apartment knowing I wouldn't be able to sleep.

CHAPTER 42

MANAGING VICTORY

T he next morning I had to be up and about by 6.30am for the 'managing victory' process. I'd still been awake when the other girls got in from the Team GB house at around four or five in the morning. By the time my alarm went off at six, I hadn't been able to snatch even one minute of sleep as people in the UK were now awake and I was busy responding to messages.

Katie and I went to do our media appearances, Elinor went to bed, declaring it was too early and she would join us later. The two of us met our press officer, Abby Burton. As usual, Abby had managed everything to well-oiled perfection, which would make the morning incredibly easy for us.

We began with radio interviews, before moving on to ITN and Sky. We finished late afternoon back at the velodrome with Clare Balding and Chris Hoy from the BBC. Katie had ducked out somewhere in the middle and Elinor joined me for that one. Meanwhile Laura Trott was focussed on her forthcoming performance in the omnium.

We did a quick interview with Clare and Chris before being told we were free to go back to the stands in the velodrome and watch the racing. It was nice, not to mention liberating, not to have to worry about my protein intake, or how my legs were feeling, or whether anyone around me had germs. It was the first time I'd felt completely free and at ease for four years.

That evening, we went to watch the athletics. Elinor's boyfriend worked for Adidas and he had managed to score us some tickets. By that stage I was so tired, having not slept for pretty much forty-eight hours, that I began to nod off in the stands. The atmosphere was fantastic, but I was simply too tired to enjoy it. I slumped back to our apartment and enjoyed the best night's sleep I'd had in a long time – it lasted a whole twelve hours.

At some point, I was made aware of a mini-scandal happening at home, involving one of the country's most-read newspapers. They had plastered our victory across their front page but cropped me out of the photo, as well as Katie. Laura and Elinor smiled out above the headline 'Golden Girls (And Boys!)' making the two of them effectively the covergirls representing all of Team GB's victories in Rio.

The *Rochdale Herald* wrote a piece about it, pointing out that Laura and Elinor are both conventionally pretty with long hair, whereas Katie and I are both less petite and dainty (and Katie had pink hair at the time). They, as well as several others, thought it spectacularly unfair that we had all put an equal amount into winning, yet I had been excluded, in their opinion, on the basis of being tall and having no hair.

The *Herald* editor was quoting from the editor of the *Daily Mail*, who had apparently said, 'Well, it's obvious really, isn't it? Most of our readers read the paper with their breakfast. We can't put a bald woman, regardless of what a magnificent example of female athleticism and achievement she is, on [our] cover… people are eating.'

If that had happened four years ago, after London, I would have been devastated. Yet in 2016, I can honestly say it didn't bother me one jot. I was beginning to understand how the media operated. Yes, it was unfair, but I wasn't going to let that spoil the part I had played in our victory – I understood that my performance on the track was what really mattered. I got texts from friends saying, 'I'm so sorry about the newspapers' and it was nice to think people had my back, but I had genuinely reached a point where I was beyond worrying about that sort of thing.

Laura's omnium was on Monday. Abby Burton asked if I wanted to join the BBC the same afternoon for another interview. I thought it would be the usual sort of affair, lasting around five minutes, but when I got there I was given a seat next to Chris Hoy and was told I was going to be a pundit. It was very last minute, but I enjoyed it immensely.

I often find it difficult to speak about my own performances and wins, probably because it is hard to put into words all the overwhelming emotions of the moment, but I found it easy to give insight into other riders. To me it was something which came quite naturally, analysing the track from afar.

We had been issued with some very short shorts as part of our Team GB kit issue and that was what I ended up wearing for that surprise TV appearance. I received tweets telling me I was showing 'too much leg' and I replied saying I'd worked damned hard for those legs and had earned the right to show them off. I found the whole thing very amusing. Imagine being so outraged as to get in touch with someone telling them off about their legs… The mind positively boggles.

That evening I was asked by Radio 5 Live if I was willing to work with them the following day. I said yes, since I had nothing else planned. Unbeknownst to me, Abby Burton had arranged TV appearances for me at the same time so I ended up spending the day racing between the radio commentary positions and the TV set with Clare Balding and Chris Hoy. I was commentating during the races live on the radio, then dashing back upstairs to do after-race punditry. It might sound stressful, but I was really enjoying myself.

The following day, Wednesday, was my last day in Rio. I took the opportunity to go to the beach with Katie. It wasn't far from the Olympic Village and had beautiful white sands and clear waters. We sat and reflected merrily on how well our trip had gone. That evening, I flew back to the UK.

We hadn't been booked into business class seats for the journey home since we'd done our job, won our medals and no longer needed to be looked after in the same way. When we got to check in, one of the lads asked if there was any chance of a cheeky upgrade whilst flashing his medal, but he was given a firm no. In fairness, I think the flight was genuinely full.

I did, however, manage to commandeer an extra leg-room seat meaning I was able to sleep for the entire flight. Ciara came home with me, whilst Katie and Elinor chose to stay on in Rio for the closing ceremony. Ciara was, understandably, very emotional. It was nice to be able to give her an extra hug at Heathrow as we said goodbye.

Ciara was, understandably, very emotional. Despite her being an amazing friend to me during the whole two years before Rio, and us both supporting each other through the ups and downs of training, I failed to be there for her when she needed me most after missing out on competing. In the whirlwind of media interviews and excitement, I'd neglected my close friend, who was hurting so much. I apologised and gave her an extra tight hug at Heathrow as we said goodbye. She said she was so happy that I had achieved my dream. I said the gold medal wasn't a dream come true, as it didn't include her on the podium with me. We both cried again before agreeing friendship was more important than any medals, and not to let it come between us anymore.

I'm often asked why I flew back early. My main reason was that Dan and my family hadn't been able to come out to Rio. I'd been away for over a month by this point and I was missing everyone terribly.

That Saturday, my parents had arranged a party for me back at home. After London, I'd told my family I didn't want any fuss. This time, I felt totally different. As I saw all the faces I'd been missing, enveloping them in hugs without spending a single second worrying about whether or not they might have a cold, I couldn't have been more content.

CHAPTER 43

A CHANGING PERSPECTIVE

Dan's Mum, Jeannette, had been admitted to hospital whilst I was in Newport during July 2016. I had known this basic detail, i.e. that she was in hospital, but nothing more. Every time I spoke to Dan on the phone and asked after her, he said she was 'fine'. I later realised he was trying to keep the truth from me, so I wouldn't worry and be distracted during the Games.

The first thing I did after I landed in Manchester following the Olympics was to go and see Jeannette in hospital. Her condition was far worse than I had imagined. She looked weak and thin and was awaiting surgery. The visit certainly gave me a shock, as well as a new perspective on things.

Jeannette had her surgery but became very unwell afterwards. She was in hospital for two months and wasn't making a good recovery. Dan and I were upset by the way things had turned out, having been told that surgery would be the answer when in reality it had made her even more poorly in the short term. Jeannette came home for a week at one stage but had to be re-admitted to hospital with sepsis, which is a severe infection. She recovered, but because she was so weak, her wounds wouldn't heal.

It was at this point that I started to question how important riding around in circles really was, in the scheme of life. Jeannette had always been so supportive of me and I felt totally helpless in the face of her illness. I tried to help her by passing on what I had learned about nutrition over the years. I bought her protein drinks and made her smoothies, which I hoped would build her up during a time when she had no appetite for food.

As I write, Jeannette has made a full recovery and has gone back to work as a nurse, but it was touch-and-go for a while and it really shook me up. If that wasn't enough to deal with, my dad also ended up in hospital following an accident causing him to break both his kneecaps. Dad had never even spent a night in hospital before but now found himself bed-bound in the orthopaedic ward for over a week and requiring surgery, and initially we were worried about his prospects for a full recovery. When he could travel home to begin with he required a great deal of care due to his limited mobility so I was glad time away from training meant I was able to spend a few weeks living at my parents' house to help my mum at this difficult time. Overall, life after Rio was a balancing act of spending as much time as I could with my family, in and around media commitments and any other opportunities, as well as seeing friends I hadn't seen properly in ages.

I visited Dan's sister, Keeley, and her children, Maddox and Maizie. I am godmother to Maizie, who was born in 2010. I felt very honoured and proud to be given such an important title. The christening had been held in September 2012 in Cheshire. It was a beautiful day. Dan and I had been together for three years at that point and weren't yet engaged so this felt like my official acceptance into the family, who had always been so welcoming to me.

I spent the late August bank holiday at Keeley's house. Maddox and Maizie wanted to go on bike rides with me and show me how fast they could pedal. Their enthusiasm was a glorious thing to behold. Up until this point I'd never had much energy to play with the kids since I had to rest fully in between training sessions, so this felt like special, quality time.

I was also able to spend a lot more time with Natalie, Dan's twin sister, and assist her by babysitting her son, Jude. He had been born on 2 January 2016, but in the build-up to Rio my time spent with him had been very limited.

Media-wise, I'd been booked to do *Sunday Brunch*, a British TV show where chefs cook with celebrity guests whilst chatting to them about their work. I was one of the three 'tasters' who get to look on, laugh at the funny bits and sample all the dishes at the end. This suited me down to the ground. As I may have mentioned once or twice previously, I love eating!

Mark Cavendish was also on *Sunday Brunch* and gave a really funny interview about how appalling the Olympic Village in Rio was. During this rant, he kept turning to me as if for confirmation and, whilst I nodded and smiled, I did wonder whether we should technically be criticising the Village so publicly. Eventually, I put it to the back of my mind. I figured everything he was saying was out there in the public domain, anyway, and it was good that he was being honest.

I appeared on the *Lorraine* chat show the following morning with Gaby Roslin. The vibe of the interview was very much 'Yay, you won!' so it wasn't too taxing for me to do it alone. I joined Katie and El later that week at Media City and we did the rounds at the BBC, including *Breakfast*, *Newsround* and Radio 5 Live.

I remember it being quite surreal at the time. In my head, my calendar had finished on 13 August and I felt as though I was living on borrowed energy.

One of the first events I attended after Rio was the premiere of the film *Bridget Jones's Baby*. With Dan in hospital after London 2012, I hadn't been able to attend things like this so I was incredibly excited.

As I stepped onto the carpet, hand on hip, turning this way and that in response to my name being called and the flashing of camera bulbs, I realised I was getting more comfortable with my photo being taken. Having said that, I still haven't fully nailed my red carpet pose – I look back at photos and think I seem a bit awkward.

The night after *Bridget Jones* I went to the GQ Awards. The event was full of A-Listers, meaning I felt like a small fish in a big pond filled with astronomically famous faces. Team GB were presented with an award at the end of the night to mark our achievements. We were given a thunderous applause and a standing ovation and I remember thinking how incredible it was that people like Amy Schumer and Elton John were getting to their feet for us.

In September I went on the BBC's children's TV show *Blue Peter* and that was one of my personal highlights. For anyone my age, *Blue Peter* was a fundamental part of our childhood and if you managed to get a coveted Blue Peter badge, you were the coolest human in the universe. To be in the iconic studio felt momentous. I had to do a piece to camera announcing a competition winner. Afterwards, to my astonishment, I was given a Blue Peter badge. Whenever I tell people this, it always gets the biggest reaction – sometimes larger than for my Olympic golds or indeed anything else I've done before or since.

I also filmed *A Question of Sport* again and this time I was nowhere near as nervous. Something had definitely shifted in me, in the four years between London and Rio.

The weirdest thing I did was to attend a track day at a place called Palmer Sport in Bedford – Chris Hoy is mates with the owner and had invited us all along to try out racing cars. I brought Dan as my guest, since I knew he had always wanted to try something like that.

As the day drew near, I began getting really nervous. My feelings of trepidation were somewhat magnified when we arrived and were told that it was a competition (not just a leisurely jaunt around the track, as I'd imagined), we were going to be working in teams and all of our individual times counted towards the final result. I was mortified at the prospect of letting down the legend that is Sir Chris Hoy. I'm a particularly careful and slow driver and everyone kept saying to me they couldn't believe I was there as it really didn't seem like my thing.

I came into my own during the very last activity, which was off-road skills, and more of a case of slow and steady wins the race. Whilst my performance in the other vehicles had been pretty crap, taking part in the event was symbolic. It was just for fun and I'd spent so long saying no to things like that because they weren't strictly necessary and would have impacted my training, it was fun being a 'yes' person.

Lizzie married Phil in September 2016 in her hometown of Otley, north of Leeds. I couldn't have been happier for her – I was so pleased to see her with someone who clearly cares for and respects her so much. The day was a lot of fun and I was honoured to be a bridesmaid.

Best of all, Dan and I finally managed to have a proper honeymoon – three weeks in America. We landed in New York, before taking a train to Boston, where we hired a car and drove up through New England to Niagara Falls, then Washington. We then flew down to Florida for ten days and finally back to New York.

Florida was my highlight. It was warm and sunny and I got to visit the Harry Potter theme park at Universal Studios. It was, I am sorry to say, one hundred times better than the one in London. We visited out-of-season so the park was very quiet in general, but the Harry Potter world was by far the busiest.

I wasn't wearing a wig at the theme park (they can be impractical for rollercoasters!) and just wore a hat, which I took off for the rides. At one point, a man came up to me and asked if he could give me a hug. I was completely confused by this so I said no and felt very uncomfortable. He apologised and told me he knew what I was going through, living with cancer.

I was mortified, as I explained that I didn't have cancer and that my hair loss was because of alopecia. He just gave me a funny look, one I took to mean that he didn't really believe me and thought I was in denial. It isn't the only time something like that has happened. When you suffer from hair loss people do tend to make an assumption that you have cancer. In fact, that's one of the reasons I'm so determined to raise awareness about alopecia. People with this condition don't want you to feel sorry for them. Living with alopecia and explaining it to other people would be a lot easier if there was more public knowledge about it.

Whilst in general I am now far happier talking about alopecia, insensitive comments do occasionally get to me. In October it was the British Cycling Gala Dinner, an event that is held only once every four years, to celebrate international success. I was surprised to see a huge banner with a photo of me and

Elinor Barker, celebrating after winning in Rio, at the front of the room set out for dinner. The whole room and bar area had been decorated with photos, which brought back some lovely memories from all the international success enjoyed by British riders that year. The huge photo of me and El right at the front was of us hugging in delight after winning the final. We had both taken our helmets off so my head was fully on show. It's a lovely photo, which captured a special moment. It didn't bother me I wasn't wearing a wig in the photo, until late in the evening when another rider, who'd had too much to drink, said to me loudly, 'Why have they used that photo of you? They could have used a nicer one! Why did we all sit and look at you with no hair?'

I responded calmly by saying it captured a special moment. His response was, 'Yeah, you are a bit special. Still not a nice photo, don't know why they used it.' It put a downer on the evening and I went straight up to my room in the hotel without mingling with anyone anymore. I felt embarrassed and wondered if everyone else had been thinking the same thing. Was it really that horrible to look at?

I know he'd had too much to drink and wouldn't have said the same sober, but it is little moments like that which can really dent your confidence. Fortunately I got over this quickly and wasn't bothered about it for very long. I reminded myself it really was a beautiful photo capturing a special moment. Neither of us looked our best covered in sweat, but we'd just ridden our bikes faster than any other women in the world have ever ridden for 4km, and that was far more important to celebrate: we are real women and we had achieved something amazing.

The way I feel now is that if my hair grew back, I don't think it would change my life at all. I spent years wishing for it to grow again, believing that was the only thing that would make me truly happy. But now, in 2017, if I had the option of using my life savings to pay for a guaranteed treatment for it to grow back, I wouldn't do it. I have learnt to live with the condition in a way that suits me and I enjoy wearing the fabulous wigs I now wear. If my own hair grew back, I may even still continue to wear wigs as I love the colour and the volume they have.

I only realised this relatively recently – I had stopped wishing for it. There were more important things in my life. I am lucky to have found a wonderful husband who sees past the condition and I feel confident enough now in myself not to let it hold me back from anything. Of course I still have bad days, but I know my hair growing back wouldn't actually change my life now.

I'd told my coaches I wanted a break following Rio until the end of November, which was by far the longest I'd had since my full-time cycling career began, nearly ten years earlier. This was accepted no problem at all and there were a few other riders intending to take extended breaks. What I didn't tell them was that during this time I'd been debating with myself whether returning to the sport was something I really wanted to do.

Dan's mum's illness, my dad's accident, seeing friends and family properly, saying yes to things when I'd had a lifetime of having to say no was a revelation as to how much I'd missed out on and made me question what was important.

I was beginning to feel as though I had come full circle.

CHAPTER 44

FULL CIRCLE

I returned to training in December 2016, but deep down I knew that my heart just wasn't in it in the same way it had been before. I was determined to persevere though, recognising that December isn't the easiest month to start a training regime, partly due to the weather but also all the temptations of Christmas celebrations. However, I was beginning to realise I wanted something different from my life.

I had so enjoyed the freedom to say yes over the winter and, as much as I liked the idea of competing in Tokyo in 2020, I realised there were things I wanted more. The past decade had required a huge amount of commitment and sacrifice – not just from me but from Dan and the rest of my family too.

I remember being at an event with some retired athletes in late February 2017 and listening to them talk about how hard it had been for them to retire. They were also saying that nothing they had done during their careers had seemed like a sacrifice because of the huge reward you get at the end of it all. Yet I couldn't agree.

There are moments – christenings, hen-dos, weddings, family barbecues, children growing up, lazy lie-ins with your partner, spontaneous nights out with your mates – that you can never recapture and money can't buy. I realised that having another gold medal wouldn't actually make me any happier. It was at that moment I knew I wanted to retire and that I didn't see it as 'quitting' – my career had simply come to a natural end and I felt very lucky I was able to end it on my own terms.

I still found it hard to admit that I wanted to leave professional sport, even to myself. It had been central to my identity for so long. When I went to tell the British Cycling coaches, I couldn't even bring myself to say the word 'retirement' – I had to call it 'the R word' instead. I knew in my heart I'd made the right decision, but there was a part of me screaming that I couldn't believe I would no longer be a part of the GB Cycling Team, especially when they were working towards something so momentous as the Olympics.

Yet stronger than the desire to carry on winning medals was the desire I had to be 'normal'. In particular, I knew I wanted to start a family with Dan. I had felt as though my body was on its last legs in the run-up to Rio and I needed to listen to those signs.

When I told the coaches, they didn't give much indication as to whether they were particularly surprised or not. I left the meeting and went to see the doctor, Richard Freeman, who I trusted completely, and told him my plans and suddenly became very emotional. I then went straight to my car and burst into tears. I probably sat there for about fifteen minutes before I pulled myself together for the short drive home.

In that moment I forgot every bad day of training, every epic tough session and every cold, rainy morning and just remembered all the good times that I would be walking away from. I wouldn't be going to another Olympic Games and I wouldn't be winning any more medals.

Dan just wanted me to be happy. He'd played a significant role in my training, providing me with support, analysis and distraction when I needed it, but there was never a point when he put pressure on me, either to stop or to continue. He had, however, warned me I would find the decision to retire difficult. I'd spent my whole career thinking retirement would be an easy decision and something that would come naturally, but now I was realising he was completely right. For the few days after I told British Cycling staff I suddenly felt completely lost and at sea. I spent this time wallowing in my sadness – moping around the house and weeping – but tellingly, I didn't touch my bike.

We made plans to put an announcement to the media which I was nervous about, particularly as it happened to coincide with a time when there was a lot of negative press about British Cycling.

My perspective on the whole thing was this: as an athlete, you have to get used to being scrutinised and criticised. Yes, some harsh decisions are made, but that's the nature of the game. I wouldn't call myself thick-skinned but I would prefer a coach to be honest with me if I wasn't on track than to beat around the bush or say nothing at all. Elite sport is a hard environment to be in, but I don't see how it can be any other way.

But the biggest pressure in my career always came from myself, never from a coach or a manager. I was the one who always questioned my performance and always wanted more; I craved analysis and understanding. The most important thing for me was a fair chance to prove myself. If I wasn't good enough, I would have been able to take that as long as I'd known I'd had a fair chance at selection. After a poor performance, the key was always looking ahead to the next target; treating a bad race as a learning experience and then looking for new ways to improve.

I think this attitude can work well in life in general. We all face challenges, but it's how we handle setbacks that defines us. A positive attitude, looking for solutions rather than problems, can go a long way.

Cycling internationally, and professional sport generally, is unquestionably sexist. After all, London was the first Olympics in history where we had an equal number of events for men and women in track cycling. I'd questioned the wisdom behind that since school. But I couldn't help feeling that British Cycling were being blamed for things which were both international and institutional. The support we had as a team pursuit group going into both Olympic Games was incredible and I honestly believe my medal was worth just as much as the men's equivalent.

In addition, British Cycling does a lot for grass roots sport. Their activity and events have got more families and women into cycling, with incredible statistics showing the huge boom in participation in the UK. It's a shame no one mentioned that when the press was trying to bring them down. The organisation isn't perfect, and I hope in my retirement to do even more to help more people, especially women, overcome the barriers they may face when it comes to getting on their bikes. But I had the feeling in the media storm British Cycling were being made out to be the enemy in order to generate sensationalist headlines.

In terms of bullying, if you claim to be the victim of bullying then clearly someone has upset you enough for that to be a legitimate claim and that should be taken seriously. I would never dismiss accusations of bullying as just banter. But in response to debates about the culture, my belief is that situations are what you make of them. Something which seems negative at first can either be perceived as a threat or as an opportunity. A lot of riders couldn't handle the intensity of scrutiny as part of the GB Cycling Team, and I admit there were times when I craved more freedom rather than being under the microscope of the velodrome, but I tried to embrace this as a fantastic opportunity to be the best athlete I could be. I was part of an incredible set-up, with some of the best support staff in the world (who went way above and beyond), excellent training facilities, and the latest technology for performance analysis. Not every day was fun and games, but the rewards of hard work and perseverance could be massive.

It's human nature to want to blame someone else when things aren't going your way, but I've learnt to put my hands up and take blame when I haven't performed at my best. I believe the best athletes always can.

***

At 8:30am on Tuesday, 14 March 2017, I released my retirement statement. I had already told the members of staff and riders I had worked with closely during the Rio cycle as I felt it was important they found out from me rather than via social media. I'd also told Lizzie, Sarah, Ed Clancy and Andy Tennant, being the riders I was most closest to. I was completely overwhelmed by the incredible response on social media. My phone was having a meltdown from all the messages across Twitter, Instagram and Facebook, as well as emails and texts. It took me a few days to actually read them all. I sat down in sessions and went through and read them in chunks. I really wanted to read everyone's kind words but the messages had been coming in quicker than I could read them. There were lots of tears, but tears of happiness.

I looked back fondly on my career, not just because of the medals I'd won, but because of my personal transformation during that time. I have learnt the power of sport. How it can bring people together and how it can give you confidence. I will always be involved in sport in some capacity, and my natural competitive nature will, I'm sure, surface in whatever route my life takes me next. But most importantly, I want people to know there is no reason to let an inhibition hold you back. I had to dive straight into cycling at a time when I was too shy to even speak to new people, but I have now blossomed into a confident young woman, unashamed of my alopecia, keen to raise awareness of the condition and eager to help people recognise the power of sport.

Upon announcing my retirement, there was an interesting gender divide in terms of people's reaction to the news. Women tended to say, 'Fair enough. You've achieved a lot, time for a new chapter.' Men, conversely, tended to express total incredulity that I'd even consider leaving at what they perceived to be the top of my game. I heard that opinion everywhere, from armchair experts to random Twitter users to cabbies. Yet I'd challenge those people to think about everything you have to miss out on when you are training at an elite level and whether they'd be prepared to make those sacrifices.

I wanted to go to family dos and eat things that may or may not have been touched briefly by people with germs without fear of becoming sick. I wanted to spend time playing with my niece and nephews. I wanted to be able to agree to a last-minute night out with my husband. I wanted to eat for pleasure and not worry about my protein intake and go for a walk without being concerned that I was supposed to be resting. I wanted to live in ways that other people took for granted.

After so many years riding around in circles, I was ready to move forward.

CHAPTER 45

TAKEAWAY

Reader, thank you so much for reading my story, one of a life which is equal parts completely normal and total extraordinary. I hope you enjoyed it. I don't know about you, but when I read an autobiography, I always like to reflect on what I can learn from that person's life. In that spirit, here are a few takeaway pieces of wisdom I've picked up on my journey. I hope they serve you well.

Nice Girls DON'T Finish Last!
I've always been told throughout my career that I'm 'too nice'. I think this is because whilst I've always had self-belief, at times I've been lacking on the self-confidence front. Plus, I am naturally introverted.

Yet I've learned you don't have to have the stereotypical 'thick skin' to succeed. I've got a little better at accepting life's small injustices, but I'm still sensitive, I still worry about what other people think and I still despise cycling in the rain! (Although I often found it worthwhile reminding myself of the Dolly Parton quote, 'If you want the rainbow, you gotta put up with the rain!') I like who I am, and my career has taught me there is a difference between arrogance and resilience – the latter is essential, the former isn't.

Grab Opportunities

Not trying feels one hundred times worse than failing. In cycling terms, last is better than DNF (did not finish), which is better than DNS (did not start). Don't let opportunities pass you by and be open-minded enough to just see what happens.

Believe in yourself. It sounds obvious, but always worth remembering. Whenever I am struggling whilst trying to master something new, I remind myself of quite how abysmal I was at riding a bike in those early days, and I tell myself if I can conquer the velodrome, I can achieve anything.

Training

'I don't want to bulk up' is a phrase I hear all too often from people, particularly women, who are exercising. It's actually incredibly hard to 'bulk up', particularly if you're female. Doing sport doesn't have to mean a sacrifice of your femininity. I spent ten years training full-time with pretty much the sole aim of making my legs bigger and more powerful and I still look great in a mini skirt!

Mix your training up – if you do what you've always done, you'll get what you've always had. Keep your body guessing.

Focus on your own training plan and don't be distracted when it looks like other people are progressing faster than you. Your body is unique and so too should your training and your goals be.

Body Confidence

If a body confidence issue is holding you back from something you want, have a word with yourself. It's a cliché, but you really do only live once and it's worth remembering that your so-called 'flaws' are so much more noticeable for you than they are to anyone else.

If you think someone is staring at you, perhaps they are. That's human nature. Yet you can guarantee that in five minutes they will have totally forgotten about you.

Social Media

Block trolls – you don't need that kind of negativity in your life.

Remember, social media isn't real life. For every 'perfect' selfie there were at least twenty that didn't cut it, plus it probably has filters added. We all do it, and I happen to love it, but it isn't real.

Sexism

Speaking of the internet, some of the comments on social media could make you lose your faith in humanity. Far too many users seem to believe women belong in the kitchen. I've found it's best to just not read them.

Never settle for inequality, keep questioning the status quo. And men, don't allow sexism when you see it.

Teamwork

Everyone is motivated by different things and learning what drives the people around you can be the key to success when working in a team.

Communication is key to good teamwork, so create an environment where everyone feels they can speak up without judgement. Then learn who needs to be told things straight and who might need a softer approach.

Pick your battles. Learn when it's important to stand up for yourself and when to let go for the good of the team.

Motivation

Self-belief is the most powerful tool in your armour. It doesn't matter if other people don't believe in you, so long as you still believe in yourself.

It's okay to have days when you don't feel motivated, when all you want to do is lie on the sofa with a family-sized packet of Hobnobs and watch repeats of *Friends*. It happens to everyone. Don't waste time beating yourself up, just get back on track the next day.

It's easier to motivate yourself if you're helping others. Arrange to train as a group, that way you're in it together and won't want to let each other down.

Success

Don't be afraid to celebrate success. Even if you have far more left to achieve it's important to acknowledge the victories along the way.

The road to success always requires adaptation – don't be afraid of change.

Life Lessons

'Happy heads, fast legs' is one of my all-time faves – don't neglect your mental health.

'Discipline is choosing between what you want now and what you want most'. I can't tell you how many times I have said to myself, 'I want that bag of Maltesers, but not as much as I want to win the Olympics!'

'Focus on the controllables'. Process over outcome, performance over result.

'That girl who….'
Don't let other people define who you are.

Alopecia will always be a part of my identity, but it isn't the sum total of it. I'm a former professional athlete, an Olympic champion, a world record holder, a godmother, an auntie, a wife, a friend, a numbers-geek, a food-obsessive, a chocoholic, a sun-worshipper and a cat-lover.

No matter how other people define me, I won't define myself as 'that girl with alopecia'!

'Be who you are and say what you feel, because those who mind don't matter and those who matter don't mind.'

Dr. Seuss

ACKNOWLEDGEMENTS

Dan – thank you for being a source of unwavering support throughout my cycling career through all the tough times. All the days when I was incredibly sore from the gym or feeling down after a bad track session, you always had some wise words and usually an episode of *Friends* lined up to cheer me up! You have also given me incredible confidence and strength off the bike in all other forms of life, reminding me what's most important. I feel so lucky to have married my best friend and that through pure chance (and just a little meddling) our paths crossed in Belgium and my SatNav broke that day! I look forward to helping you pursue your own dreams and build the future together that we have spent so many years dreaming of.

Dad – always on the end of the phone whenever I need you. I've appreciated your unique way of looking at things and ability to think outside the box when it comes to solving problems. Your ability to hold everyone together during tough times is inspirational and I will always admire your positive attitude.

Mum – you have taught me from a young age to always be gracious, in success or defeat, and this has stood me in good stead in a career path none of us would ever have imagined. I am always refreshed by your perspective on life and way of simplifying the big occasions. Thank you for always pedalling with me on those big days.

Erick – from replacing my brake pads on my cyclo-cross bike on Boxing Day to changing my cleats on my shoes the night before the National 10. Your practical help has been invaluable, but more than that, your understanding of the reality of the job and the life of being an elite athlete has meant you were always a good person to turn to when the pressure was on.

Jeannette and Gary – thank you for all your help when I needed it most; from taking me in after a horrendous crash to looking after me after surgery. Your home was always a place I felt I could fully relax and switch off from the stresses of my job.

Kev Shand – thank you for welcoming me into the Shand family and making the girl from Surrey feel at home in Rochdale. Your cheerful personality and nature of being friends with everyone is an inspiration to me, not to mention all the hard miles you put in on your bike, regularly clocking up more miles than me over the winter in the bad weather!

Keeley and Natalie Shand – thank you for being the big sisters I never had. I can't wait to spend the rest of my life with you two to look up to as I one day hopefully start a family of my own.

Lizzie Deignan – my longest friend and person who I can rely on most to be honest with me. In a world full of nonsense you speak a lot of sense! Your results on the bike have been hugely impressive to me as we went our separate paths in the cycling world, but more than that, your strength of character in the face of adversity and ability to keep your feet on the ground and focus on the most important things in life will mean you will always be someone I look up to. You are a true role model to me.

Sarah Storey – your results as an athlete speak for themselves but your never wavering desire to continue to change the world for the better and never settling for anything less than the best will always be an inspiration to me. I am still convinced you must have a time machine in order to fit everything in that you do!

Ciara Horne – having you by my side is what kept me going throughout the last two years of my cycling career. Your perspective on life and constant desire to add balance helped me through the toughest training phases. Your bubbly personality brought out a new side to me that I'm so glad you discovered. Not having you on the podium alongside me in Rio will always hurt, but I believe you can achieve whatever you set your mind to and I truly hope to see you make it in Tokyo. However I do hope our training camp dance videos never get leaked onto the internet!

Katie Archibald – I loved sharing the journey to Rio with you, from our discussions about feminism to politics, your addition to the squad was a breath of fresh air.

El Barker – your fearlessness of speaking your mind provided a brilliant balance to our squad and your ability to talk logic in an emotional environment is something I had huge admiration for. You were mature beyond your years and it was a pleasure to race with someone so consistent and reliable.

Dani King and Laura Kenny – sharing our journey together to London will always be one of the most memorable and fun times of my life. Being the first time for all of us and all the excitement that came with it was what made that gold medal even more special, even if we were a little 'juvenile'.

Gayle Thrush – my first agent and first person to give me

confidence to tell my story. A wonderful person with a big heart. It is an honour to still call you my friend.

Len Parker Simpson and Joe Hewitt – the double act that will never be replaced. Together you made the last two years of my career far more enjoyable with your refreshing attitudes to training and ability to pick me up when I was feeling down. You are truly two of the best I have ever worked with.

Stuart Blunt – thank you for visiting my school all those years ago. Thank you for persevering with me when I turned up at Talent Team camps looking like I had no hope at all! And thank you for always being there for a chat over the years. One of the few people I could always trust for an honest opinion.

Ed Clancy – thank you for reminding me this is just riding a bike round in circles in a wooden bowl whenever the nerves got too much and what's really important in life is our pet cats!

Andy Tennant – thank you for always making me laugh and reminding me not to take life too seriously.

Richard Freeman – through all the ups and downs of my career you have been a source of unwavering support. Thank you.

The 'team behind the team' – who don't get anywhere near enough mentions or thanks for the huge amount of hard work they do – THANK YOU! Debs Sides, Kath Brown, Ruth Anderson, Emma Barton, Hannah Crowely, Phil Burt, Hanlie Fouche, Luc de Wilde, Heather Miller, Vicky Hayles, Paul Barratt, Ernie Feargrieve, Adam Bonser, Mark Ingham, Greg Stevens, Tony Purnell, Sally Cowan, Abby Burton, Angela Haig, Arabella Ashfield, Jo Harrison, Keith Reynolds, Denise Yarrow and everyone else I have worked with as part of the British Cycling support team over the last decade.

Mrs Holmes, Mrs Etheridge, Miss Treen and Mr Sides – Thank you for your support during my school years at Nonsuch. The

ACKNOWLEDGEMENTS

school gave me a fantastic start in life, not only by providing the opportunity to try cycling, but by teaching me never to settle for inequality.

Thank you to my agent Jess Henig and Lauren Gardner for having the vision for this book, to Natasha Devon for learning more about cycling then you ever thought you would, and to James Hodgkinson at John Blake who made this book a reality.

Thank you to my fantastic partners both past and present for your support. Wattbike, Sports Tours International, Adidas, CNP, Link4Life, Nelsons, Honda and to Aderans Hair Centre for my beautiful wigs.

Finally thank you to all the fans out there who have supported me throughout my career and everyone who has ever sent me a message of well wishes. Knowing I have made a difference to someone by helping them deal with alopecia or inspiring someone to get on a bike is an incredible reward that money just can't buy. It is people like you that have made all the hard work worth it.